Power Graphics
Using Turbo Pascal®

Related Titles of Interest

Turbo Language Essentials: A Programmer's Reference, Weiskamp, Shammas, and Pronk

Turbo Libraries: A Programmer's Reference, Weiskamp, Shammas, and Pronk

Turbo Algorithms: A Programmer's Reference, Weiskamp, Shammas, and Pronk

Introducing C to Pascal Programmer's, Shammas

Advanced Turbo C Programmer's Guide, Mosich, Shammas, and Flamig

The Turbo C Survival Guide, Miller and Quilici

C Programming Language: An Applied Perspective, Miller and Quilici

C Wizard's Programming Reference, Schwaderer

Turbo C DOS Utilities, Alonso

Quick C DOS Utilities, Alonso

Turbo C and Quick C Functions: Building Blocks for Efficient Code, Barden

Power Graphics Using Turbo C, Weiskamp, Heiny, and Shammas

Applying Turbo Pascal Library Units, Shammas

Programming with Macintosh Turbo Pascal, Swan

Turbo Pascal DOS Utilities, Alonso

Artificial Intelligence Programming with Turbo Prolog, Weiskamp and Hengl

Mastering HyperTalk, Weiskamp and Shammas

Power Graphics Using Turbo Pascal®

Keith Weiskamp
Loren Heiny
Namir Shammas

WILEY

John Wiley & Sons, Inc.
New York • Chichester • Brisbane • Toronto • Singapore

Publisher: Stephen Kippur
Editor: Katherine Schowalter
Managing Editor: Ruth Greif
Compositor: Loren Heiny

Library of Congress Cataloging-in-Publication Data

Weiskamp, Keith.
    Power graphics using Turbo Pascal / Keith Weiskamp, Loren Heiny, Namir
Shammas.
        p.   cm.
    Bibliography: p.
    ISBN 0-471-61841-1
    1. Computer graphics. 2. Turbo Pascal (Computer program) I. Heiny, Loren.
        I I. Shammas, Namir Clement, 1954- .   III. Title.
    T385.W46   1989
    006.6'869--dc19   89-30964
                                                    CIP

Printed in the United States of America
89 90 10 9 8 7 6 5 4 3 2

Contents

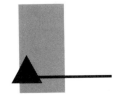

Preface

This book will show you how to get the most out of graphics programming using Turbo Pascal. If like most serious programmers you want to know how to apply graphics programming techniques, you will want a book that provides a hands-on approach to the art of developing graphics tools and applications. To fill this need, *Power Graphics Using Turbo Pascal* takes you inside Turbo Pascal's powerful graphics features and provides you with numerous useful programs.

Some of the major features of this book are:

- Hands-on approach to building graphics tools
- Techniques for designing graphics-based user interfaces
- The fundamentals of two- and three-dimensional graphics programming
- Real-time animation
- Presentation graphics
- Interactive applications including painting and Computer Aided Drafting (CAD) programs

Who Should Read This Book

If you want to learn how to create useful graphics programs with Turbo Pascal and the Borland Graphics Interface (BGI), you'll enjoy this book. Whether you're new to graphics programming or experienced with the fundamentals of graphics, this book shows you how to design tools and applications including presentation graphics, icon editors, graphics-based user interfaces, painting and CAD programs, and three-dimensional graphics viewing programs.

What You'll Need

To use this book you'll need Turbo Pascal 5.0, as well as an IBM PC XT, AT, PS/2, or a compatible computer system capable of displaying graphics. All of the programs are designed to work with Color Graphics Adapter (CGA), Enhanced Graphics Adapter (EGA), Virtual Graphics Array (VGA), or Hercules graphics adapters. Because of the flexibility of the BGI and the programs presented, you can easily customize them to run on your own system.

A Look Inside

This book has been designed so that it progresses from fundamental graphics programming techniques to more advanced topics such as three-dimensional graphics programming.

Chapter 1: *The BGI Quick Tour* presents an introduction to the BGI. This chapter will show you how to use the BGI tools to access your graphics hardware and write complete standalone graphics programs. After we cover the essentials, we'll show you how to develop a program to create fractal images.

Chapter 2: *The BGI Drawing Commands* explains how all of the major BGI drawing commands are used. You'll also learn how to fill regions with predefined and user-defined fill patterns.

Chapter 3: *BGI Fonts and Text* presents the tools for displaying text in graphics mode.

Chapter 4: *Presentation Graphics* shows you how to develop programs for generating high-quality presentation graphics. In this chapter, you'll learn how to combine the BGI fonts and drawing routines to display pie, bar and coin charts.

Chapter 5: *Graphics Techniques in Two Dimensions* covers a variety of techniques for working with two-dimensional graphics. Some of the topics presented include transformations, rotating graphic objects, and object-oriented programming.

Chapter 6: *Animation* shows you how to add animation effects to your two-dimensional graphics. You'll learn how to use the **GetImage** and **PutImage** routines to move graphics images and how to use color palettes to simulate animation.

Chapter 7: *Creating Mouse Tools* presents a hands-on discussion of how to build a set of tools to control the mouse. In later chapters, we'll use the mouse tools to support graphics drawing programs.

Chapter 8: *Working with Icons* shows you how to build a useful icon editor.

Chapter 9: *Pop-up Windows in Graphics* presents a set of tools for supporting pop-up windows in graphics mode.

Chapter 10: *Interactive Drawing Tools* shows you how to build a useful toolset of interactive drawing routines.

Chapter 11: *A Paint Program* presents a powerful painting program that includes a mouse-based user interface. With this program, you'll be able to draw images and save them to an external file.

Chapter 12: *A CAD Program* presents a two-dimensional CAD program

Chapter 13: *Three-Dimensional Graphics* explains the fundamentals of three-dimensional graphics programming. In this chapter you'll learn about clipping, projection, three-dimensional representation, and much more.

The BGI Quick Tour

If you've picked up this book because you're interested in learning how to add high-quality graphics to your Turbo Pascal applications, then you've come to the right place. In the past, programming graphics has been a difficult, time-consuming task. Fortunately, with the release of Turbo Pascal versions 4.0 and 5.0, we now have a set of powerful and easy to use graphics tools called the Borland Graphics Interface (BGI) that simplify the work of creating two- and three-dimensional PC graphics.

In this chapter, we'll take a quick tour of the basic tools provided with the BGI. However, keep in mind that our tour is designed to introduce you to the major features of the BGI. In later chapters, we'll cover the tools in much greater detail and we'll show you how they can be used to develop applications such as icon editors, and CAD and painting programs. Along the way, we'll also be presenting the major concepts of two- and three-dimensional graphics programming.

We'll begin our tour by discussing the basic structure of a Turbo Pascal graphics program and then we'll show you how to use several of the BGI graphics routines. Some of the routines that we'll present include pixel plotting procedures, line drawing commands, polygon plotting routines, and text manipulation routines that work in graphics mode.

At our final destination we'll develop an interesting program that creates fractals. We'll use this program as an opportunity to combine what we've learned along the way into a very simple fractal program that displays computer generated landscapes.

Getting Started

For each graphics program that you write, there are certain steps that must always be followed. For example, at the start of every graphics program you'll need to set your video display hardware to a graphics mode. In addition, you should restore the computer's screen to its normal display mode at the end of each program. In the following section, we'll show you what basic components are required in a typical Turbo Pascal graphics program.

Initializing the BGI

The first step required in a graphics program consists of initializing the graphics hardware. By hardware we mean the video display adapter card that must be in your PC in order to display graphics. To complicate the issue, there are several different graphics cards available for the PC with each having numerous graphics modes. Fortunately, many of the graphics cards are supported by the BGI. To start out, we won't cover all of the graphics cards and modes, but rather we'll use the default mode of the BGI initialization routine that allows us to set the currently installed graphics adapter to its highest resolution mode.

The BGI procedure used to configure your computer to graphics mode is called **InitGraph** and it has the following declaration:

```
procedure InitGraph(var GraphDriver, GraphMode: integer;
                    DriverPath: string);
```

The procedure **InitGraph** is defined in the Pascal unit **Graph** which you must specify in the **uses** section of all of your graphics programs. This file contains the data structures, constants, procedures, and functions for the BGI.

Notice, in the procedure declaration for **InitGraph** that the first two parameters are var parameters. When **InitGraph** is called, they contain logical values that specify which video adapter and mode to use, respectively. The third parameter specifies the path name where the Turbo Pascal graphics driver files are stored. The driver files are the files that come with your Turbo Pascal distribution disk and end with the **.bgi** extension. The path name can be represented as a full path name such as:

```
InitGraph(GDriver, GMode, '\compilers\turbo\graphics');
```

or it can be a partial path name, such as:

```
InitGraph(GDriver, GMode, 'graphics\drivers');
```

In the second example, **InitGraph** searches the directory **drivers** which is a subdirectory of the directory **graphics** which is a subdirectory of the current directory. If the BGI graphics driver files are stored in the directory where you are executing your program, you can call **InitGraph** with:

```
InitGraph(GDriver, GMode, '');
```

Here, the path name is specified as the empty string.

Now let's learn how we can use **InitGraph** to select the graphics mode. You can instruct **InitGraph** to use a particular graphics driver and mode by setting its first two parameters to particular values. Alternatively, you can let **InitGraph** automatically configure your PC's video adapter. We'll use this option. If the first parameter is set to the constant **Detect**, a constant declared in the unit **Graph**, **InitGraph** will configure your graphics system to its highest resolution mode. In this case, the second parameter in **InitGraph** does not need to be initialized to any value, but you do need to specify an integer to hold the parameter's return value. After **InitGraph** is called, you can examine the value of this parameter to determine which graphics mode the BGI initialized. As a last requirement for setting your PC's video adapter, you'll need to specify the path to the BGI driver files.

When writing a graphics program, **InitGraph** is not complete without its companion routine **CloseGraph**. The procedure **CloseGraph**, which does not take any parameters, should be used at the end of all of your programs to shut down the BGI system and restore the monitor to the video mode it was in before the call to **InitGraph**.

Writing the Basic BGI Program

To summarize the initialization steps we have been discussing, let's write a simple graphics program that uses **InitGraph** and **CloseGraph**. The following program is probably the shortest graphics program we can write in Turbo Pascal. It's shown here to emphasize the basic structure of the typical Turbo Pascal graphics program and you can use it as a model to write your own programs.

```
program SmallestGraphicsProgram;
uses
   Graph;                            { Turbo Pascal graphics unit }
const
   GDriver: integer = Detect;        { Select the autodetect feature }
```

```
var
   GMode: integer;                  { For autodetection use a }
                                    { variable placeholder }
begin                              { for the mode }
   InitGraph(GDriver, GMode, '');  { Set the driver and mode }
   { ... put drawing commands here ... }
   CloseGraph;                      { Exit the graphics mode }
end.
```

If you run this program without adding any graphics drawing routines, you'll see a couple of flashes on the screen and that's about it. The screen flicker is caused by your PC switching from its normal text mode to graphics mode and then back again to text mode (assuming the screen was in text mode before the call to **InitGraph**).

Let's take a closer look at the program. The code begins with the **uses** section which includes the Turbo Pascal unit **Graph**. Every graphics program must contain this statement. Remember that the unit **Graph** contains various predefined constants, type definitions, and all of the BGI routines.

The call to **InitGraph** automatically sets your video adapter because **Detect** is passed as the value for the first parameter. The second parameter, which references the video mode, is not given a value; it simply acts as a placeholder in this example. After **InitGraph** is called, you can examine **GDriver** and **GMode** to see which video adapter has been loaded and which mode was initialized. Again, the third parameter specifies the directory where the BGI driver files are kept. If you don't specify the correct directory, your program will fail to be initialized to graphics mode and won't display any graphics. (We'll show you in a moment how to check for this and other potential errors when loading driver files.)

You should also be aware that our sample program does not perform any error checking with respect to the graphics initialization. Therefore, if the graphics initialization fails, the program will not be placed in graphics mode. Fortunately, the BGI provides several error handling routines. One such function, **GraphResult**, obtains the error condition of the last graphics routine called. Another BGI function, called **GraphErrorMsg**, takes the value returned by **GraphResult** and displays an appropriate error message for you. We'll use these error detection functions in the next program we write to show how to construct a much more robust version of our first program.

Error Checking

The most common error that can occur in a graphics program is caused when the Turbo graphics driver cannot be found. Remember, the third parameter of the function **InitGraph** specifies the path to the Turbo Pascal graphics driver files. If the path is incorrect and the graphics drivers can't be located, the graphics initialization will fail. In our first sample program, the path to the graphics drivers is set to the null string which indicates that the BGI drivers must be located in the current directory. If your BGI files are not in the directory where you're running your graphics programs, you'll need to set this path to the directory where they are stored.

Let's now modify our original example so that we can check for potential errors. Here is the program that you should type in, compile, and execute.

```
program GraphTest;
uses
   Graph, Crt;
const
   GDriver: integer = Detect;          { Autodetect graphics mode }
var
   GMode: integer;
   GError: integer;


begin
   InitGraph(GDriver, GMode, '');
   GError := GraphResult;               { Get error flag value }
   if GError < 0 then begin             { If negative then error }
     write('Graphics initialization error: ');
     writeln(GraphErrorMsg(GError));     { Print error message }
     halt(1);                           { Since error, quit program }
   end;
{ If no graphics error has occurred, then print a greeting }
   OutText('Hello graphics world!      Press any key to exit ...');
{ Wait for the user to strike a key, otherwise the program will
   immediately execute CloseGraph and the screen will be cleared
   and switched to text mode
}
   repeat until KeyPressed;
   CloseGraph;                          { Exit graphics mode }
end.
```

This program does a comprehensive job of error checking. If everything is okay, the message

```
Hello graphics world!      Press any key to exit ...
```

is displayed. If a problem occurs, however, an appropriate error message is displayed and the program is terminated. To ensure that your graphics environment is set up correctly, you should try running this program before going on to the next section.

One new routine in the program that we haven't seen yet is **OutText** which is used to write a text string to the screen. This is one of two specialized graphics text output routines provided with the BGI. There is also a BGI procedure called **OutTextXY** which allows you to display a text string at a specified screen location. We'll look at both of these routines in much greater detail in Chapter 3 when we present the techniques for working with BGI fonts and text.

Working with Coordinates

As is the case with most goals you wish to accomplish, it helps to know where you have been and where you are going. In graphics, we keep track of our positions by using *pixel coordinates*. Pixels are the very small dots you see on the screen, and they can be addressed by using a coordinate system that is similar to the way we access the rows and columns in an array data structure. This coordinate system is called the cartesian coordinate system. Figure 1.1 illustrates how pixels are referenced with row and column coordinates.

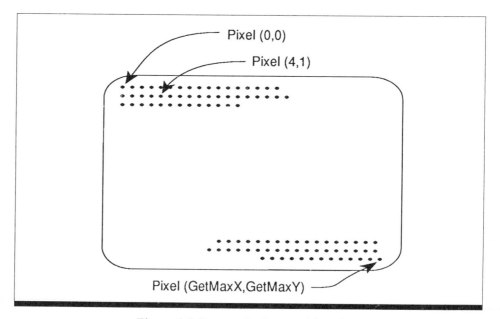

Pixel (0,0)

Pixel (4,1)

Pixel (GetMaxX,GetMaxY)

Figure 1.1. Row and column addressing

The extent of your system's coordinates is dependent on the video adapter that you are using. Fortunately, there are some standard techniques for handling pixel coordinates that you can use for any of the BGI supported video adapters. First, all graphics modes on the PC start their coordinates at the top left of the screen with the coordinate (0,0). The highest pixel coordinate is at the bottom right of the screen. Its actual value is dependent on your graphics mode; however, Turbo Pascal includes two functions, **GetMaxX** and **GetMaxY**, that you can call to get these values. They are typically used in statements such as:

```
MaxXCoordinate := GetMaxX;
MaxYCoordinate := GetMaxY;
```

It's good programming practice to exploit these function calls and create programs that can work equally well on several different graphics adapters and modes. Neither function requires a parameter to be passed to them, and they return the number of pixels in the x direction (the number of columns on the screen) and the number of pixels in the y direction (the number of rows), respectively. Therefore, the bottom, right coordinate is given by (**GetMaxX, GetMaxY**). With this information, we are now able to instruct the BGI where objects should be drawn on the screen. We'll now investigate some of the drawing routines.

Drawing Commands

Turbo Pascal supports a wide variety of drawing routines that are amazingly simple to use. These extend from pixel level screen commands to high-level routines that draw three-dimensional bar graphs.

In this part of our tour, we'll explore several of the BGI's drawing routines. We'll start with the lowest level drawing routines in the BGI, the **PutPixel/GetPixel** routines, and then we'll work our way up to the higher level ones.

Getting Down to Pixels

Both **PutPixel** and **GetPixel** can access only 1 pixel on the screen at a time. The **PutPixel** procedure sets a pixel at a specified location (coordinate) to a particular color. The **GetPixel** function, however, is used to determine the current pixel color of any location on the screen. These routines are defined as:

```
function GetPixel(x, y: integer): word;
procedure PutPixel(x, y: integer; Color: word);
```

Notice that **GetPixel** returns a word value that corresponds to the pixel's color at (x, y). Here are a few sample calls for these routines:

```
PutPixel(100, 200, Red);
Color := GetPixel(20, 50);
```

To see how both of these routines are used in the context of a real graphics program, let's write a program that randomly plots 1000 pixels on the screen using **PutPixel** and then relies on **GetPixel** to locate each pixel in order to thin them out. Here is the complete program:

```
program RandPixl;
{ This program randomly plots 1000 pixels on the screen and
  then erases every other one
}
uses
  Graph;
var
  GDriver, GMode: integer;
  MaxX, MaxY: integer;       { Maximum coordinates of screen }
  MaxColor: word;            { This mode's maximum color value }
  i, x, y: integer;
  Color: word;

begin
  GDriver := Detect;
  InitGraph(GDriver, GMode, '');
  Randomize;        { Initialize the random number generator }

{ Get the maximum x and y screen coordinates and the largest
  valid color for this mode
}
  MaxX := GetMaxX;
  MaxY := GetMaxY;
  MaxColor := GetMaxColor;

  for i := 1 to 1000 do begin
    x := Random(MaxX+1);          { Use plus for these since }
    y := Random(Maxy+1);          { random returns a value }
    Color := Random(MaxColor+1);  { between 0 and num - 1 }
```

```
        PutPixel(x, y, Color);          { Color the pixel }
    end;


{ Now scan through the screen and thin out the nonblack pixels.
  Uses the GetPixel command to locate the nonblack pixels. Every
  other pixel that is found is reset to black.
}
    i := 0;
    for y := 0 to Maxy do
      for x := 0 to MaxX do
        if GetPixel(x,y) <> black then begin
          if (i mod 2) = 0                     { Only reset every }
            then PutPixel(x, y, black);     { other pixel }
          Inc(i);
        end;
    CloseGraph;
end.
```

The program starts by initializing the graphics mode using the BGI's autoconfiguration feature. After the graphics mode is set, the maximum x and y screen coordinates are determined by calls to the functions **GetMaxX** and **GetMaxY**. In addition, a similar call is made to **GetMaxColor** which retrieves the highest color value that the currently installed video adapter can produce. This function gives us the full range of valid color values for the active video mode, since all colors lie between 0 and this number. The **GetMaxColor** function works much like **GetMaxX** and **GetMaxY** and is invaluable for writing device independent programs. One final part of the initialization process involves a call to **Randomize** that seeds the random number generator we'll be using later.

You may have noticed that no error checking is done in this program. Although it is good practice to check and ensure that the graphics system has successfully initialized itself, for the sake of brevity we'll ignore this possibility for now.

The first **for** loop generates the randomly drawn pixels. They are plotted throughout the screen in random locations and colors. The color values used range from 0 (black) to the value returned in **GetMaxColor** (often white). After this loop, your screen will portray an impressive looking night sky filled with stars.

The next **for** loop travels through these stars and erases every other one by resetting them to black. To locate the randomly drawn stars, a search is made of the screen pixels. This is accomplished by calls to the **GetPixel** function. Every other time this **GetPixel** encounters a pixel other than black, **PutPixel** is called to reset it to black. The thinning process is assured by the variable **i** which allows **PutPixel** to plot its black pixels on every even occurrence of **i**. The indexing of the screen is limited by the variables **MaxX** and **MaxY** that hold the maximum screen coordinates. These variables were set at the beginning of the program with calls to **GetMaxX** and **GetMaxY**.

Drawing Figures

Now that we've seen how to plot and read pixels, let's move on and take a look at how some of the Turbo Pascal BGI routines are used to draw figures. We'll start with the drawing routines that create outlines of figures and shapes. These are the **Arc**, **Circle**, **DrawPoly**, **Ellipse**, **Line**, and **Rectangle** routines. Each one of these six procedures has its own unique features and peculiarities and rather than go into them now, we'll simply develop a program that will serve to briefly introduce you to them.

Each of these procedures have rather intuitive names and operate much as you might expect. For example, **Arc** draws an arc and **Circle** draws a circle. The **Circle** procedure requires three parameters: the x and y coordinates of its center, and the radius of the circle. The other procedures are similar. The only odd one is **DrawPoly**. This routine takes an array of x and y points and the number of points in the array and plots line segments connecting the points. As long as the first coordinate in the list of points matches with the last, then a closed polygon is drawn.

The basic BGI drawing routines are powerful for drawing figures. You can control the color that figures are drawn in, the type of line style used to make their perimeter, and the aspect ratio used (in the case of the **Arc** and **Circle** procedures). In Chapter 2, we'll explore each of the drawing routines in much greater detail.

For now, let's write a program that illustrates how the six drawing procedures previously discussed are used. The program is somewhat encumbered by the need to keep all of the indexes to the drawing routines device independent, but this is often the cost of generality.

The screen is divided into six sections in which figures are drawn for each of the drawing commands. In addition, it uses the **OutTextXY** text display function to write labels for each of the figures. Here is the program:

```
program Draw;
{ Shows you most of the simple drawing routines in the BGI. These do
  not include the fill routines or the various line styles that are
  available.
}
uses
  Graph, Crt;
```

```
var
   GDriver, GMode: integer;
   MaxX, MaxY: integer;
   Color: word;
   Points: array[1..5] of PointType;

begin
   GDriver := Detect;
   InitGraph(GDriver, GMode, '');
   MaxX := GetMaxX;     MaxY := GetMaxY;

{ Draw an arc, circle, and polygon on the top portion of the screen
  and an ellipse, line, and rectangle on the lower portion
}
   Arc(MaxX div 6, MaxY div 4, 0, 135, 50);
   OutTextXY(MaxX div 6-TextWidth('Arc') div 2, 0, 'Arc');
   Circle(MaxX div 2, MaxY div 4, 60);
   OutTextXY(MaxX div 2-TextWidth('Circle') div 2, 0, 'Circle');
   Points[1].x := MaxX * 5 div 6 - 20;
   Points[1].y := MaxY div 4 - 20;
   Points[2].x := MaxX * 5 div 6 - 30;
   Points[2].y := MaxY div 4 + 25;
   Points[3].x := MaxX * 5 div 6 + 40;
   Points[3].y := MaxY div 4 + 15;
   Points[4].x := MaxX * 5 div 6 + 20;
   Points[4].y := MaxY div 4 - 30;
   Points[5].x := Points[1].x;
   Points[5].y := Points[1].y;
   DrawPoly(5, Points);
   OutTextXY(MaxX*5 div 6-TextWidth('DrawPoly') div 2, 0,'DrawPoly');
   Ellipse(MaxX div 6, MaxY*3 div 4, 0, 360, 75, 20);
   OutTextXY(MaxX div 6-TextWidth('Ellipse') div 2,
             MaxY-TextHeight('l'), 'Ellipse');
   Line(MaxX div 2-25, MaxY*3 div 4-25, MaxX div 2+25,MaxY*3 div 4+25);
   OutTextXY(MaxX div 2-TextWidth('Line') div 2,
             MaxY-TextHeight('L'), 'Line');
   Rectangle(MaxX*5 div 6-30, MaxY*3 div 4-20,
             MaxX*5 div 6+30, MaxY*3 div 4+20);
   OutTextXY(MaxX*5 div 6-TextWidth('Rectangle') div 2,
             MaxY-TextHeight('R'), 'Rectangle');
```

```
    repeat until KeyPressed;
    CloseGraph;
end.
```

The display produced by this program is shown in Figure 1.2. The main drawing routines spotlighted are the calls to the drawing routines of the form:

```
Arc(x, y, StAngle, EndAngle, Radius);
Circle(x, y, Radius);
DrawPoly(NumberOfPoints, ArrayOfXYPoints);
Ellipse(x, y, StAngle, EndAngle, XRadius, YRadius);
Line(x1, y1, x2, y2);
Rectangle(Left, Top, Right, Bottom);
```

The different calculations and offsets are included in the program so that you can see what type of code is typically needed to generate device independent scenes in Turbo Pascal. In particular, note that we are using the **TextHeight** and **TextWidth** functions to determine the size of the text strings that are displayed. We'll look at both of these functions in more detail in Chapter 3.

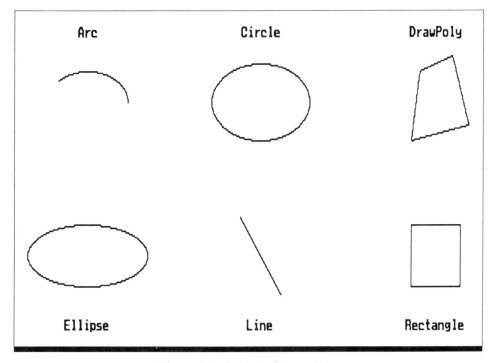

Figure 1.2. Output of Draw.Pas

Keep in mind that we are showing only some of the powerful features of these drawing routines in our sample program. For example, several of the routines shown earlier let you set their line styles and all of them let you control the color used to draw them. However, we've avoided these for now so that we can show you their basic features in our quick tour.

Filling Figures

In the previous section we experimented with routines to draw outlines of objects. Turbo Pascal also has a set of graphics routines that can draw and paint solid objects or objects filled with patterns. These routines are **Bar, Bar3D, FillPoly, FillEllipse, PieSlice**, and **Sector**. As in the figure drawing routines, these procedures are very flexible. Most of these procedures support different fill patterns, colors, and even different line styles. Here are the procedural declarations for each of these routines:

```
procedure Bar(Left, Top, Right, Bottom: integer);
procedure Bar3D(Left, Top, Right, Bottom: integer;
                Depth: word; TopFlag: Boolean);
procedure FillEllipse(x, y: integer; XRadius, YRadius: word);
procedure FillPoly(NumberOfPoints: integer; var ArrayOfXYPoints);
procedure PieSlice(x, y: integer; StartAngle, EndAngle, Radius: word);
procedure Sector(x, y: integer; StartAngle, EndAngle,
                XRadius, YRadius: word);
```

The procedures **Bar, Bar3D, PieSlice, FillEllipse,** and **Sector** are useful routines for creating impressive looking graphs and charts. In Chapter 4 we'll explore these and other routines in much greater detail when we develop several presentation graphics applications. The remaining routine, **FillPoly**, works much like its companion routine **DrawPoly**, except that it both draws and fills a polygon using the current drawing color and fill pattern.

Now let's write a program that uses each of these routines to draw some basic graphic objects. The program divides the screen into six regions and draws a different object in each region. Since there are actually only five routines, but six regions on the screen, we'll use the sixth region to show how the **PieSlice** procedure can be used to display a filled circle. The display produced by the program is shown in Figure 1.3. The offset calculations make the code a bit cumbersome, but once again this is the cost of the generality. Here is the complete program:

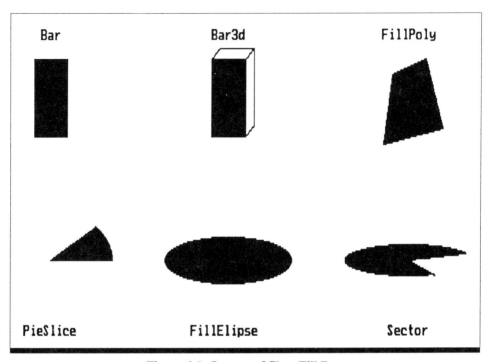

Figure 1.3. Output of ShowFill.Pas

```
program ShowFill;
{ This program uses most of the simple fill functions in the BGI }
uses
   Graph, Crt;
var
   GDriver, GMode: integer;
   MaxX, MaxY: integer;
   Color: word;
   Points: array[1..5] of PointType;

begin
   GDriver := Detect;
   InitGraph(GDriver, GMode, '');
   MaxX := GetMaxX;
   MaxY := GetMaxY;

{ Draw a bar, a 3d bar, and a filled polygon on the top portion of
  the screen and a pieslice, a filled ellipse, and a filled
```

```
      elliptical region on the bottom portion. Each object will be
      drawn in a different color.
}
    Bar(MaxX div 6-20,MaxY div 4-30, MaxX div 6+20, MaxY div 4+20);
    OutTextXY(MaxX div 6-TextWidth('Bar') div 2, 0, 'Bar');
    Bar3d(MaxX div 2-20, MaxY div 4-30, MaxX div 2+20,
          MaxY div 4+20, 10, true);
    OutTextXY(MaxX div 2-TextWidth('Bar3d') div 2, 0, 'Bar3d');
    Points[1].x := MaxX*5 div 6-20;
    Points[1].y := MaxY div 4-20;
    Points[2].x := MaxX*5 div 6-30;
    Points[2].y := MaxY div 4+25;
    Points[3].x := MaxX*5 div 6+40;
    Points[3].y := MaxY div 4+15;
    Points[4].x := MaxX*5 div 6+20;
    Points[4].y := MaxY div 4-30;
    Points[5].x := Points[1].x;
    Points[5].y := Points[1].y;
    FillPoly(5, Points);
    OutTextXY(MaxX*5 div 6-TextWidth('FillPoly') div 2,0, 'FillPoly');
    PieSlice(MaxX div 6, MaxY*3 div 4, 0, 45, 75);
    OutTextXY(MaxX div 6-TextWidth('PieSlice') div 2,
            MaxY-TextHeight('l'), 'PieSlice');
    FillEllipse(MaxX div 2, MaxY * 3 div 4, 75, 15);
    OutTextXY(MaxX div 2-TextWidth('FillEllipse') div 2,
            MaxY-TextHeight('F'), 'FillElipse');
    Sector(MaxX*5 div 6, MaxY*3 div 4, 25, 295, 75, 10);
    OutTextXY(MaxX*5 div 6-TextWidth('Sector') div 2,
            MaxY-TextHeight('l'), 'Sector');
    repeat until KeyPressed;
    CloseGraph;
end.
```

You may now be wondering, how do the fill commands know what type of fill pattern to use? Basically, each time you call one of the fill commands it uses the current fill style and color. In our program, we did not explicitly set the fill style, so the program defaults to a solid fill painted in the maximum color available on the video adapter. Turbo Pascal provides a procedure called **SetFillStyle** which is used to change the fill style. As an example, if we added the statement:

```
SetFillStyle(HatchFill, Blue);
```

immediately after the call to **InitGraph**, our program would have drawn all of the objects with a blue (on an EGA system) hatch pattern. The values for **HatchFill** and **Blue**, along with other colors and fill styles, are predefined in the **Graph** unit file. In Chapter 2 we'll show you how you can create your own fill patterns.

You may also be wondering whether Borland has provided enough fill commands in their BGI toolset. For example, there isn't a circle fill command; or is there? Actually, several of the Turbo Pascal graphics commands serve dual roles. In the case of a circle, the **PieSlice** procedure can be used to paint a filled circle as shown in the previous program. The trick is to call **PieSlice** with a start and end angle that ranges a full 360 degrees. The **FillPoly** procedure is the real powerhouse, however. It has a tremendous amount of flexibility because you can use it to fill objects of any shape. We'll use this feature later in this chapter in the section "Fractal Landscapes" when we discuss fractals.

Text and Fonts

When it comes to fonts and text output, the BGI is quite impressive. Traditionally, text output in graphics mode on an IBM PC has been a bit of a disappointment. For example, in graphics mode the IBM PC provides only characters of a fixed size which are in some cases of poor quality. However, with the BGI tools you can easily add high-quality text to your graphics displays.

The BGI includes a stroke font package that is well suited for drawing characters of various heights and widths. In addition, it is also capable of drawing vertical text.

Our next task is to write a program that displays a single line of text at varying scales and in both horizontal and vertical orientations. The program uses the sans serif stroke font to display the message "Turbo Pascal Fonts" centered on your screen. The program will allow you to interactively rescale the size of the text. The s key is used to shrink the text, and the g key to make the text grow in size. The space bar will switch the text between a horizontal and a vertical format. Finally, pressing the q key will quit the program.

```
program ShowText;
{ Displays the statement 'Turbo Pascal Fonts' centered on
  the screen which you can scale or have displayed vertically
  or horizontally. The following user interaction is supported:
    Key    Action
    ---------------------------------------------
    g      Grows the size of the text
    s      Shrinks the text size
```

```
        space   Toggles between vertical and horizontal text
        q       Quits program
}
uses
   Graph, Crt;                               .
const
   Incr: integer = 10;
   GDriver: integer = Detect;        { Use autodetect mode }
   TextStr: string[18] = 'Turbo Pascal Fonts';
var
   GMode: integer;
   ch: char;
   cx, cy: integer;                  { Text is centered to this point }
   sw, sh: integer;                  { String height/width }
   MultX, DivX: integer;             { BGI scaling factors }
   MultY, DivY: integer;
   Dir: integer;                     { Orientation to display text }

begin
   InitGraph(GDriver, GMode, '');
   SetFillStyle(SolidFill, Black);
   cx := GetMaxX div 2;              { Calculate center of screen }
   cy := GetMaxY div 2;
   MultX := 100;      DivX := 100;   { Set scaling ratio 1:1 }
   MultY := 100;      DivY := 100;
   Dir := HorizDir;                  { Start with horizontal text }
   SetTextJustify(CenterText, CenterText);
   SetTextStyle(SansSerifFont, Dir, UserCharSize);
   OutTextXY(cx, cy, TextStr);       { Write the string out }
   ch := ReadKey;                    { Get user input }
   while ch <> 'q' do begin          { Loop until q pressed }
   { Erase the existing string. Use a solid black bar
     to write over the text and erase it.
   }
      sw := TextWidth(TextStr) div 2;
      sh := TextHeight(TextStr) * 3 div 2;
      if Dir = HorizDir then begin
         if sw > cx then sw := cx + 1;      { Clips erase region }
         if sh > cy then sh := cy + 1;      { to screen }
         Bar(cx-sw, cy-sh, cx+sw, cy+sh);   { Erase text if horizontal }
      end
```

```
      else begin
        if sh > cx then sh := cx + 1;        { Clips erase region }
        if sw > cy then sw := cy + 1;        { to screen }
        Bar(cx-sh, cy-sw, cx+sh, cy+sw);     { Erase text if vertical }
      end;
      { Resize the text }
      if ch = 'g' then begin                 { Grow the text }
        if DivX > Incr then begin
          Dec(DivX,Incr);   Inc(MultX,Incr);
        end;
        if DivY > Incr then begin
          Dec(DivY,Incr);   Inc(MultY,Incr);
        end
      end
      else if ch = 's' then begin            { Shrink the text }
        if MultX > Incr then begin
          Dec(MultX,Incr);   Inc(DivX,Incr);
        end;
        if MultY > Incr then begin
          Dec(MultY,Incr);   Inc(DivY,Incr);
        end
      end
      else if ch = ' ' then                  { Switch text orientation }
        if Dir = HorizDir then Dir := VertDir
        else Dir := HorizDir;
      SetUserCharSize(MultX, DivX, MultY, DivY);
      SetTextStyle(SansSerifFont, Dir, UserCharSize);
      OutTextXY(cx, cy, TextStr);            { Rewrite the text }
      ch := ReadKey;                         { Get user input }
    end;
    CloseGraph;
  end.
```

Fractal Landscapes

Our tour of the BGI is almost over, but before we finish let's put together a program that uses many of the BGI features that we have been discussing. Of course, this program won't demonstrate everything that we have learned in this chapter, but it will show you the simplicity and the power of graphics programming with the BGI.

The program uses BGI tools to draw landscape scenes that are generated using fractal geometry. Each scene is designed with a mountain skyline and an ocean shoreline topped off with a glowing red sun. A sample scene created by the program is shown in Figure 1.4. The contours of the mountains and the shoreline are both created with fractals. We'll discuss fractals shortly, but first let's look at an important BGI function used in the program that we have not yet discussed.

The sky, the water, and the sun are all painted using a procedure called **FloodFill**. This routine simply fills a bounded region of any size or shape with the current fill settings and drawing color. The procedure declaration for **FloodFill** is:

```
procedure FloodFill(x, y: integer; BorderColor: word);
```

Here the parameters **x** and **y** specify what is called a *seed point* and the parameter **BorderColor** indicates the color of the border of the bounded region. The seed point should be a coordinate point that is somewhere inside the bounded region.

Now let's take a quick look at fractal geometry. Fractal technology was created by mathematical researchers who were attempting to efficiently model the complexity of nature. By using mathematical formulas, these researchers found it possible to create realistic three-dimensional scenes of mountains complete with trees, lakes, bolts of lightning, and many other natural objects.

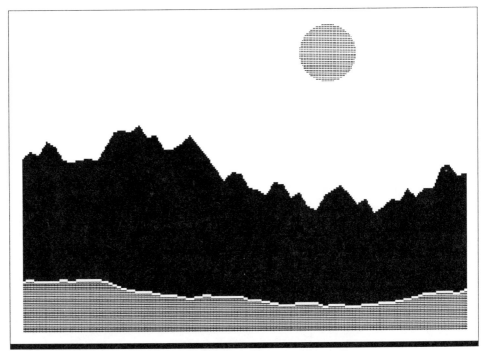

Figure 1.4. Sample output of Fractal.Pas

Our example program uses a fractal routine to generate a view of a coastal range against a shoreline. The contour lines of the mountains and the ocean actually begin as straight horizontal lines that extend across the screen. A procedure called **Fractal** is invoked to contort these lines so that they take on the jaggedness of a mountain skyline or the meanderings of a shoreline.

The **Fractal** procedure calls the routine **Subdivide** which actually performs the *fractalization*. This routine takes a line segment, which is passed to it as two endpoints, calculates the midpoint for the line segment, and then uses the midpoint to *bend* the line up or down. The line is bent by a random amount. This adjusted midpoint, which will later correspond to the y value to be used when drawing the line at that point, is saved in a global array called **Frctl**. The fractalization continues by taking the line segments to the left and right of the midpoint and bending them at their midpoints, too. Their segments are subdivided and bent in a similar fashion and the process is repeated until the segments become too small to subdivide. The resulting line is a connected series of small segments that vary in the y direction. Figure 1.5 shows the stages of the fractalization on a sample line segment. Note that the amount the line segment is bent decreases as the line segment is subdivided into smaller pieces.

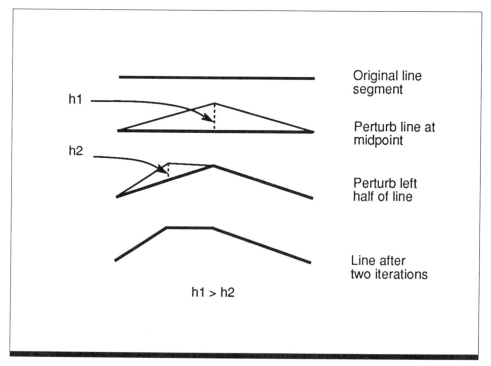

Figure 1.5. The process of fractalizing a line

The amount that the midpoint is bent, or perturbed, is randomly calculated. This gives the line a reasonably natural look. However, there are several variables that we'll be using to help control the way that the lines are generated. Let's start by examining the parameters used with the **Fractal** procedure. Here is its declaration:

```
procedure Fractal(y1, y2, MaxLevel: integer; H, Scale: real);
```

The last parameter in **Fractal**, called **Scale**, partially defines the amount of the perturbation at each step in the fractalization. In addition, the preceding parameter called **H** specifies a decay factor that is multiplied against the current perturbation value in **Scale** at each subdivision of the line to reduce the size of **Scale** with each smaller and smaller line segment. In other words, initially, line segments vary greatly, but as they get smaller, they are perturbed less and less. This creates a realistic roughness in many scenes. In fact, it is the combination of these two values, **Scale** and **H**, that we'll use to control the outcome of the fractal line. For example, the mountain skyline is much rougher than the shoreline so its **H** decay factor is set to only 0.5 (1 is the smoothest and close to 0 is the roughest). In addition, the mountains should be large, so **Scale** is initially set to a rather large value of 50. The shoreline, however, is supposed to be much smoother, so its **H** factor is 0.9, and **Scale** is assigned a value of 30.0.

The key to fractal geometry is the randomness that is applied to the line, surface, or shape that is being fractalized. Here, the Turbo Pascal routines **Random** and **Randomize** are combined to return a random value based on the clock in the PC. These random values are used to determine how much to perturb each line segment. Since the clock is used in the random number process, the program generates a different landscape scene each time it is run.

Finally, you may also want to try experimenting with the **H** and **Scale** values passed to the fractal routine for the mountains and shoreline in order to see what effect these parameters have on the fractalized surface.

```
program FractalProgram;
{ This program combines several of the features of the BGI with a
  fractal routine to create a fractalized landscape scene. The scene
  will be slightly different each time you run it. Press any key to
  quit the program after the scene is displayed.
}
uses
  Graph, Crt;
const
  MaxSize  = 1000;     { The fractalized array has this room }
```

```
     MaxLevel = 6;         { Number of times line is cut in half }
     Water    = 1;         { Color of the water  on CGAC3 = blue }
     Sun      = 2;         { Color of the sun -- on CGAC3 = red }
     Sky      = 3;         { Color of the sky -- on CGAC3 = white }
  var                      { Array used to hold fractalized lines }
     Frctl: array[1..MaxSize] of real;
     GDriver, GMode: integer;


function Power(Num, Pow: real): real;
{ Returns Num to the Pow }
begin
   if Num = 0 then Power := 0
   else Power := Exp(Pow * Ln(Num));
end;


procedure Subdivide(P1, P2: integer; Std, Ratio: real);
{ This is the workhorse routine for the fractalization process.
  It computes the midpoint between the two points: p1 and p2,
  and then perturbs it by a random factor which is scaled by std.
  Then it calls itself, to fractalize the line segments to the
  left and right of the midpoint. This process continues until
  no more divisions can be made.
}
var
   MidPnt: integer;
   StdMid: real;


begin                                 { Break the line at the midpoint }
   MidPnt := (P1 + P2) div 2;         { of point 1 and point 2 }
{ If midpoint is unique from point 1 and point 2, then perturb it
  randomly according to the equation shown
}
   if (MidPnt <> P1) and (MidPnt <> P2) then begin
      Frctl[MidPnt] := (Frctl[P1] + Frctl[P2]) / 2 +
                    (Random(16) - 8.0) / 8.0 * Std;
{ Then fractalize the line segments to the left and right
  of the midpoint by calling subdivide again. Note that the
  scale factor used to perturb each fractalized point, is
  decreased each call by the amount in ratio.
}
```

```
      StdMid := Std * Ratio;
      Subdivide(P1,MidPnt,StdMid,Ratio);  { Fractalize left side }
      Subdivide(MidPnt,P2,Stdmid,Ratio);  { Fractalize right side }
    end
end;


procedure Fractal(Y1, Y2, MaxLevel: integer; H, Scale: real);
{ This is the main fractal routine. It fractalizes a line in one
  dimension only. In this case, the y dimension. The fractalized line
  is put into the global array: frctl. The parameter maxlevel specifies
  how much to break up the line, and h is a number between 0 and 1
  which specifies the roughness of the line (1 is smoothest), and scale
  is a scale factor which tells how much to perturb each line segment.
}
var
   First, Last: integer;
   Ratio, Std: real;

begin
   First := 1;                          { Determine the bounds of }
   Last := Round(Power(2.0,MaxLevel));{ array that will be used }
   Frctl[First] := Y1;                  { Use y1 and y2 as start }
   Frctl[Last] := Y2;                   { and end points of line }
   Ratio := 1.0 / Power(2.0,H);         { Defines fractalization }
   Std := Scale * Ratio;                { decays at each level }
   Subdivide(First,Last,Std,Ratio);   { Begin the fractalization }
end;


procedure DrawFractal;
{ This routine displays a fractalized line. The frctl array
  holds y values. The x values are equally spaced across the
  screen depending on the number of levels calculated.
}
var
   i, x, XInc, l: integer;

begin
   { Number of points in Frctl used }
   l := Round(Power(2.0,MaxLevel));
```

```
      XInc := GetMaxX div 1 * 3 div 2;      { Calculate the x increment }
      MoveTo(0,100);                        { used to draw each line }
      x := 0;
      for i := 1 to 1 do begin             { Draw the lines, one at a time }
        LineTo(x,Round(Frctl[i]));          { using the y values in frctl }
        Inc(x,XInc);
      end
  end;

begin
    GDriver := CGA;                  { Sets the screen to CGAC3 which has }
    GMode := CGAC3;                  { black=0, cyan=1, magenta=2, white=3 }
    InitGraph(GDriver, GMode, '');

    Randomize;                               { Initialize random function }
    Rectangle(0,0,GetMaxX,GetMaxY);          { Draw a frame for picture }
    SetColor(Sky);                           { Prepare to draw the sky }
    Fractal(100,100,MaxLevel,0.5,50.0);  { Fractalize the skyline }
    DrawFractal;                             { and then display it }
    SetFillStyle(SolidFill,Sky);             { Use floodfill to draw }
    FloodFill(1,1,Sky);                      { color in the sky }

    SetColor(White);                         { Draw shoreline with white }
    Fractal(170,170,MaxLevel,0.9,30.0);  { line. Use smoother }
    DrawFractal;                             { settings. Color the screen }
    SetFillStyle(SolidFill,Water);           { below the shoreline with }
    FloodFill(1,GetMaxY-1,White);            { the color Water. }

    SetFillStyle(SolidFill,Sun);             { Draw a sun with }
    SetColor(Sun);                           { a circle floodfilled with }
    Circle(GetMaxX-100,40,20);               { the color Sun }
    FloodFill(GetMaxX-100,50,Sun);
    repeat until KeyPressed;                 { Hold screen until key hit }
    CloseGraph;                              { Exit graphics mode }
  end.
```

The BGI Drawing Functions

The heart of any graphics system consists of its drawing routines. As we saw in Chapter 1, the BGI provides a rich set of drawing procedures and functions that support several graphics hardware and video modes. In this chapter we're going to show you how you can use the basic drawing functions in your Turbo Pascal programs.

We'll begin with the fundamental BGI drawing routines—the pixel-oriented routines. We'll then work with the more general drawing procedures that include routines to draw rectangles, circles, ellipses, polygons, and other shapes. In addition, we'll explore region filling techniques and develop a program to help us experiment with our own fill patterns and designs. Along the way, we'll take a close look at the **PutImage** and **GetImage** procedures which we'll use to introduce programming techniques for creating animation.

Working with Pixels

As we've seen in Chapter 1, the pixel is the basic building block for PC graphics. By grouping pixels, we can draw lines, figures, textures, and other graphics objects. Of course, if we were to construct all our graphics scenes at the pixel level, we'd have a tremendous programming task before us. Nevertheless, pixels and the routines that can manipulate them are an essential element of a graphics toolkit.

The BGI includes two pixel routines, **PutPixel** and **GetPixel**, which we briefly introduced in our quick tour in Chapter 1. To refresh your memory, **PutPixel** displays one pixel at a specified screen location and **GetPixel** returns the current color of any pixel on the screen. In the following section we'll use both of these to illustrate how pixels are accessed and displayed.

Plotting a Single Pixel

The **PutPixel** procedure plots a pixel at an x and y coordinate using a specified color. It is declared as:

```
procedure PutPixel(x, y: integer; PixelColor: word);
```

The location where the pixel is displayed is relative to the origin of the current viewport. Although the valid range of x and y depend on the size of the viewport, initially the full screen is used. Therefore, the functions **GetMaxX** and **GetMaxY** can be used to determine the maximum extents of x and y, respectively.

The **PixelColor** parameter specifies the pixel's color. Actually, the **PixelColor** parameter specifies the index location of the palette from which the color is chosen. This parameter, like the x and y coordinates, has a restricted range of values for each video mode. This range extends from zero to the maximum color value returned by the **GetMaxColor** function. In actuality, **GetMaxColor** returns the valid range of indexes into the palette table.

General Drawing Commands

Although you can draw almost anything using pixels, Turbo Pascal furnishes numerous drawing procedures and functions that simplify the task. These drawing routines can be divided into the following categories:

- Lines
- Rectangles
- Polygons
- Arcs, circles and ellipses

We'll now take a closer look at each of these categories.

Drawing Lines

Although a line is always the shortest distance between two points, Turbo Pascal provides three different ways of drawing one. Table 2.1 presents a list of the line

Table 2.1. Line drawing and positioning routines

Routines	Description
Line	Draws a line from (x1,y1) to (x2,y2)
LineTo	Draws a line from the current position to the point (x,y)
LineRel	Draws a line from the current position in the relative direction (dx,dy)
MoveRel	Moves the current position a relative amount
MoveTo	Moves the current position to the point (x,y)

drawing and related positioning routines. As shown in Table 2.1, there are essentially two types of line drawing procedures: absolute and relative. Both, however, always use the current drawing color and line style when drawing a line.

Drawing Lines with Absolute Coordinates

We'll start our discussion of the line drawing routines by looking at the two procedures, **Line** and **LineTo**, which use absolute coordinates. Let's begin by looking at the procedure **Line**. It takes two x and y coordinate pairs that specify the endpoints of the line that it is to draw. A typical call to **Line** is:

```
Line(5, 30, 200, 180);
```

This statement, if executed, will draw a line from the point (5,30) to the point (200,180). Similarly, a triangle can be drawn with the following code sequence

```
Line(x1, y1, x2, y2);
Line(x2, y2, x3, y3);
Line(x3, y3, x1, y1);
```

where (x1,y1), (x2,y2), and (x3,y3) are the vertices of the triangle.

An alternative technique for drawing lines consists of using the **LineTo** and **MoveTo** procedures that allow you to draw lines by moving in discrete steps. Both of these routines take one coordinate pair as a parameter. The **LineTo** procedure is used to draw a line from the current position to a coordinate specified by **LineTo**. After a call to **LineTo**, the current position is updated to the coordinate pair specified with **LineTo**.

The **MoveTo** procedure is used to move the current position as needed. Normally, it is used when setting the beginning of a line segment. The current position may be effected by other graphics functions, too. For example, when you open a viewport the current position is always set to (0,0).

To draw the same triangle that was presented in our previous example using **MoveTo** and **LineTo**, you would use:

```
MoveTo(x1, y1);
LineTo(x2, y2);
LineTo(x3, y3);
LineTo(x1, y1);
```

In some cases, **LineTo** provides a more convenient way of drawing line figures. For example, if you are calculating points for a figure while you are drawing it but are not saving them as you go, the **MoveTo** and **LineTo** pair may be an ideal way of drawing the lines.

Drawing Lines with Relative Coordinates

In some of your applications, you may need to draw lines using relative coordinates. For instance, you may want to draw lines relative to other points or lines. The **LineRel** and **MoveRel** procedures are provided for this reason.

By way of an example, our triangle can be drawn using:

```
MoveTo(x1, y1);
LineRel(x2-x1, y2-y1);
LineRel(x3-x2, y3-y2);
LineRel(x1-x3, y1-y3);
```

Of course, this example is rather poor, since it leads to a lot of extra operations, so clearly it's not the best solution for this case. However, if we were calculating our way along a curved surface, the **LineRel** routine might be the best choice.

Setting a Line Style

In the previous section we explored several ways to draw lines using the BGI. The BGI also allows us to specify its thickness and its style. By default, all lines are drawn as solid lines, 1 pixel wide using the current drawing color. However, we can change each of these drawing parameters.

For instance, in Chapter 1 we learned how to change the current drawing color with the **SetColor** procedure. In addition, the BGI supports four predefined line patterns as well as user-defined line styles. In the next section, we'll look at how we can change the line style and its thickness.

Predefined Line Patterns

The BGI provides the **SetLineStyle** procedure to alter the line type and width of all lines drawn. Its declaration is:

```
procedure SetLineStyle(LineStyle, Pattern, Thickness: word);
```

The **LineStyle** parameter, which can be set to one of five values as defined in the unit **Graph**, specifies the line type that is used when a line is drawn. Its possible values are:

Constant	Value
SolidLn	0
DottedLn	1
CenterLn	2
DashedLn	3
UserBitLn	4

The first four constants specify predefined line patterns and are shown in Figure 2.1. These enable you to draw solid lines, dotted lines, and dashed lines. You can also create your own line style by using the **UserBitLn** constant.

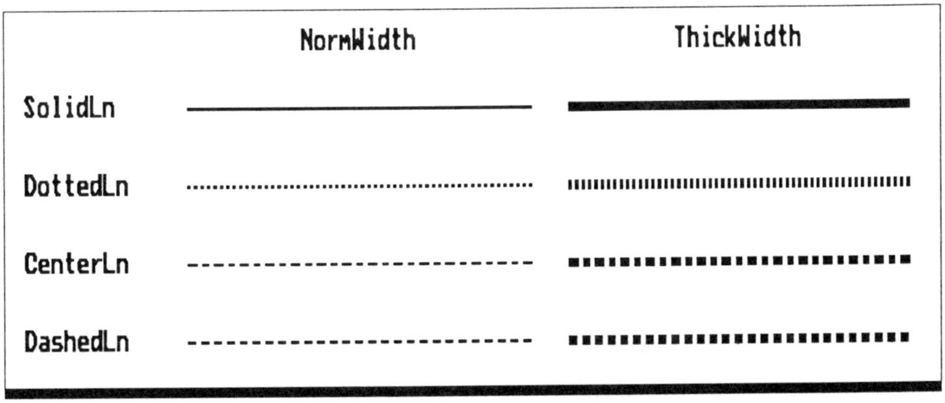

Figure 2.1. The four predefined line styles

The second parameter in **SetLineStyle** is used when a user-defined line pattern is desired. If, however, you're using one of the four predefined patterns, you should use a value of 0 for this parameter. The last parameter, **Thickness**, specifies the thickness that all lines are to be drawn. There are two possibilities here:

Constant	Value	Line Thickness
NormWidth	1	1 pixel thick
ThickWidth	3	3 pixels thick

Combining this information, suppose we want to draw a series of dashed, thick lines using the current drawing color. In order to do this, we must first make a call to **SetLineStyle**:

```
SetLineStyle(DashedLn,0,ThickWidth);
```

Once this is done, all lines that are drawn will use these line settings.

Determining the Current Line Style

Now let's look at how the BGI enables us to determine the current line settings. This feature is particularly useful when we need to save the current line settings so that they can be changed and later restored. Fortunately, the BGI provides the procedure **GetLineSettings** which is specifically designed for this task. To understand how it works, we must introduce the record type **LineSettingsType** that is used for storing the current line settings. It is defined in the **Graph** as:

```
LineSettingsType = record
   LineStyle: word;
   Pattern: word;
   Thickness: word;
end;
```

This record type is important because **GetLineSettings** expects a record of this type to be passed to it and will return the various line parameters within its fields. The procedural declaration for **GetLineSettings** is:

```
procedure GetLineSettings(var LineInfo: LineSettingsType);
```

Therefore, to retrieve the current line settings, you can use the statements:

```
SavedLineInfo: LineSettingsType;     { Declare line record }
GetLineSettings(SavedLineInfo);      { Save line settings }
```

Later, to restore the line settings, you can use the **SetLineStyle** procedure:

```
SetLineStyle(SavedLineInfo.LineStyle,
            SavedLineInfo.Pattern, SavedLineInfo.Thickness);
```

User-Defined Line Styles

Besides the four predefined line styles shown in Figure 2.1, the BGI also provides us with a way of defining our own line styles. This is accomplished with the **SetLineStyle** procedure and the first two of its three parameters.

As mentioned before, the leftmost parameter of **SetLineStyle** declares the type of line that is used and must in this case be set to **UserBitLn** or a value of 4. The second parameter, however, actually defines the line pattern. It is a 16-bit binary pattern that encodes the way that lines are to be drawn. Each bit in the pattern is equivalent to 1 pixel along a 16 pixel stretch of a line. If the bit is on, all pixels in its corresponding position on the line are displayed with the current drawing color. If the bit is a 0, its corresponding pixels are not painted or changed. Therefore, a user-defined line pattern that defines a solid line can be created by the procedure call:

```
SetLineStyle(UserBitLn, $FFFF, NormWidth);
```

The hex value $FFFF will turn all pixels on along the 16-bit line pattern and will effectively cause solid lines to be drawn. Similarly, to draw a dashed line where every other pixel is on, you merely need to use a bit pattern with every other bit set to a 1. This can be accomplished with the line:

```
SetLineStyle(UserBitLn, $AAAA, NormWidth);
```

Figure 2.2 shows several line patterns that can be generated by varying the user-defined line pattern.

Drawing Rectangles

All the PC graphics that we'll create throughout this book could be produced with the pixel and line drawing procedures that we've already presented. The BGI, however, also provides several higher-level drawing routines that can help us

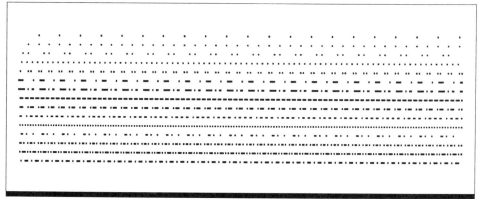

Figure 2.2. Several user-defined line patterns

generate graphics. The first of these procedures we'll present is **Rectangle**. As you can probably guess, it is used for drawing rectangles. Its declaration as given in **Graph** is:

```
procedure Rectangle(Left, Top, Right, Bottom: integer);
```

The four parameters specify the pixel coordinates of the top-left and bottom-right corners of the rectangle. When using **Rectangle**, keep in mind that it draws only the perimeter of a rectangle. In later sections of this chapter, we'll see how the **Bar** and **Bar3D** procedures can be used to draw filled rectangles. Like most of the procedures we'll cover from this point on, **Rectangle** uses the current drawing color and line style settings and is drawn relative to the current viewport.

Working with Polygons

The BGI also includes a generic routine to draw polygons, appropriately called **DrawPoly**. It takes an array of points and draws line segments between the points using the current line style and drawing color. In effect, **DrawPoly** is comparable to making a series of calls to a line routine. Here is how it is declared in **Graph**:

```
procedure DrawPoly(NumPoints: word, var PolyPoints);
```

The first parameter specifies the number of *coordinates* that are sent to **DrawPoly**. The second parameter, **PolyPoints**, is an untyped parameter which points to an array of records of type **PointType** that specify x and y coordinates that are to be joined by line segments. The record **PointType** is defined in the unit **Graph** as:

```
PointType = record
   x, y: integer;
end;
```

Therefore, if we want to draw an open three-sided figure, **NumPoints** should be set to a value of 3 and the array of coordinate points should contain three PointType structures that specify the three line endpoints. For example, let's say that the three points are (10, 30), (300, 30), and (100, 90). The following lines of code would draw this figure for us.

```
Points: array[1..3] of PointType = ((x:10,  y:30), (x:300, y:30),
                                    (x:100, y:90));
DrawPoly(3,Points);
```

The **DrawPoly** procedure does not automatically close off the polygon. If you want a closed polygon, you must add a point to the end of the **Points** array which is the same as the first point. Therefore, to close the polygon presented in the previous example, we can use the following code:

```
Points: array[1..4] of PointType = ((x:10,  y:30), (x:300, y:30),
                                    (x:100, y:90), (x:10,  y:30));
DrawPoly(4,Points);
```

Note that the first and last coordinate pairs in the points array are the same and that the **NumPoints** parameter has been increased by one to accommodate this.

Arcs, Circles, and Ellipses

By now you're probably wondering if the BGI can do more than draw lines. Fortunately, it can. The BGI provides the procedures **Arc**, **Circle**, **Ellipse**, **PieSlice**, **FillEllipse**, and **Sector** that can each draw curved figures. We'll begin by looking at the first three of these. The **PieSlice**, **FillEllipse**, and **Sector** procedures will be presented later in the "Filling Regions" section later in this chapter.

Each of the curve drawing routines uses the current drawing color. They are, however, not completely affected by the line styles. In particular, the perimeters of the objects are always drawn solid, yet they are affected by the current setting of the line thickness. In addition, like all the procedures thus far, the coordinates of these routines are taken relative to the current viewport. Let's now look at the **Arc** procedure.

Drawing Arcs

The **Arc** procedure draws a portion of a circle or a complete circle. It is defined as:

```
procedure Arc(x, y: integer; StAngle, EndAngle, Radius: word);
```

The first two parameters specify a screen coordinate for the center point of the arc. The **StAngle** and **EndAngle** parameters are angles that specify the sweep of the arc. These values are in degrees and are measured counterclockwise starting from the 3 o'clock position. The last parameter dictates the radius of the circle. This value is measured in pixels from the center of the arc along the current row until it intersects the arc or the location on the screen where it would intersect the arc if it were swept to its 0 angle. This description is important when you consider that the aspect ratio of a given screen mode may cause the radius to actually be a different number of pixels in size and in length at different angles along the circle.

For example, suppose we want to draw an arc that extends 15 degrees from the horizon. For the sake of this example, let's center the arc at (200, 100) and give it a radius of 100. The line of code that will produce this arc is:

```
Arc(200, 100, 0, 15, 100);
```

If you count the pixels along the radius of this arc, you'll be able to verify that the radius is 100 pixels along its horizon.

Arc Endpoints

Sometimes it is useful to be able to tell where the endpoints of an arc are located. For example, there are times when you may want to connect a line with the end points of an arc or link a series of arcs together. To accomplish this, the BGI provides the procedure **GetArcCoords**. Its procedural declaration is:

```
procedure GetArcCoords(var ArcCoords: ArcCoordsType);
```

The only parameter of **GetArcCoords** is a record of type **ArcCoordsType**. This record stores the endpoints of the last arc drawn and its center location. It is defined in **Graph** as:

```
ArcCoordsType = record
  X, Y: integer;
```

```
    XStart, YStart: integer;
    XEnd, YEnd: integer;
end;
```

By way of example, suppose we want to draw the perimeter of a hemisphere. To do this we can use a combination of the **Arc** and **Line** procedures. To properly connect the arc with a line segment, we'll use **GetArcCoords** to determine exactly where the endpoints of the arc are and consequently where the line should be drawn. The following program demonstrates this process by drawing a hemisphere at the center of the screen with a radius one fourth its width.

```
program HemiSphere;
{ Draws a hemisphere at the center of the screen }
uses
  Graph;
const
  GDriver: integer = Detect;
var
  GMode: integer;
  ArcCoords: ArcCoordsType;

begin
  InitGraph(GDriver,GMode,'');
  Arc(GetMaxX div 2,GetMaxY div 2, 0, 180,GetMaxX div 4);
  GetArcCoords(ArcCoords);
  Line(ArcCoords.XStart, ArcCoords.YStart,
       ArcCoords.XEnd,ArcCoords.YEnd);
  Readln;
  CloseGraph;
end.
```

Circles and Ellipses

Although **Arc** can be used to draw a complete circle (by specifying a start angle of 0 degrees and an ending angle of 360 degrees), a better method of accomplishing the same task is to use the BGI's **Circle** procedure. It is declared as:

```
procedure Circle(x, y: integer; Radius: word);
```

The **x** and **y** parameters specify the center of the circle and the last parameter—its radius. As is the case with **Arc**, the radius of the circle refers to the number of pixels from the center of the circle along its horizontal axis to its perimeter.

Note that **Circle** only draws the perimeter of a circle. In order to draw a filled circle, you must use **PieSlice** or alternatively flood fill the region as we will see later.

Another curved shape supported by the BGI is an ellipse. This shape is drawn with the procedure **Ellipse** which operates much like **Arc**, since it can be used to draw a portion of an ellipse or the whole thing. The procedural declaration for **Ellipse** is:

```
procedure Ellipse(x, y: integer; StAngle, EndAngle: word;
                  XRadius, YRadius: word);
```

Most of these parameters function in the same manner as those from the previous two routines. However, in order to achieve a wide variety of elliptic shapes **Ellipse** allows you to specify the radius in both the y and x direction. The **Ellipse** procedure does not affect the interior of each ellipse that it draws. As we'll see, the **Sector** and **FillEllipse** procedures are used to draw filled elliptic regions.

Fundamentals of Animation

Let's take a break from the drawing commands so that we can focus on the **GetImage** and **PutImage** procedures. These procedures will be needed in the next section when we develop an interactive program to create our own fill patterns.

Basically, **GetImage** and **PutImage** are used to manipulate rectangular regions of the graphics screen. Using these procedures, we can easily cut, paste, move, or change regions of the screen without having to worry about screen memory addresses. We can, therefore, concentrate on using **GetImage** and **PutImage** for tasks such as animation effects, supporting pop-up windows, or allowing graphics objects to be easily edited and moved.

The declaration for **GetImage** is:

```
procedure GetImage(Left, Top, Right, Bottom: integer; var BitMap);
```

The first four parameters of the procedure specify the top-left and bottom-right pixel boundaries of a rectangular region on the screen that is to be copied. This copied image is saved in an array pointed to by its last parameter, **BitMap**. The size of the **BitMap** array is dependent on the size of the screen image being saved and the current graphics mode. Remember that each mode supports a different screen resolution that requires different amounts of memory. To determine the size of a screen image, the BGI provides the **ImageSize** function. This function takes the same pixel boundaries as **GetImage** to calculate the size of the screen that is to be saved. Based on these boundaries, the function returns the number of bytes that should be allocated for the **BitMap** array. For example, suppose we want to copy the region of the screen bounded by (10,10) and (100,100). First, we need to declare and allocate space for the **BitMap** as shown:

```
ScreenImage: pointer;
GetMem(ScreenImage, ImageSize(10, 10, 100, 100));
```

Next, the image can be copied into the **ScreenImage** block of memory by a call to **GetImage**:

```
GetImage(10, 10, 100, 100, ScreenImage^);
```

Note that the ^ symbol must be used to properly reference the **ScreenImage** memory when calling **GetImage**. Now that we have a copy of the screen image in **BitMap**, we can copy it to a different screen location with **PutImage**. The declaration for **PutImage** is:

```
procedure PutImage(Left, Top: integer; var BitMap; Op: word);
```

The first two parameters specify the top-left location where the image passed to the procedure is supposed to be aligned to. Note that **PutImage** does not require the bottom-right boundaries, since this information is actually saved within **BitMap**. The last parameter of **PutImage**, called **Op**, specifies how **BitMap** is supposed to be copied to the screen. It can take on the following values:

Constant	Value	Description
CopyPut	0	Copy bit image to screen as is
XorPut	1	Exclusive-or bit image and screen
OrPut	2	Inclusive-or bit image and screen
AndPut	3	And bit image and screen
NotPut	4	Copy inverse of bitmap to screen

Therefore in our example, if we want to copy the bit map image to the location (110, 10) on the screen, we could use the statement:

```
PutImage(110, 10, ScreenImage^, CopyPut);
```

Once again note that the ^ symbol must be used to properly access the **ScreenImage** memory. Similarly, if we want to invert the portion of the image that we saved earlier we could use the statement:

```
PutImage(10, 10, ScreenImage^, NotPut);
```

This can be useful in highlighting portions of a screen. Figure 2.3 shows the effects produced by each of the image copying options listed previously.

Another extremely useful possibility with **PutImage** is to use the **XorPut** operation. It exclusive-ORs the bit-map image with the screen image. At a binary level the exclusive-OR operation sets all bits in the screen memory to a one if either but not both corresponding bits in the bit image and screen image are a 1. If both bits are 0 or 1, then the corresponding bit in the screen image is set to a 0. What makes this particular feature so useful is that copying an image over itself, in many cases, will erase any objects in the region and then repeating the process will make it reappear. This can be valuable for some types of animation. For example, in a program later in this chapter we'll use the **XorPut** option to help move a cursor across the screen without having to worry about modifying the screen as it is moved.

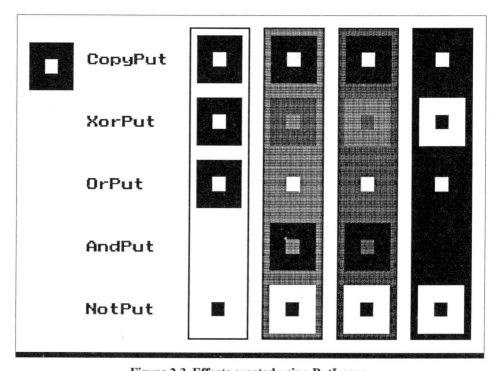

Figure 2.3. Effects created using PutImage

Note that the results of a **PutImage** operation using the exclusive-OR function will depend on the current colors on the screen and the colors in **BitMap**.

The other two operations supported by **PutImage** are the **AndPut** and **OrPut** selections. These can be used to achieve various special effects and can even be combined to produce other types of results not directly possible with any of the predefined operations.

Finally, there are a few considerations that you should keep in mind while using **GetImage** and **PutImage**. First, although these procedures are positioned relative to the current viewport coordinates, they are not affected by viewport clipping. However, if any portion of the **BitMap** image extends beyond the screen boundaries, the whole image operation may be clipped. Both conditions may cause problems when moving objects about a region; however, most of the time this is what you want.

Another area that may lead to a restriction when using **GetImage** and **PutImage** is related to the maximum size allowed for any bit-map array. These procedures are designed to accept images that are 64k in size or smaller. This may seem like more than enough memory for any situation; however, when dealing with graphics screens this memory restriction can quickly become a problem. For example, in many of the 640 by 200 modes we would be unable to save the entire screen at once, since it would require more than 64k for the bit-map memory.

Filling Regions

Thus far we have looked only at the graphics routines that draw the outlines of objects. Turbo Pascal also provides several procedures that can draw figures filled with either one of several predefined patterns or a user-defined pattern. These procedures are listed in Table 2.2.

Table 2.2. The BGI draw and fill routines

Routine	Description
Bar	Draws a filled bar without an outline
Bar3D	Draws a three-dimensional filled bar with an outline
FillPoly	Draws a filled polygon
FillEllipse	Draws a filled elliptic region
PieSlice	Draws a pie slice and can be used to draw a filled circle
Sector	Draws a filled elliptically filled region

Before we proceed, let's take a quick look at the procedures listed in Table 2.2. (Refer to the program **ShowFill.PAS** in the section "Filling Figures," Chapter 1, for a demonstration of how these routines work.) The **Bar** and **Bar3D** procedures are similar. There are two key differences, however. The **Bar3D** procedure draws a three-dimensional bar while the **Bar** routine simply draws a filled rectangular region. We'll explore this more in Chapter 5. Actually, **Bar3D** can also be used to draw a two-dimensional bar also, by setting its depth to zero. However—and here is the other major difference—**Bar3D** draws an outline to its region in the current drawing color while **Bar** does not have any outline. This distinction will become important at many times throughout this book. You should also be aware that **Bar3D** has an additional parameter called **TopFlag** which indicates whether a three-dimensional bar should be topped-off. If **True,** the procedure shades the top of the three-dimensional bar. Drawing a three-dimensional bar without a top can be useful if you want to stack several bars on top of one another.

The procedure **FillPoly** is also much like its counterpart **DrawPoly.** Both are used the same way. The only difference is that **FillPoly** draws the polygon passed to it, as well as filling its interior.

Finally, **PieSlice** and **Sector** can draw filled pie slices and filled elliptical shapes, respectively. Each has parameters to specify where the pie slice or sector is supposed to start and end. Both angles begin at the 3 o'clock position relative to the center point (x, y) of the figures.

A final note on **PieSlice, FillEllipse,** and **Sector** is in order. Recall that the BGI does not directly include a procedure that can draw a filled circle. We've suggested that the **PieSlice** and **Sector** procedures can be used. The idea is to use a start angle of 0 degrees and an end angle of 360 degrees to draw a completely filled circle. However, note that both of these routines draw a perimeter in the current drawing color which will surround the shape as well as extend into its center. If the interior and border are different colors you will see a line extending from the center of the circle to the 3 o'clock position on the border of the circle. The only way to avoid this is to make the border and the fill pattern the same color. The other approach is to use the **FloodFill** procedure as we will discuss in the section "Working with Flood Fills" later in this chapter.

Now let's get back to the fill patterns. The BGI supplies 12 predefined fill patterns that the procedures listed in Table 2.2 can use. They are enumerated in **Graph** and are listed in Table 2.3. Figure 2.4 displays each of these fill patterns as they appear in a filled rectangle. Besides the predefined fill patterns, you can use **UserFill** to add your own fill pattern. We'll soon look at this. By default all fill operations use **SolidFill** and paint the interior regions with the color returned by **GetMaxColor**—most often this will be white.

Table 2.3. Predefined fill patterns

Constant	Value	Description
EmptyFill	0	Fill with background color
SolidFill	1	FIll with fill color
LineFill	2	Fill with horizontal lines
LtSlashFill	3	Fill with thin left to right slashes
SlashFill	4	Fill with thick left to right slashes
BkSlashFill	5	Fill with thick right to left slashes
LtBkSlashFill	6	Fill with thin right to left slashes
HatchFill	7	Fill with a light hatch pattern
XHatchFill	8	Fill with a heavy crosshatch
InterleaveFill	9	Fill with interleaving lines
WideDotFill	10	Fill with widely spaced dots
CloseDotFill	11	Fill with closely spaced dots

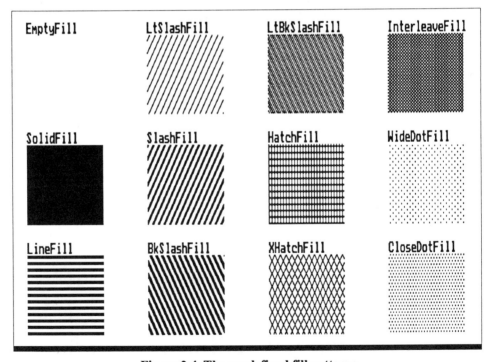

Figure 2.4. The predefined fill patterns

Setting the Fill Pattern

The fill pattern is selected by the **SetFillStyle** procedure. The declaration for this routine is:

```
procedure SetFillStyle(Pattern, Color: word);
```

The **Pattern** parameter is one of the fill styles listed in Table 2.3. The **Color** parameter is the color to be used when drawing the interior. All parts of the interior that are not part of the pattern are painted with the background color. One quirk that you may run across here is that in CGA high-resolution mode, all black patterns are drawn the same as white patterns.

User-Defined Fill Patterns

Defining a user-defined fill pattern is not done through **SetFillStyle**. Instead, the procedure **SetFillPattern** is used. As shown below, **SetFillPattern** is passed an 8 by 8 binary pattern representing the fill pattern to use and the color that it is to be drawn as. Its declaration is:

```
procedure SetFillPattern(Pattern: FillPatternType; Color: word);
```

The first parameter, called **Pattern**, is a byte array that specifies the pattern to use in the fill operation. Its type, **FillPatternType**, is predefined in the unit **Graph** as:

```
FillPatternType: array[1..8] of byte;
```

It is an array 8 bytes long where each byte represents one row of 8 pixels in the pattern. For example, a solid fill pattern can be defined as:

```
FillPattern: FillPatternType = ($FF, $FF, $FF, $FF, $FF, $FF, $FF, $FF);
```

Similarly, a checker pattern of alternating on and off pixels can be declared as:

```
FillPattern: FillPatternType = ($AA, $55, $AA, $55, $AA, $55, $AA, $55);
```

To set the current fill pattern to one of these user-defined patterns you can use a statement such as:

```
SetFillPattern(FillPattern, GetMaxColor);
```

Getting the Fill Pattern

As is the case with line styles, it is sometimes useful to be able to retrieve and save the current fill settings. This is often invaluable when you want to temporarily alter the fill settings. The procedure to access the current fill settings is:

```
procedure GetFillSettings(var FillInfo: FillSettingsType);
```

As you can see, it uses a record of type **FillSettingsType** to return the fill settings. This record is defined in the unit **Graph** as:

```
FillSettingsType = record
  Pattern: word;
  Color: word;
end;
```

Retrieving the fill settings is somewhat complicated by the user-defined fill patterns. If you are not using user-defined fill patterns all you need to do is call **GetFillSettings** and it will return the pattern style and the fill color. However, if the current fill style is a user-defined fill pattern, the **Pattern** field in the record will be set to **UserFill**. Clearly, this can be used to tell that a user-defined pattern is being used, however, it doesn't tell what the pattern is. Thus whenever you want to save a user-defined pattern you must make an additional call to a procedure called **GetFillPattern** to retrieve the user-defined fill pattern.

The procedure **GetFillPattern** is defined as:

```
procedure GetFillPattern(var FillPattern: FillPatternType);
```

It copies the user-defined fill pattern that is currently being used into the array **FillPattern** (of type **FillPatternType** defined earlier) which is passed to it.

Finally, let's say that we want to save the current fill settings, no matter what they are, perform some operations, and then restore the settings. To accomplish this, the following excerpted lines of code can be used:

```
SaveUserPtrn: FillPatternType;      { Declare space for the }
SaveFill: FillSettingsType;         { user-defined pattern }
                                    { and the fill settings }
GetFillSettings(SaveFill);          { Retrieve fill settings }

if SaveFill.Pattern = Userfill then { If user-defined fill }
   GetFillPattern(SaveUserPtrn);    { pattern, save it }
```

```
{ ... code which can change fill settings ... }
if SaveFill.Pattern = Userfill then { Restore fill settings }
   SetFillPattern(SaveUserPtrn, SaveFill.Color)
else
   SetFillStyle(SaveFill.Pattern, SaveFill.Color);
```

Experimenting with User-Defined Fill Patterns

There are many possible user-defined fill patterns. Visualizing these patterns is a rather complicated thing to do; so instead, we'll develop a stand-alone program that will enable us to interactively explore different fill patterns.

The **UserFill.Pas** program (see Listing 2.1) has three main components. First, there is a rectangular polygon drawn on the upper-right portion of the screen that shows a user-defined fill pattern. Adjacent to it is an exploded view of an 8 by 8 pixel pattern that you can edit using the arrow keys on the PC keypad by moving a cursor through this pattern and toggling its pixels on and off by pressing the space bar. Each time the space bar is pressed the current fill pattern is automatically updated in the polygon on the right side of the screen so you can see what the fill pattern looks like. In addition, along the lower portion of the screen you will see a valid Pascal declaration that you can use in a program to declare the pattern you see on the screen. You won't have to figure out the bit patterns by hand.

Using the Arrow Keys

The **UserFill.Pas** program relies on the keyboard for user input. More specifically, the arrow keys on the keypad are used to move the cursor around the enlarged fill pattern. These keys require special handling because each of the arrow keys generates a 2 byte sequence rather than the normal single character that most of the keyboard keys produce. Consequently, it takes two calls to **ReadKey** to acquire the full key code for the arrow keys. The question then becomes, how can we tell if we have an extended key code where we must make two calls to **ReadKey** or a normal character in the keyboard buffer? Luckily, for the keys that we are interested in, this is not much of a problem. It turns out that the first byte of each of the arrow keys is always a zero and that none of the other regular keys on the keyboard generates a single character equal to zero. Consequently, when our program reads a zero character, it knows that an extended key code is in the buffer and that it must read another byte from the keyboard buffer. This second byte can be used to decipher which arrow key was pressed. A list of these values is shown in Table 2.4.

In the mainline of **UserFill.Pas** the **case** statement tests for the extended key codes by checking for a zero value in the character that is read by **ReadKey** at the beginning of the **while** loop. If this value is zero, it anticipates that an arrow key was pressed, and reads another character from the keyboard buffer. This is the value that is actually used in the **case** statement to decide which arrow key was pressed and which action to take. These are the values listed in the third column of Table 2.4.

Table 2.4. Extended key codes for arrow keys

Arrow Key	First Byte	Second Byte
Home	$00	$47
Up	$00	$48
PGUP	$00	$49
Left	$00	$4b
Right	$00	$4d
End	$00	$4f
Down	$00	$50
PGDN	$00	$51

• Listing 2.1

```pascal
program UserFill;
{ This program enables the user to interactively experiment with various user-defined
    fill patterns. The user actually manipulates an 8 by 8 enlarged version of the
    pattern which is drawn on the left side of the screen. On the right side of the
    screen is a rectangle filled with the current fill pattern. At the bottom of the
    screen is the Pascal code for an array declaration that could be used to generate
    the current fill pattern. The user interaction allowed is:
      Arrow keys on keypad -- moves the cursor in an enlarged fill pattern
      Space bar            -- toggles the current pixel under the cursor
      ESC                  -- terminates the program
}
uses
    Graph, Crt;
const
    GDriver: integer = Detect;
```

```
   PLeft = 20;                        { Left column of the big pattern }
   PTop = 50;                         { Top row of the big pattern }
   BigPixelSize = 8;                  { The big pixels are 8 by 8 in size }
   { A few titles: }
   BigPatternTitle: string[17] = 'User Fill Pattern';
   PolyTitle: string[12] = 'Test Polygon';
   { Contains the fill pattern. Initially, it is all set off. }
   Fill: FillPatternType = ($0, $0, $0, $0, $0, $0, $0, $0);
var
   BigPixel: pointer;                 { Image used to hold a big pixel }
   Cursor: pointer;                   { Cursor image }
   ch: char;
   x, y: integer;
   GMode: integer;


procedure InitImages;
{ This initialization routine is called once to create the images
  that are used for the big pixel and the cursor
}
var
   px, py: integer;
   i, j: integer;
   Size: word;


begin
{ Create the image of a big pixel. Do this at the top-left corner of the big pattern.
  Once it is created, erase it by exclusive ORing its own image with itself.
}
   px := PLeft;
   py := PTop;
   for j := py+1 to py+BigPixelSize do begin
     for i := px+1 to px+2*BigPixelSize do begin
       PutPixel(i,j,GetMaxColor);
     end
   end;
   Size := ImageSize(px+1,py+1,px+2*BigPixelSize,py+BigPixelSize);
   GetMem(BigPixel,Size);
   GetImage(px+1,py+1,px+2*BigPixelSize,py+BigPixelSize,BigPixel^);
   PutImage(px+1,py+1,BigPixel^,XorPut);       { Erase the big pixel }
   { Next, create a small cursor image where the big pixel just was }
```

```
    px := px + 3;
    py := py + 3;
    for j := py to py+BigPixelSize-5 do begin
      for i := px to px+2*BigPixelSize-5 do begin
        PutPixel(i,j,GetMaxColor);
      end
    end;
    Size := ImageSize(px,py,px+BigPixelSize*2-5,py+BigPixelSize-5);
    GetMem(Cursor,Size);
    GetImage(px,py,px+2*BigPixelSize-5,py+BigPixelSize-5,Cursor^);
end;

procedure DrawEnlargedPattern;
{ Using a series of horizontal and vertical lines, draw an outline for the 8 by 8
  large pattern on the left side of the screen. Use dotted lines for these and when
  done, call InitImages to create the bigpixel and cursor images.
}
var
    i: integer, Right, Bottom: integer;

begin
    SetLineStyle(DottedLn,0,NormWidth);
    Right := 2 * (PLeft + (BigPixelSize-1) * (BigPixelSize + NormWidth));
    Bottom := PTop + 8 * (BigPixelSize + NormWidth);
    for i := 0 to 8 do begin                  { Draw outline of big pixels }
      Line(PLeft,PTop+i*(BigPixelSize+NormWidth),Right,
          PTop+i*(BigPixelSize+NormWidth));
      Line(PLeft+2*(i*(BigPixelSize+NormWidth)),PTop,
          PLeft+2*(i*(BigPixelSize+NormWidth)),Bottom);
    end;
    InitImages;                               { Initialize the big pixel and cursor }
end;

procedure DrawTestPolygon;
{ This routine draws a rectangular region on the right-hand side of the screen using
  the current user-defined fill pattern. Before it displays the pattern it erases the
  existing rectangle on the screen by drawing a black rectangle.
}
begin
    SetLineStyle(SolidLn,0,NormWidth);        { Erase the old filled }
    SetFillStyle(SolidFill,Black);            { rectangle }
```

```pascal
   Bar3D(400,PTop,500,PTop+50,0,false);
   SetFillPattern(Fill,GetMaxColor);           { Set to the new fill }
   Bar3D(400,PTop,500,PTop+50,0,false);        { Fill pattern and show it }
end;

function IntToStr(L : longint) : string;
{ Convert an integer into a string }
var
   S : string;

begin
   Str(L,S);
   IntToStr := S;
end;


procedure ShowPatternCode;
{ Show Pascal code that can be used to declare the fill pattern currently shown }
const
   x: integer = 20;
   y: integer = 150;
var
   Buffer: string[80];

begin
{ Erase the old text on the screen by drawing a black filled rectangle. The rectangle
  extends across the screen and is 8 pixels high since the default font is used.
}
   SetColor(Black);
   SetLineStyle(SolidLn,0,NormWidth);
   SetFillStyle(SolidFill,Black);
   Bar3D(x,y,GetMaxX,y+8,0,False);
   { Convert the values to a string that can be printed out by OutTextXY }
   Buffer := 'Fill: FillPatternType = ($' + IntToStr(fill[1]) +
      ' $' + IntToStr(fill[2]) + ' $' + IntToStr(fill[3]) +
      ' $' + IntToStr(fill[4]) + ' $' + IntToStr(fill[5]) +
      ' $' + IntToStr(fill[6]) + ' $' + IntToStr(fill[7]) +
      ' $' + IntToStr(fill[8]) + ');';
   SetColor(White);                      { Restore the drawing color to white  }
  OutTextXY(x,y,Buffer);                 { Write the Pascal code for the pattern }
end;
```

```
procedure TogglePixel(x, y: integer);
{ Toggle the value for the indicated pixel stored in the user-defined pattern }
var
   mask : byte;

begin
   mask := $01;
   mask := mask shl (8-x);
   fill[y] := fill[y] xor mask;
end;

procedure ToggleBigPixel(x, y: integer);
{ This routine should be called each time a pixel in the user-defined pattern is
   toggled. It will toggle the current big pixel by exclusive ORing the current cell
   with the bigpixel image. It then calls TogglePixel to toggle the pixel in the
   pattern array.
}
var
   px, py: integer;

begin
   px := PLeft + (x-1) * 2 * (BigPixelSize + NormWidth) + 1;
   py := PTop + (y-1) * (BigPixelSize + NormWidth) + 1;
   PutImage(px,py,BigPixel^,XorPut);
   TogglePixel(x,y);
end;

procedure ToggleCursor(x, y: integer);
{ Toggle the cursor image on the screen by using the exclusive-OR
   feature of the PutImage command
}
var
   px, py : integer;

begin
   { Calculate screen location of cursor }
   px := PLeft + (x-1) * 2 * (BigPixelSize + NormWidth) + 3;
   py := PTop + (y-1) * (BigPixelSize + NormWidth) + 3;
   PutImage(px,py,Cursor^,XorPut);        { Toggle cursor }
end;
```

```pascal
begin
  x := 1;
  y := 1;
  InitGraph(GDriver,GMode,'');
  OutTextXY(PLeft,PTop-20,BigPatternTitle);          { Write the titles }
  OutTextXY(400,PTop-20,PolyTitle);

  DrawEnlargedPattern;                               { Create the enlarged pattern }
  DrawTestPolygon;                                   { Draw the test filled polygon }
  ShowPatternCode;                                   { Show the code for the pattern }
  ch := ReadKey;
  while (ch <> #27) do begin                         { While person doesn't type ESC }
    if ch = ' ' then begin                           { If it is a space, then toggle }
      ToggleBigPixel(x,y);                           { the big pixel and update the }
      DrawTestPolygon;                               { polygon and code which shows }
      ShowPatternCode;                               { the pattern }
    end
    else if ch = #0 then begin                       { If character was a 0, then it }
      ch := ReadKey;                                 { may be an extended code for }
      ToggleCursor(x,y);                             { an arrow key, get next ch }
  { Move the cursor through the big pixel pattern according to the
    arrow key that is pressed
  }
      case ch of
        #75 : if x > 1 then Dec(x);                  { Left arrow }
        #77 : if x < 8 then Inc(x);                  { Right arrow }
        #72 : if y > 1 then Dec(y);                  { Up arrow }
        #80 : if y < 8 then Inc(y);                  { Down arrow }
        #71 : begin
          if x > 1 then Dec(x);                      { Home key }
          if y > 1 then Dec(y);
          end;
        #73 : begin
          if x < 8 then Inc(x);                      { PGUP key }
          if y > 1 then Dec(y);
          end;
        #81 : begin
          if x < 8 then Inc(x);                      { PGDN key }
          if y < 8 then Inc(y);
          end;
```

```
    #79 : begin
        if x > 1 then Dec(x);                  { End key }
        if y < 8 then Inc(y);
        end;
    end;
    ToggleCursor(x,y);                         { Restore cursor to screen }
  end;
  ch := ReadKey;
  end;
  CloseGraph;                                  { Exit graphics mode }
end.
```

Working with Flood Fills

So far all of the fill operations that we have discussed have been oriented around various shapes. Sometimes, you may just want to fill a region with a particular fill pattern that is bounded by a set of lines or objects. To accomplish this, you can use an operation called a flood fill where you specify a location to begin filling and then the filling process floods an area until the border of the object has been reached.

The declaration for the BGI flood fill operation is:

```
procedure FloodFill(x, y: integer; Border: word);
```

Here, the values of **x** and **y** specify the starting location of the fill operation, commonly called the *seed point*. The **Border** parameter indicates the color that the **FloodFill** uses to determine when it has reached the border of the region it is filling. The procedure uses the current fill settings when filling the region.

One place where the flood fill operation may come in handy is when you want to draw a filled circle. This can be done with **PieSlice**, **FillEllipse**, or **Sector**; however, we can also draw a filled circle by first drawing a circle and then filling it with a call to **FloodFill**. The following code performs this sequence of operations.

```
SetColor(White);           { Use White for the circle }
Circle(100,100,50);        { Draw a circle }
FloodFill(100,100,White);  { Fill the circle starting }
                           { from its center }
```

Note that the color of the circle must be the same as the border color specified in the **FloodFill** procedure in order for this process to work correctly.

The BGI Fonts and Text

This chapter continues our in-depth examination of the BGI with a closer inspection of its text manipulation routines. Although the BGI has several unique and powerful drawing and filling features, its character generation capabilities are some of its most distinguished.

We'll begin by outlining the two forms of character generation supported by the BGI: bit-mapped characters and stroke fonts. We'll then demonstrate how you can exploit these two techniques in a typical graphics program. We'll continue by discussing the complete set of routines that are used to specify the font style, set the character magnification, determine the text dimensions, define the text justification, and more.

In this chapter we'll also develop a useful unit containing enhanced text manipulation tools. These new routines will perform such tasks as automatically enclosing text within a border, sizing text to fit in an existing window, and supporting text input with screen echo.

Text in Graphics Mode

The BGI provides two methods for writing characters to the screen in graphics mode. The default text scheme uses bit-mapped characters. An optional, more powerful, approach uses *stroke* fonts. The method that you select for an application will depend on the size of the text you want to write, the degree of quality of text you need, and the font style you desire. In the following sections, we'll look at both methods for displaying text.

The Bit-Mapped Font

A bit-mapped font is automatically built into every program that you write under the BGI. By default, bit-mapped characters are displayed whenever you perform text output operations to the screen with one of the BGI text functions.

Each character in the default bit-mapped font is represented with an 8 by 8 pixel pattern where each bit in the pattern corresponds to a screen pixel. If the bit in the pattern is a one, a corresponding pixel is displayed on the screen in the current drawing color. If the bit is a zero, the pixel is set to the background color. Since all characters are stored and displayed in the same manner, the bit-mapped characters are easy to work with and can be displayed quickly. Figure 3.1 presents an exploded view of a bit-mapped character.

By default, these bit-mapped patterns produce characters that are 8 pixels wide and 8 pixels high. Later, we'll see how we can change the size of bit-mapped characters and even write them vertically.

The Four Stroke Fonts

Although bit-mapped characters are adequate for most applications, the BGI also provides stroke fonts that are invaluable for displaying high-quality text output in graphics mode. Stroke fonts are not stored as bit patterns; instead, each character is defined as a series of line segments called strokes. The size of a character's description depends on its complexity. For example, the character "M" requires more strokes than the character "T." Therefore, characters with curves or numerous segments may take dozens of strokes to be properly defined. Figure 3.2 displays a

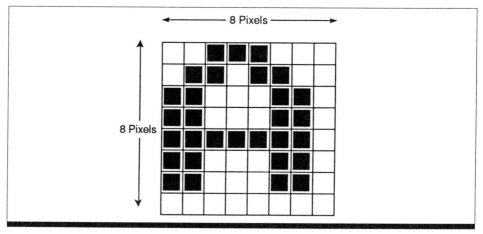

Figure 3.1. An exploded view of a bit-mapped character

Figure 3.2. A stroke font character is made up of line segments

sample stroke character. You should compare this character to the bit-mapped character in Figure 3.1.

The BGI includes four different stroke font styles called: Small Font, Sans Serif, Triplex, and Gothic. You'll find that these font styles will supply you with enough flexibility for most applications. Figure 3.3 presents a sample of each of these fonts.

The BGI Text Functions

In addition to the fonts, the BGI provides nine text related routines which are listed in Table 3.1. Throughout this chapter we'll be discussing most of these routines in detail and we'll present different techniques for using them. As you can see by

Figure 3.3. Letter "A" in each of the BGI fonts

studying the table, the text processing routines furnish a great deal of flexibility for working with both bit-mapped and stroke font styles. Keep in mind that two of the routines, **SetUserCharSize** and **RegisterBGIFont**, work only with stroke fonts.

Table 3.1. The BGI text related routines

Routines	Description
GetTextSettings	Retrieves the current font, direction, size, and justification of the text
OutText	Displays a string of text at the current position
OutTextXY	Displays a string of text at the location (x, y)
RegisterBGIFont	Used to link a font file into the program's executable file
SetTextJustify	Defines the justification style used by OutText and OutTextXY
SetTextStyle	Sets the font style, direction, and character magnification
SetUserCharSize	Sets the magnification factor used by stroke fonts
TextHeight	Returns the height of a string in pixels
TextWidth	Returns the width of a string in pixels

Writing Text to the Screen

Since the BGI supports several different video modes, multiple font styles, and variable sized text, it provides its own text routines that should be used to display all screen output. The two routines for displaying text are **OutText** and **Out-TextXY**.

The routine **OutText** displays an ASCII string at the current screen position in the current viewport. It is declared in the unit **Graph** as:

```
procedure OutText(TextString: string);
```

The parameter **TextString** is the character string that is displayed. By default, all text is written horizontally and is left justified with respect to the current position. When the default settings are used, a call to **OutText** updates the current position to the rightmost side of the text. Therefore, the next call to **OutText** places its string immediately to the right of the previously displayed string.

You'll see later that if you switch between fonts or use a text arrangement other than the one specified earlier, then **OutText** will not automatically update the current position after each call and you must keep track of its position yourself. We'll describe this process in the section "Determining Character Dimensions."

Writing Text to a Pixel Location

A companion text output routine of **OutText** is **OutTextXY**. It displays a string of text to the screen, just as **OutText** does; however, with **OutTextXY**, the text is displayed with respect to a pixel coordinate that you specify. Here is the declaration for **OutTextXY**:

```
procedure OutTextXY(x, y: integer; TextString: string);
```

The first two parameters specify the pixel coordinate about which the string is justified. As before, **TextString** is the string displayed. When using **OutTextXY**, keep in mind that this routine does not change the current drawing position after a text string has been displayed.

An Example of Text Display

The program shown in this section, called **TextTest.Pas**, demonstrates how text is displayed with the **OutText** and **OutTextXY** routines. It begins by initializing the graphics mode using Turbo Pascal's autodetect feature. As long as the initialization succeeds, several strings are displayed on the screen. The program uses the default settings for all the displayed text. Consequently, bit-mapped characters are used and the text is left justified and written horizontally. Here is the complete program:

```
program TextTest;
{ This program demonstrates the BGI OutText and OutTextXY functions }
uses
  Graph;
const
  GDriver: integer = Detect;
var
  GMode: integer;

begin
  InitGraph(GDriver,GMode,'');
```

```
    if (GDriver < 0) then begin
      writeln('Graphics initialization failure.');
      halt(1);
    end;
    OutText('This sentence is printed using OutText ');
    OutText('in the default font. ');
    OutTextXY(GetMaxX div 2, GetMaxY div 2,'OutTextXY printed this.');
    OutText('This sentence is also printed using OutText.');
    OutTextXY(0,GetMaxY-20,'Press Return ...');
    Readln;
    CloseGraph;
end.
```

The first two text strings are displayed with **OutText**. Since this program uses the default justification, **OutText** updates the current position after each call. As a result, the two strings are displayed next to each other. The next statement is **OutTextXY** which is used to display a string originating at the middle of the screen. The functions **GetMaxX** and **GetMaxY** retrieve the width of the screen and are used to calculate the screen midpoint. This is accomplished by the line:

```
OutTextXY(GetMaxX div 2, GetMaxY div 2, 'OutTextXY printed this.');
```

The next call is to **OutText**. Since **OutTextXY** does not update the current drawing position, note that its string is displayed after the last string printed by **OutText** and not the string printed by **OutTextXY**. Finally, the program calls **OutTextXY** to display a status line at the bottom-left corner of the screen, informing you to press any key to continue.

How Turbo Pascal Accesses Fonts

Unlike the default bit-mapped characters, the stroke fonts are not automatically built into every graphics program. In addition, only one stroke font is normally available in memory at once while your program is running. Turbo Pascal does this to avoid excessive use of memory, but it has several implications.

First, each stroke font is stored in a separate font file. These files are included with your Turbo Pascal disks and end with a **.chr** extension (see Table 3.2).

If you plan to use the stroke fonts, the stroke font files must be accessible to your program at run time. If they are not accessible, an error will occur. In addition, if you use more than one stroke font, the program must have access to the stroke files each time a different font style is selected.

Table 3.2. The BGI stroke font files

Filename	Description
goth.chr	Stroked gothic font
litt.chr	Stroked font of small characters
sans.chr	Stroked sans serif font
trip.chr	Stroked triplex font

Selecting and Loading a Font

To use one of the stroke fonts you must explicitly load a font file. This is done with the **SetTextStyle** procedure. It's declared as:

```
procedure SetTextStyle(Font, Direction, CharSize: word);
```

The **font** parameter is a numeric value which specifies the font file to be loaded. To represent the codes for font files, the BGI provides the following set of constants which are defined in the unit **Graph**:

Constant	Value
DefaultFont	0
TriplexFont	1
SmallFont	2
SansSerifFont	3
GothicFont	4

The second parameter, **Direction**, specifies whether the text should be written horizontally or vertically. It can be set to one of two valid values which are also represented by constants defined in **Graph** as:

Constant	Value
HorizDir	0
VertDir	1

The last parameter, **CharSize**, specifies the character magnification factor which is used when text is displayed with **OutText** or **OutTextXY**. This parameter can be set to any integer value from 0 to 10. The effects of these various values in **CharSize** will be discussed shortly.

Before we leave this topic, let's look at a few examples of how **SetTextStyle** is called. The following sample statement loads the gothic stroke font file, defines the direction flag so that all text is written horizontally, and sets the character magnification to a factor of 4:

```
SetTextStyle(GothicFont, HorizDir, 4);
```

The next statement selects the triplex font, forces all text to be displayed vertically, and sets the character size to the largest possible size, 10:

```
SetTextStyle(TriplexFont, VertDir, 10);
```

Errors in Loading a Font

If the appropriate font file cannot be found or loaded, an error state is initiated. After the call to **SetTextStyle**, you can make a call to **GraphResult** to check for an error. The possible error conditions are listed in Table 3.3.

Table 3.3. Possible errors from loading a font

Return Value	Description
-8	Font file not found
-9	Not enough memory to load font
-11	General error condition
-12	Graphics input/output error
-13	Invalid font file
-14	Invalid font number

The following excerpt of code could be used to change the currently used font, but will catch any errors if they occur. If there is a problem, the routine calls **GraphErrorMsg** to print out the reason for the error and the program terminates. Note, **grOk** is a constant defined in **Graph** for the value 0. It will be the value returned in **GraphResult** if no error occurs in **SetTextStyle**.

```
procedure ChangeTextStyle(Font, Direction, CharSize: word);
var ErrorNum: integer;
```

```
begin
  GraphResult;
  SetTextStyle(Font, Direction, CharSize);
  ErrorNum := GraphResult;
  if ErrorNum <> grOk then begin
    CloseGraph;
    writeln('Graphics Error: ', GraphErrorMsg(ErrorNum));
    halt(1);
  end
end;
```

Working with **Text Justification**

The BGI provides a handful of text justification settings that can be used to customize your graphics displays. These settings are used by the **OutText** and **OutTextXY** routines to determine how the text should be displayed relative to the current drawing position. By default, all text is left justified and displayed above the current position. These default settings can easily be changed by calling the **SetTextJustify** routine. Here is its declaration:

```
procedure SetTextJustify(Horiz, Vert: word);
```

The first parameter, **Horiz**, sets the horizontal justification style. It can be set to one of the following values:

Constant	Value
LeftText	0
CenterText	1
RightText	2

Similarly, the **Vert** parameter defines the vertical justification that is used in all calls to **OutText** and **OutTextXY**. Its range of values is:

Constant	Value
BottomText	0
CenterText	1
TopText	2

Figures 3.4 and 3.5 display a set of strings in both horizontal and vertical formats by using various combinations of the justification settings.

Determining the Current Text Settings

Turbo Pascal provides the procedure **GetTextSettings** which can retrieve the current text settings. This routine is convenient to use when you want to temporarily change the text style and then restore them to their previous settings. The procedure is defined in **GetTextSettings** as:

```
procedure GetTextSettings(var TextInfo: TextSettingsInfo);
```

To store information about a text font, a special data record named **TextSettingsType** is used. You'll find this record defined in the unit **Graph** as:

```
TextSettingsType = record
   Font: word;
   Direction: word;
```

Figure 3.4. Horizontal text justifications

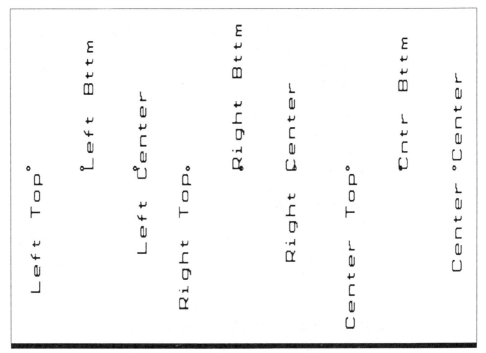

Figure 3.5. Vertical text justifications

```
    CharSize: word;
    Horiz: word;
    Vert: word;
end;
```

The record field **Font** contains the numeric code for the active font style. Remember that Turbo Pascal provides one default style and four stroke fonts; thus the range of values that are stored in this component span from zero to four. The second field, **Direction**, indicates whether the current text is to be displayed in a horizontal or vertical direction. Moving down the list, the component **CharSize** stores the magnification factor used to scale any text that is displayed.

The scale factor will be covered in greater detail later; but briefly, it can range from 0 to 10 where a value of one selects the standard size for bit-mapped characters (8 by 8), two dictates bit-mapped characters twice the size (16 by 16), and so on. Similarly, larger values of **CharSize** create larger stroke font characters. A **Char-Size** of zero is reserved for stroke fonts only and is used to select a secondary form of character magnification which we'll also see later. Finally, the last two fields, **Horiz** and **Vert,** define the justification attributes used for displaying text in the horizontal and vertical directions.

As you can see, a call to **GetTextSettings** will retrieve the font style, the direction flag, the character magnification, and the text justification settings and store this information in the **TextSettingsType** record. As an example, the following lines of code save the text settings, change them, and then restore the text specifications.

```
{ Declare a structure to save the settings in }
OldText: TextSettingsType;

{ Previous code ... }
GetTextSettings(OldText);
{ Change the text settings here ... }
{ Restore the text settings }
SetTextStyle(OldText.Font,OldText.Direction,OldText.CharSize);
SetTextJustify(OldText.Horiz, OldText.Vert);
{ Rest of the code ... }
```

Determining Character Dimensions

Since the BGI allows characters to be magnified to different sizes, it is necessary to be able to determine the actual pixel sizes of any text written to the screen. This is particularly important when you are trying to align text or enclose a text string within a window. The BGI provides two functions to determine the text dimensions of a string. These routines are:

```
function TextHeight(TextString: string): word;
function TextWidth(TextString: string): word;
```

Individually, they return the height and width in pixels of the character string when it is displayed on the screen. The values returned by these functions are always determined with respect to the orientation of the characters and not the screen axes. In other words, **TextHeight** and **TextWidth** return the same values whether the text is displayed horizontally or vertically.

A bit-mapped character (remember that they are derived from an 8 by 8 bit pattern) with the default character magnification of 1, has a text width of 8 pixels. Similarly, its height is also 8 pixels. To better understand the effects that magnification has on the dimensions of a bit-mapped character see Figure 3.6. Here we are showing the dimensions of the letter A with magnifications of 1 through 10 times the default size.

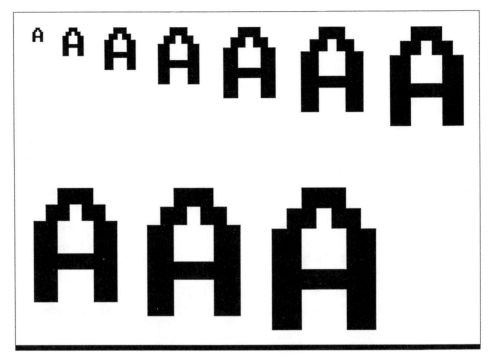

Figure 3.6. Magnification of a bit-mapped character

A Note about Vertical Character Dimensions

Although **TextHeight** and **TextWidth** operate similarly whether text is written horizontally or vertically, they may confuse you when you are writing code. Remember that these functions return pixel dimensions that are oriented with respect to the character strings. For example, when a string is displayed horizontally, **TextWidth** returns the number of pixel columns that the text spans. However, when the text is displayed vertically, **TextWidth** returns the number of pixel rows that the text stretches across. You will need to be careful with **TextWidth** and **TextHeight** when writing routines that are designed to handle horizontal and vertical text equally.

Magnifying Characters

The BGI provides two methods for altering the size of text displayed by **OutText** and **OutTextXY**. The approach to use depends on whether bit-mapped or stroke fonts are being displayed.

The simplest way to change the size of text that is displayed is by altering the **CharSize** field in the **TextSettingsType** record introduced earlier. The **CharSize** component can be set by a call to the procedure **SetTextStyle**. Remember, it defines the scale factor that is applied to all text that is displayed by **OutText** and **OutTextXY** and can range from 0 to 10. If the **CharSize** value is between 1 and 10, it will affect both the default bit-mapped characters and the stroke fonts. In the case of bit-mapped characters, a **CharSize** of 1 will produce characters the default size of 8 by 8. Bit-mapped text written with a **CharSize** of 2 are twice as big as the default size (16 by 16) and so on up to a **CharSize** of 10 which produces characters 80 by 80 pixels in size.

The larger values of **CharSize** also serve to magnify the stroke fonts although they do not always generate characters of the same size as the bit-mapped characters. Figure 3.7 shows each of the stroke fonts and the default font using the **CharSize**'s of 1, 2, 3, and 4.

The one remaining value of **CharSize**, 0, is reserved exclusively for stroke fonts. If it is used, a second group of scale factors, specified by calls to the procedure **SetUserCharSize**, are employed. These allow finer control over the stroke fonts so that you can adjust the height and width of the text independently. For instance, you

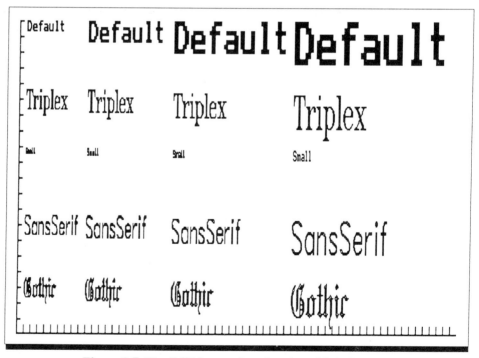

Figure 3.7. The BGI fonts using charsize of 1, 2, 3, and 4

can use the scale factors in **SetUserCharSize** to fit a text string precisely to a rectangular window.

The routine **SetUserCharSize** is defined in **Graph** as:

```
procedure SetUserCharSize(MultX, DivX, MultY, DivY: word);
```

where the four parameters represent the scale factors to be applied to the default size of the text displayed (a **CharSize** of 4 for the stroke fonts). The first two parameters indicate the amount that the text is to be stretched or compressed in the horizontal direction. These parameters work as a pair and it is the ratio of these values that defines the scale factor that is applied. For example, to double the width of all text **MultX** can be set to 2 and **DivX** to 1. Similarly, to reduce the height of all text to one third its default height, we can set **MultY** to 1 and **DivY** to 3. These numbers can take on any ratio of integers up to the screen width of the graphics mode being used. Therefore, in the CGA high-resolution mode (640 by 200), the ratio **MultX/DivX** cannot exceed 639 and similarly the ratio **MultY/DivY** cannot be larger than 199. Figure 3.8 shows how the scale factor ratios influence a stroke font character.

You should be aware that when using vertical text, the four parameters of **SetUserCharSize** are relative to the text itself and not the screen. Therefore, changing **MultX** and **DivX** when the text is vertical will change the number of rows that the text stretches across.

Fitting Text Inside a Box

By way of example, let's now see how we can scale a stroke font text string so that it fits into a rectangular region. The program **AutoScal.Pas**, shown in Listing 3.1,

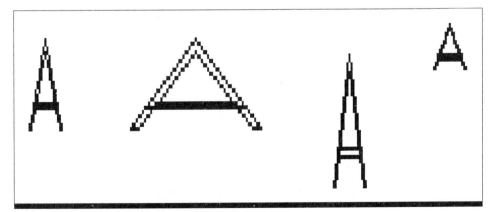

Figure 3.8. Scale factors influence stroke fonts

allows us to specify the dimensions of a rectangular region and a string which is to be centered inside it. The program automatically scales the text string so that it completely fills the inside of this region as shown in Figure 3.9. This program is worth looking over because of its use of the **SetUserCharSize** procedure.

The program includes two routines, **ScaleText** and **ScaleVertText**. The first routine, scales the text so that it fits horizontally into the window specified in its parameters. The latter routine operates the same except that it places the text vertically in the window.

In each procedure, the parameters **Left, Top, Right,** and **Bottom** specify the bounds of the region in which the text is to be displayed. The text to display is contained in the array called **String**. The two routines center the text in both the horizontal and vertical directions so each contains the statement:

```
SetTextJustify(CenterText, CenterText);
```

Now let's take a closer look at how **SetUserCharSize** is used to scale the text string to fit inside the window specified. This is performed in the following statements included in each of the routines:

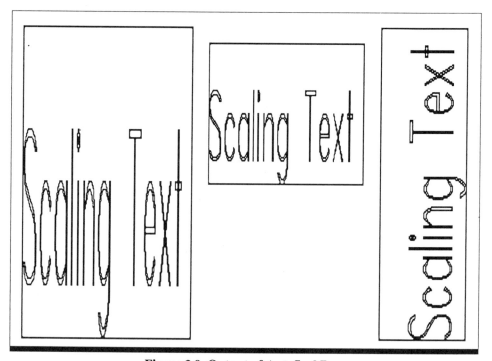

Figure 3.9. Output of AutoScal.Pas

```
SetUserCharSize(1, 1, 1, 1);
SetTextStyle(Font, HorizDir, UserCharSize);
{ Note the order of the box coordinates. Compare them with the
  ordering for vertical text.
}
SetUserCharSize(Right-Left, TextWidth(Str),
                Bottom-Top, TextHeight(Str) * 3 div 2);
```

You'll probably first notice that there are two calls to **SetUserCharSize**. Let's start with the second one. As mentioned earlier, the *ratios* of the parameters in **SetUser-CharSize** define the scale factors applied to the text string. Since we want the text to stretch across the window, we can set **MultX** to **Right-Left** and **DivX** to the length of the string. Actually, we need to ensure that the length of the string is calculated using the default text magnification, not the current settings, so this explains the earlier use of:

```
SetUserCharSize(1, 1, 1, 1);
```

The height is similarly scaled to fit into the window. However, you'll note that the height returned from **TextHeight** is scaled by one and one half. This factor must be used in order to squeeze the characters into the box so that letters like p, g, and y, which extend below the text line, do not protrude from the bottom of the box.

• Listing 3.1

```
program AutoScal;
{ Given a box of a particular size, scale the text so that it fits inside it. This
  routine guarantees that the text string will fit in the box, but it doesn't
  guarantee that the text will look good or that it will be readable. This can happen
  if the box is too small for the text.
}
uses
   Graph, Crt;
const
   Str: string[12] = 'Scaling Text';
var
   GDriver: integer;
   GMode: integer;
```

```
procedure ScaleText(Left, Top, Right, Bottom: integer; Font: integer; Str: string);
{ Scale Horizontal text to fit in a rectangle }
begin
{ Reset usercharsize to all ones, so that the textwidth and textheight functions will
  return the number of pixels on the screen that the default font size uses, not the
  current size, whatever it may be
}
  SetUserCharSize(1, 1, 1, 1);
  SetTextStyle(Font, HorizDir, UserCharSize);
{ Note the order of the box coordinates. Compare them with the ordering
  for vertical text.
}
  SetUserCharSize(Right-Left,TextWidth(Str),
          Bottom-Top,TextHeight(Str) * 3 div 2);
  SetTextJustify(CenterText, CenterText);
  { Clear screen and draw a box where text is to be displayed }
  SetFillStyle(SolidFill, GetBkColor);
  Bar3D(Left, Top, Right, Bottom, 0, False);
  { Write text string centered in the box }
  OutTextXY((Right+Left) div 2, (Bottom+Top) div 2, Str);
end;


procedure ScaleVertText(Left, Top, Right, Bottom: integer;
                        Font: integer; Str: string);
{ Scale vertical text to fit in a box }
begin
{ Reset usercharsize to all ones, so that the textwidth and textheight functions will
  return the number of pixels on the screen that the default font size uses, not the
  current size, whatever it may be
}
  SetUserCharSize(1, 1, 1, 1);
  SetTextStyle(Font, VertDir, UserCharSize);
  SetUserCharSize(Bottom-Top, TextWidth(Str), Right-Left, TextHeight(Str) * 3 div 2);
  SetTextJustify(CenterText, CenterText);
  { Clear screen and draw a box where text is to be displayed }
  SetFillStyle(SolidFill, GetBkColor);
  Bar3D(Left, Top, Right, Bottom, 0, False);
  { Write string centered in the box }
  OutTextXY((Right+Left) div 2, (Bottom+Top) div 2, Str);
end;
```

```
begin
   GDriver := Detect;
   InitGraph(GDriver, GMode, '');
   ScaleText(0, 0, 200, GetMaxY, SansSerifFont, Str);
   ScaleText(220, 10, 400, 100, SansSerifFont, Str);
   ScaleVertText(420, 0, 520, GetMaxY, SansSerifFont, Str);
   repeat until KeyPressed;
   CloseGraph;
end.
```

A Note on Clipping Text

Although the BGI supports clipping for both bit-mapped and stroke fonts, it handles the two slightly differently. If clipping is set for the current viewport, a bit-mapped character will be completely clipped if any portion of it extends beyond the borders of the viewport. A stroke font character, however, will have only that portion of the character that extends beyond the viewport clipped.

Displaying Characters and Numbers

Thus far we have only talked about writing text strings to the screen in graphics mode. You may be wondering how numeric values and the like can be displayed in graphics mode. After all, **OutText** and **OutTextXY** can only display text strings. The trick is to convert all values you want to display into ASCII strings and then display these strings through calls to **OutText** and **OutTextXY**. This can be accomplished for integers or real values using the Turbo Pascal's **Str** function and its other string manipulation features. In the next section we'll look at this and other routines in detail.

Extended Text Manipulation Routines

Although the BGI text manipulation routines have great power, they do lack sufficient capabilities to perform interactive text input and output. For example, we need text output routines in graphics mode that have the versatility of the **write** procedure and input routines that operate like their counterparts in text mode.

In the forthcoming sections, we'll be developing a set of enhanced text routines which we'll be using throughout the rest of this book when displaying text to the screen. These routines are all combined into a Turbo Pascal unit called **GText.Pas** (see Listing 3.2). A list of the routines in **GText.Pas** is shown in Table 3.4.

Table 3.4. Routines in GText.Pas

Routine	Description
GWrite	Graphics print utility which mimics **write**
GWriteXY	Graphics **write** routine which displays text at the location (x, y)
GWriteCh	Puts a single character on the graphics screen
IntToStr	Converts an integer to a string
RealToStr	Converts a real value to a string
GReadStr	Allows user to enter a text in graphics mode
GReadReal	Allows user to enter real numbers in graphics

Graphics Version of write

At first glance, both **OutText** and **OutTextXY** seem adequate for applications that manipulate text in graphics mode, but their limitations become apparent when we compare them to the Pascal routine **write**. In particular, they only accept string arguments and they do not clear the screen where they write to the screen. In this section we'll develop a graphics version of the **write** routine that will support the text features of the BGI. This routine will be called **GWrite** and is included in **GText.Pas**.

The greatest difficulty in creating a routine that mimics **write** comes from the fact that the routine will have to be able to process a variable number of parameters. Since Turbo Pascal doesn't provide an easy way for us to do this, we will limit our **GWrite** routine so that it only takes a single string parameter. Instead, we'll use support routines that assist us in converting any integer or real values that we wish to display, into string values.

The unit **GText** includes two such support routines. They are called **IntToStr** and **RealToStr**. The first one converts an integer value into a string and the second similarly converts a real value into an equivalent string representation. The strings that these functions generate can then be concatenated to other strings or simply passed along to **OutText** or **OutTextXY** to be displayed.

As an example, let's look at the function **RealToStr**. It requires three parameters which correspond to the real value to be converted, the total character width that the conversion should have, and the number of decimal positions that should appear in the string. The string is returned in the function name. Here is the complete listing of the **RealToStr** function:

```
function RealToStr(n: real; width, decimals: integer): string;
{ Converts a real number to a string }
var
   s: string;

begin
   Str(n:width:decimals, s);
   RealToStr := s;
end;
```

Now let's see how we can use this routine to display the value 3.1 which is stored in the variable **x**. To accomplish this we can use the following statement:

```
OutText('The value of x='+RealToStr(x,3,1));
```

It will display the line

```
The value of x=3.1
```

on the graphics screen. The **IntToStr** function works in a similar fashion.

Now that we've seen how to write numeric values to a graphics screen, let's continue to see how we can improve on **OutText** and **OutTextXY**. One thing that is annoying about the BGI stroke fonts is that they make a mess when they overwrite graphics already displayed on the screen. The reason for this is that stroke fonts only draw a series of line segments, they do not clear the space below the character as it is displayed. A way around this problem is to erase the screen where each character is to appear before it is displayed. This can be done by drawing a filled rectangular region the size of each character with the background color prior to writing the character. If you examine the **GWrite** routine in **GText.Pas**, you'll see that **Bar** is used in conjunction with a **SolidFill** set to the background color to clear the screen underneath the string that is displayed.

Finally, in our **GWrite** routine, **OutText** is used to display the formatted ASCII string. Note that the text will be displayed and justified relative to the current position. If left justification and horizontal text styles are in force, then the current position will automatically be updated after a call to **GWrite**.

In addition to **GWrite**, **GText.Pas** includes **GWriteXY** which is routine similar to **GWrite**. The main difference is that **GWriteXY** writes a character string at an (x, y) coordinate position. Like the BGI **OutTextXY**, **GWriteXY** does not update the current position. Since the routine is similar to **GWrite** we will not cover it in any detail.

One other text output routine in **GText** that you'll often find useful is the routine **GWriteCh**. It simply displays a single character to the graphics screen. It is often convenient when echoing user input when using a function such as **ReadKey**. Actually, all it does is load a string with the single character and pass it along to **GWrite**.

Working with Text Input

Another area that the BGI does not directly support is text input. Fortunately, we can easily build tools to provide text input features. One important input routine to have is a character input function that echos the input to the graphics screen. As mentioned in the last section we could retrieve user input using the Turbo Pascal routine **ReadKey**, however, it does not support the backspace character or a cursor. We must handle these ourselves. This is the purpose of our next routine, **GReadStr**.

The routine **GReadStr** requires a string to be passed to it in which it will place all text typed until a carriage return is entered. While the text is typed, it will provide an underbar as a cursor and will support the backspace character. When using this **GReadStr**, you must ensure there is enough room in the character buffer passed to **GReadStr** to accept the whole string typed in.

The routine is rather lengthy but it only has two main elements. The first is a **while** loop which continually accepts any text typed by the user until a carriage return is pressed. Every character that is typed is entered into the string, **S**, passed to it by the statements:

```
Inc(CurrLoc);
S[0] := Chr(CurrLoc);
S[CurrLoc] := ch;
```

where **CurrLoc** is the next location in the string. Remember that the 0 location in a string holds its length. This explains the purpose of the second statement in the code above.

The backspace character, which has a value of $08, is handled as a special case. It causes the last character to be rewritten in the background color which effectively erases it, the current position to be moved left to where the character used to reside, and the **CurrLoc** index to be decremented.

When you enter a carriage return the **while** terminates and **GReadStr** erases the cursor and exits with a value of True. If the string entered is empty, then the function will return False.

Entering Numeric Values

Just as displaying numeric values in graphics mode is a problem, so is entering numeric values. The **GText.Pas** source file also includes the routine **GReadReal** that can read real values typed while in graphics mode. It is much like an inverse of the **GWriteReal** function that we saw earlier. In particular, it uses the **GReadStr** function to retrieve an input text string and then calls the Turbo Pascal function **Val** to have it converted into a real value. Like **GReadStr**, it too is a Boolean function that only returns True if the user has entered an appropriate real value.

• Listing 3.2

```
unit GText;
{ An extended set of text routines for graphics mode }
interface
const
  CR  = #13;
  ESC = #27;
  BS  = #08;
{ These routines are available to any programs that "use" this unit }
function IntToStr(Num: longint): string;
function RealToStr(n: real; width, decimals: integer): string;
procedure GWrite(S: string);
procedure GWriteXY(x, y: integer; S: string);
procedure GWriteCh(ch: char);
function GReadReal(var Num: real): boolean;
function GReadStr(var S: string): boolean;
implementation
uses
   Graph, Crt;

function IntToStr(Num: longint): string;
{ Converts an integer to a string }
var
   S: string;
```

```
begin
  Str(Num, S);
  IntToStr := S;
end;

function RealToStr(n: real; width, decimals: integer): string;
{ Converts a real number to a string }
var
  s: string;

begin
  Str(n:width:decimals, s);
  RealToStr := s;
end;

procedure GWrite(S: string);
{ Write a string to the screen. Clear the screen below the text before writing the
  string. It will update the current position. It assumes that you are using the
  HorizDir and LeftText settings.
}
var
  x, y: integer;
  SaveFill: FillSettingsType;

begin
  GetFillSettings(SaveFill);
  x := GetX;  y := GetY;
  SetFillStyle(SolidFill, Black);
  Bar(x, y, x+TextWidth(S), y+TextHeight(S));
  SetFillStyle(SaveFill.Pattern, SaveFill.Color);
  OutText(S);
end;

procedure GWriteXY(x, y: integer; S: string);
{ Write a string to the location (x,y). It does not update the current position,
  but it does clear the screen where it will write the text. It assumes that you are
  using the HorizDir and LeftText settings.
}
var
  SaveFill: FillSettingsType;
```

```pascal
begin
  GetFillSettings(SaveFill);
  SetFillStyle(SolidFill, Black);
  Bar(x, y, x+TextWidth(S), y+TextHeight(S));
  OutTextXY(x, y, S);
  SetFillStyle(SaveFill.Pattern, SaveFill.Color);
end;

procedure GWriteCh(ch: char);
{ Writes a single character to the screen }
var
  S: string;

begin
  S[0] := #1; S[1] := ch;
  GWrite(S);
end;

function GReadReal(var Num: real): boolean;
{ Read a single real number followed by a carriage return from the graphics screen }
var
  S: string;
  Code: integer;
  t: boolean;

begin
  if GReadStr(S) then begin
    Val(S, Num, Code);
    if Code <> 0 then GReadReal := False
      else GReadReal := True;
  end
  else GReadReal := False;
end;

function GReadStr(var S: string): boolean;
{ A graphics based text input routine. It returns the string entered. Echos
  text as it is entered. It supports the backspace character and provides a
  cursor for easy typing.
}
const
  Buff2: string[2] = 'c_';
```

```pascal
var
   i, CurrLoc, MaxChars, OldColor: integer;
   View: ViewPortType;
   CharBuff: string[2];
   ch: char;

begin
   S[0] := #0;
   CurrLoc := 0;
   CharBuff[0] := #1;
   GetViewSettings(View);
   MaxChars := (View.x2 - GetX) div TextWidth('M') - 1;
   if MaxChars <= 0 then Exit;
   GWriteXY(GetX, GetY, '_');
   ch := ReadKey;
   while ch <> CR do begin
      if ch = BS then begin
         if CurrLoc > 0 then begin
            if CurrLoc <= MaxChars then begin
               OldColor := GetColor;
               SetColor(GetBkColor);
               CharBuff[1] := S[CurrLoc];
               Buff2[1] := S[CurrLoc];              { Erase last character }
               GWriteXY(GetX-TextWidth(CharBuff), GetY, Buff2);
               SetColor(OldColor);
               MoveTo(GetX-TextWidth(CharBuff), GetY);
               Dec(CurrLoc);
            end;
         end;
      end
      else begin                              { Show this character if room permits }
         if CurrLoc < MaxChars then begin
            OldColor := GetColor;
            SetColor(GetBkColor);
            GWriteXY(GetX, GetY, '_');         { Erase cursor }
            SetColor(OldColor);
            Inc(CurrLoc);
            S[0] := Chr(CurrLoc);
            S[CurrLoc] := ch;
            GWriteCh(ch);
         end
```

```
        else begin
            Sound(220); Delay(200); NoSound;   { Beep! No room. }
        end
    end;
    if CurrLoc < MaxChars then GWriteXY(GetX, GetY, '_');
    ch := ReadKey;
  end;
  if Currloc <= MaxChars then begin
    OldColor := GetColor;
    SetColor(GetBkColor);
    GWriteXY(GetX, GetY, '_');                     { Erase cursor upon exit }
    SetColor(OldColor);
  end;
  if Length(S) = 0 then GReadStr := False
    else GReadStr := True;
end;


end.
```

4

Presentation Graphics

A wise philosopher once said a picture is worth a thousand words, and if you have ever experienced a good art gallery, you'll probably agree with this popular saying. Of course, when it comes to communication, pictures not only have a place in the art world but in the fast moving business world as well. And that's where microcomputers come in.

In the early days, most microcomputer users found it downright cumbersome to create useful and attractive presentations. Fortunately, the situation has changed. Now with the latest generation of fast PCs equipped with high-resolution video cards and displays, the field of presentation graphics has emerged. By presentation graphics we mean the technology of using the computer to represent complex information in the forms of charts, graphs, and pictures.

In this chapter we'll show you how to use Turbo Pascal's graphics capabilities to produce high-quality business and scientific charts and graphs. In particular, we'll explore techniques for drawing pie charts, bar graphs, coin graphs, and animated charts. We will not be able to cover all of the types of graphs and charts that can be generated with the BGI tools, but by the end of the chapter, you'll learn enough to be able to customize your own Pascal applications with presentation graphics.

The Basic Graph Types

The BGI provides three specialized routines for generating graphs and charts. These include a pie chart routine, a bar graph routine and a three-dimensional bar graph procedure. With these high-level routines we can create professional looking charts and graphs with a minimum of effort. We'll explore each one of these in detail, and, in addition, we'll use several of the other tools in the BGI to generate other types of charts and graphs including coin graphs and animated charts.

Getting Started

If you're looking for hard and fast rules for developing charts and graphs, you won't find any here. After all, a picture doesn't always tell the same story to everyone. Our major goal is to display information in a consistent and meaningful manner. However, meaningful does not mean boring. In fact, a good graph or chart is one that is visually pleasing. Therefore, along the way, you may want to experiment with various colors, backdrops, and the layout of the graphs. This chapter will give you a few sample programs that will help you get started; however, feel free to experiment with your own ideas.

Pie Charts

If you pick up almost any magazine or newspaper, you're bound to see pie charts. In fact you'll also find them in popular software applications such as Borland's Quattro. In this section we'll develop a utility called **Pie.Pas** that can automatically create a complete pie chart like that shown in Figure 4.1. All we'll need to do is provide **Pie.Pas** with the data and titles for the pie slices. It automatically sizes the pie chart to fit on the screen, creates a legend, and writes a title. The program, shown in Listing 4.1, is designed around Turbo Pascal's **PieSlice** procedure and a set of our own custom routines. Let's take a close look at **Pie.Pas**.

Drawing a Slice

In Chapter 2, we introduced the **PieSlice** procedure. We'll use it to draw the pie slices in our pie charts. Our task then is to determine how to relate a set of data to the various slices in the pie chart. Typically, each slice represents the proportion of a particular group of data in relation to the whole chart. In other words, each slice represents a percentage of the whole pie.

For our program, we'll assume that a series of percentage values are available for us to use. Each percentage value corresponds to one pie slice and all the slices total to 100 percent. In some applications, a set of raw data is used from which the program must calculate appropriate percentage values. To keep our program simple, we'll assume that these percentages are already available.

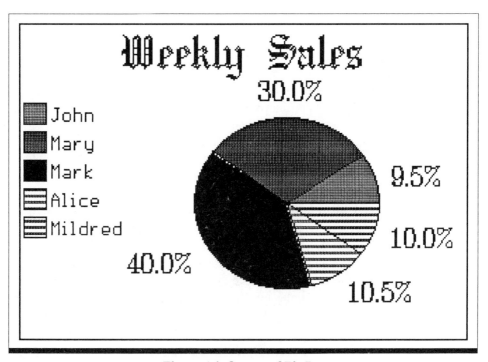

Figure 4.1. Output of Pie.Pas

Our enhanced version of the **PieSlice** procedure is called **PieceOfPie**. We'll invoke this custom routine for each pie slice of the chart that we need to draw. Here is the code for a simplified version of this procedure:

```
const
   StartPercentage: real = 0.0;
procedure PieceOfPie(x, y, Radius: integer; SlicePercentage: real;
                     Color, Fill: integer);
var
   StartAngle, EndAngle: integer;

begin
   SetFillStyle(Fill, Color);
   StartAngle := Round(StartPercentage / 100.0 * 360.0);
   EndAngle := Round((StartPercentage+SlicePercentage) / 100.0 * 360.0);
   PieSlice(x, y, StartAngle, EndAngle, Radius);
   StartPercentage := StartPercentage + SlicePercentage;
end;
```

The first three parameters to **PieceOfPie** define the center point and radius of the pie slice to be drawn. From the code, you can see that these values are simply passed along to the Turbo Pascal **PieSlice** procedure. However, we still need to determine the overall size of the pie slice which is dependent on the value in **SlicePercentage**. But first, let's see how we determine the starting angle to begin drawing the current pie slice. This is the purpose of the real constant **StartPercentage**. It keeps a running total of the percentage of the circle that has already been displayed. The declaration initializes it to zero as shown:

StartPercentage: real = 0.0;

Each time **PieceOfPie** is called, **SlicePercentage** is added to the running total. The next pie slice is then drawn starting at this location. Therefore, **StartPercentage** specifies the starting angle for drawing the pie slice and **SlicePercentage** instructs the routine on how big to make the slice. Actually, these percentage values must be converted to angles before they can be used. The Turbo Pascal **PieSlice** procedure is expecting angles to be passed to it, not percentages. Therefore, we must convert these values to angles. This is accomplished by the two statements:

```
StartAngle := Round(StartPercentage / 100.0 * 360.0);
EndAngle := Round((StartPercentage+SlicePercentage) / 100.0 * 360.0);
```

Both of these statements are similar. Each is based on the following ratio:

$$\frac{\text{angle desired}}{360 \text{ degrees}} = \frac{\text{percentage}}{100 \text{ percent}}$$

Note that this procedure sets the current fill style and color to the values specified with the last two parameters that are passed to it. These drawing parameters are set so that each pie slice can be drawn differently.

As it stands, our procedure, **PieceOfPie**, is ready to be called to create a pie chart. However, let's modify it slightly so that it will add labels for the percentage values alongside each pie slice.

Labeling Pie Slices

There are many different ways to add labels to a pie chart. We'll write the percentage value of each pie slice off to the slice's side. This technique makes it easy for the viewer to determine the sizes of the pie slices. Some other possibilities are to write titles next to the pie slices or even write the titles or percentage values over the pie slices themselves. Listing 4.1 includes the updated listing of this procedure as well as the rest of the source code for our pie chart program.

When looking at the **PieceOfPie** procedure the first thing to note is that it contains a new variable called **LRadius**. This variable is used to determine the distance from the center of the pie chart to where the labels are written. For our application, the **LRadius** is set to be 1.2 times the radius of the pie chart by the statement:

```
LRadius := Radius * 1.2;    { Varies with char size }
```

This calculation depends on how much room you have on the screen for the labels and the size of the text that you are using. You can derive a general equation for this, but to keep things simple we'll just use the multiplication constant 1.2.

By convention, each of the labels are placed at the middle of the pie slice. This angle is stored in **LabelAngle** and is half way between the start angle of the pie slice and its ending angle. In order to be used by the Turbo Pascal trigonometric functions, this value is converted into radians by the function **ToRadians**.

```
LabelAngle := (StartAngle + EndAngle) div 2;
LabelLoc := ToRadians(LabelAngle);
```

Next, the x and y coordinates of where the label is to be written are calculated by the following lines of code. Note that the y value must be adjusted for the aspect ratio of the screen.

```
x := x + cos(LabelLoc) * LRadius;
y := y - sin(LabelLoc) * LRadius * AspectRatio;
```

The following statements set the text parameters. First, the font style is set to the triplex stroke font. Next you'll find a series of nested if-then-else statements that determine which type of text justification to use. For instance, if the label is to be printed to the right of the pie slice, then its justification is set to **LeftText** and **CenterText**. However, if the text is to be written on the left side of the pie chart, its justification is set to **RightText** and **CenterText**. Finally, the text is written to the screen by the **OutTextXY**.

```
SetTextStyle(TriplexFont, HorizDir, 1);
if (LabelAngle >= 300) or (LabelAngle < 60) then
   SetTextJustify(LeftText, CenterText)
```

```
else if (LabelAngle >= 60) and (LabelAngle < 120) then
   SetTextJustify(CenterText, BottomText)
else if (LabelAngle >= 120) and (LabelAngle < 240) then
   SetTextJustify(RightText, CenterText)
else
   SetTextJustify(CenterText, TopText);
OutTextXY(x, y, RealToStr(ShowPercentage,3,1));
```

Up to this point, we've seen how to draw each slice in a pie chart. To draw a complete pie chart we merely need to call **PieceOfPie** repetitively with the appropriate values.

Making Each Slice Different

One thing that you will probably want to do is draw each pie slice a different color or at least fill it with a different fill pattern. To accomplish this we'll sequence through the colors supported by the current graphics mode and 11 of the fill patterns. (We won't use the empty fill pattern since it doesn't generate a unique fill pattern in CGA high-resolution mode.)

The program in Listing 4.1 uses the procedure **NextColorAndFill** to sequence through each of the fill patterns and color combinations. It uses global variables to begin the fill patterns at 1 and the fill color at 0. When all of the combinations are used up, the procedure is written so that the program will exit. You may want to change this so that it cycles through the values again.

Creating a Legend

At the end of **PieceOfPie**, the **ShowKey** procedure is called to write out an entry in a color key on the left side of the screen. This legend shows each color and fill pattern used in the pie chart along with its corresponding label. The procedure **ShowKey** draws one rectangle for each pie slice starting from the top-left of the screen and working down. The **Bar3D** procedure is used with a depth of 0 in order to draw the filled region. The boxes are 16 pixels in width by 16 pixels in height times the aspect ratio. This correction is made in order to make the region square. The location of the square is maintained by the global integer constants **Keyx** and **Keyy**. The **Keyx** value is always equal to 3. However, the **Keyy** position is incremented by 18 pixels each time **ShowKey** is called.

• Listing 4.1

```pascal
program Pie;
{ This is a demonstration of the pie chart capabilities of the BGI }
uses
  Graph, Crt;
const
  PercentValues: array[1..5] of real = (9.5, 30, 40, 10.5, 10);
  Labels: array[1..5] of string =  ('John', 'Mary', 'Mark', 'Alice', 'Mildred');
  NumValues: integer = 5;
  Title: string[12] = 'Weekly Sales';
  GDriver: integer = CGA;
  GMode: integer = CGAC3;
  StartPercentage: real = 0.0;
  Keyx: integer = 3;
  Keyy: integer = 50;
  FFill: integer = 1;
  FColor: integer = 0;
var
  AspectRatio: real;
  i, x, y, Radius, Color, Fill: integer;
  XAsp, YAsp: word;

function ToRadians(d: integer): real;
{ Convert degrees to radians }
begin
  ToRadians := d * Pi / 180.0;
end;

function RealToStr(n: real; width, decimals: integer): string;
var
  s: string;
begin
  Str(n:width:decimals, s);
  RealToStr := s;
end;

procedure ShowKey(Color, Fill: integer; TheLabel: string);
{ Each pie slice has an entry in a key on the left side of the screen which shows the
  fill pattern used for the pie slice and a corresponding label for it
}
```

```
begin
   SetFillStyle(Fill, Color);
   Bar3D(Keyx, Keyy, Keyx+16, Round(Keyy+16.0*AspectRatio), 0, False);
   SetTextJustify(LeftText, CenterText);
   SetTextStyle(SmallFont, HorizDir, 5);
   OutTextXY(Keyx+20, Round(Keyy+8*AspectRatio), TheLabel);
   Keyy := Keyy + 18;
end;


procedure PieceOfPie(x, y, radius: integer; ShowPercentage: real;
                     Color, Fill: integer; TheLabel: string);
{ Draw a single pie slice in the pie chart }
var
   StartAngle, EndAngle, LabelAngle: integer;
   LabelLoc, LRadius: real;

begin
   LRadius := Radius * 1.2;     { Dependent on size of characters }
   SetFillStyle(Fill, Color);
   StartAngle := Round(StartPercentage / 100.0 * 360.0);
   EndAngle := Round((StartPercentage + ShowPercentage) / 100.0 * 360.0);
   LabelAngle := (StartAngle + EndAngle) div 2;
   LabelLoc := ToRadians(LabelAngle);
   PieSlice(x, y, StartAngle, EndAngle, Radius);
   x := x + Round(cos(LabelLoc) * LRadius);
   y := y - Round(sin(LabelLoc) * LRadius * AspectRatio);
   SetTextStyle(TriplexFont, HorizDir, 1);
   { Set text justification depending on location of pie slice }
   if (LabelAngle >= 300) or (LabelAngle < 60) then
     SetTextJustify(LeftText, CenterText)
   else if (LabelAngle >= 60) and (LabelAngle < 120) then
     SetTextJustify(CenterText, BottomText)
   else if (LabelAngle >= 120) and (LabelAngle < 240) then
     SetTextJustify(RightText, CenterText)
   else
     SetTextJustify(CenterText, TopText);
   OutTextXY(x, y, RealToStr(ShowPercentage,3,1));
   StartPercentage := StartPercentage + ShowPercentage;
   ShowKey(Color, Fill, TheLabel);
end;
```

```
procedure NextColorAndFill(var Color: integer; var Fill: integer);
{ Sequence through each of the fill patterns and colors possible }
begin
   Inc(FColor);
   if FColor > GetMaxColor then begin
     FColor := 1;
     Inc(FFill);
     if FFill > 11 then begin
        CloseGraph;
        Writeln('Too many calls to nextcolor ...');
        Halt(1);
     end
   end;
   Fill := FFill;
   Color := FColor;
end;

begin
   InitGraph(GDriver, GMode, '');
   Rectangle(0, 0, GetMaxX, GetMaxY);
   { Write a header to the graph }
   SetTextJustify(LeftText, TopText);
   SetTextStyle(GothicFont, HorizDir, 4);
   OutTextXY((GetMaxX - TextWidth(Title)) div 2, 0, Title);
   x := GetMaxX div 2;
   y := GetMaxY div 2;
   GetAspectRatio(XAsp, YAsp);
   AspectRatio := XAsp / YAsp;
   Radius := Round(y * 5.0 / 9.0 / AspectRatio);
   y := y + TextHeight(Title) div 2;
   x :=  Round(x * 6.0 / 5.0);
   NextColorAndFill(Color, Fill);
   for i := 1 to NumValues do begin
     PieceOfPie(x, y, Radius, PercentValues[i], Color, Fill, Labels[i]);
     NextColorAndFill(Color, Fill);
   end;
   repeat until KeyPressed;
   CloseGraph;
 end.
```

Emphasizing a Slice

In some of your pie chart presentations you might need to emphasize one or more pie slices. There are several ways to accomplish this. One approach is to offset the pie slice from the rest of the pie chart by a small amount as shown in Figure 4.2. Although we won't add this feature to our previous example, we'll develop a procedure to implement it.

To offset the pie slice, we'll remove it from the rest of the pie chart by extending it out along the radius of the circle. For instance, let's offset the pie slice by a multiple of its radius. This offset must be added to the x and y coordinates that mark the "center" of the pie slice and its label. The amount that must be added to the x versus the y location depends on where the pie slice is to be drawn. We also need to take into account the aspect ratio of the screen. Figure 4.3 shows the scaling and offset calculations for a moved pie slice.

A procedure that generates an offset pie slice is presented next; it is called **PieceOfPie2** and is similar to **PieceOfPie**—our previous routine. The key difference is that **PieceOfPie2** contains an additional parameter—**OffsetFlag**. When this boolean parameter is true, the procedure draws a pie slice offset from the rest of the

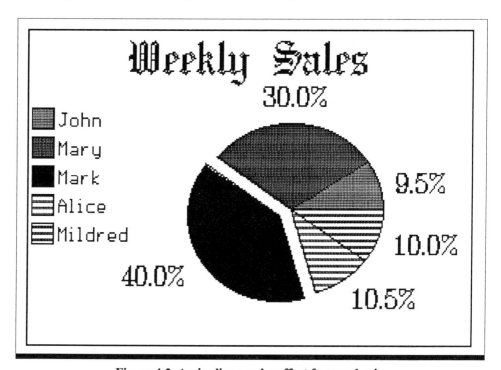

Figure 4.2. A pie slice can be offset for emphasis

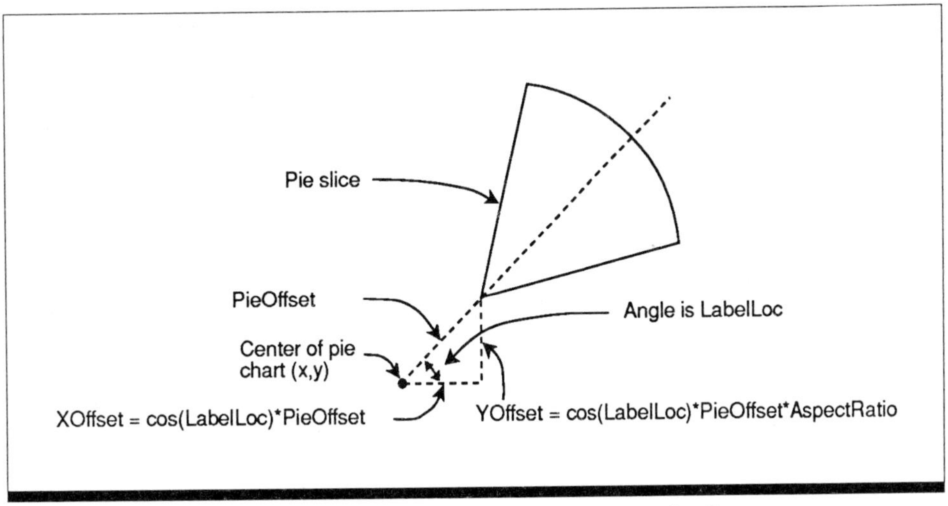

Figure 4.3. Calculations for offsetting a pie slice

pie chart as shown by the following statements. First, the amount of the offset is calculated by:

```
XOffset := cos(LabelLoc) * PieOffset;
YOffset := sin(LabelLoc) * PieOffset * AspectRatio;
```

where PieSlice is an integer constant set to a value of 10. It defines how much offset will be used. Note that these statements are similar to the ones used to calculate the location of the label.

The call to **PieSlice** must be changed to reflect this offset:

```
PieSlice(x+XOffset,y-YOffset,StartAngle,EndAngle,Radius);
```

In addition, the call to **OutTextXY** to write the text label must be changed to use the offset values as well:

```
OutTextXY(x+XOffset,y-YOffset,RealToStr(ShowPercentage,3,1));
```

The complete procedure is listed next. You can use the procedure like the last routine except that when you want to offset a particular pie slice all you need do is set the offset flag to true. Otherwise, if **OffsetFlag** is false, the pie slice is drawn as before.

```
procedure PieceOfPie(x, y, radius: integer; ShowPercentage: real;
                Color, Fill: integer; TheLabel: string;
                OffsetFlag: boolean);
```

```pascal
  const PieOffset = 20;     { Amount a pie slice may be offset }
  var
     StartAngle, EndAngle, LabelAngle: integer;
     LabelLoc: real;
     LRadius: real;
     XOffset, YOffset: integer;

begin
   LRadius := Radius * 1.2;     { Dependent on size of characters }
   SetFillStyle(Fill, Color);
   StartAngle := Round(StartPercentage / 100.0 * 360.0);
   EndAngle := Round((StartPercentage+ShowPercentage) / 100.0 * 360.0);
   LabelAngle := (StartAngle + EndAngle) div 2;
   LabelLoc := ToRadians(LabelAngle);
   if OffsetFlag then begin
      XOffset := Round(cos(LabelLoc) * PieOffset);
      YOffset := Round(sin(LabelLoc) * PieOffset * AspectRatio);
      PieSlice(x+XOffset, y-YOffset, StartAngle, EndAngle, Radius);
   end
   else PieSlice(x, y, StartAngle, EndAngle, Radius);
   x := x + Round(cos(LabelLoc) * LRadius);
   y := y - Round(sin(LabelLoc) * LRadius * AspectRatio);
   SetTextStyle(TriplexFont, HorizDir, 1);

   { Set text justification depending on location of pie slice }
   if (LabelAngle >= 300) or (LabelAngle < 60) then
      SetTextJustify(LeftText, CenterText)
   else if (LabelAngle >= 60) and (LabelAngle < 120) then
      SetTextJustify(CenterText, BottomText)
   else if (LabelAngle >= 120) and (LabelAngle < 240) then
      SetTextJustify(RightText, CenterText)
   else
      SetTextJustify(CenterText, TopText);
   if OffsetFlag then
      OutTextXY(x+XOffset, y-YOffset, RealToStr(ShowPercentage,3,1))
   else
      OutTextXY(x, y, RealToStr(ShowPercentage,3,1));
   StartPercentage := StartPercentage + ShowPercentage;
   ShowKey(Color, Fill, TheLabel);
end;
```

Creating Bar Graphs

The BGI provides two specialized procedures for drawing bar charts: **Bar** and **Bar3D**. We briefly visited these two procedures in Chapter 2 and now we'll take a closer look at how we can actually use them to create presentation bar charts.

Creating a bar chart is in itself simple. The complexity arises, however, when we try to add in various embellishments to make a professional looking bar chart or to automate the chart generation process. This section presents a bar chart program that automatically generates a bar chart from a set of data; however, it sacrifices some generality for the sake of brevity. More specifically, the program uses the BGI **Bar** procedure to create bar charts like the one pictured in Figure 4.4. A complete listing of the program is shown in Listing 4.2. The data that is displayed is contained in the three variables shown here:

```
type
    ListOfStrings = array[1..4] of string;
    ListOfNums = array[1..4] of integer;
const
    YValues: ListOfNums = (5,4,7,6);
```

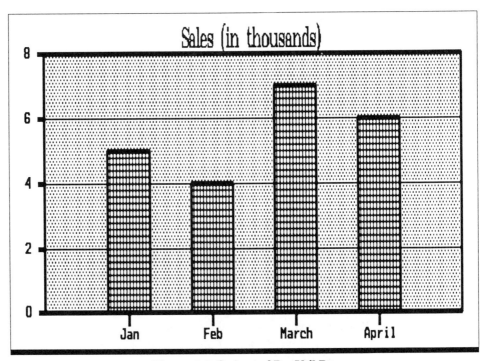

Figure 4.4. Output of BarUtil.Pas

```
XStrings: ListOfStrings = ('Jan', 'Feb', 'March', 'April');
Title: string[36] = ' Monthly Sales (in thousands) ';
```

In this example, the bar chart depicts the first quarter sales for a business. The title of the chart is stored in the string **Title**. The data for the chart corresponds to the first four months of the year. The labels for these are listed in the array of characters stored in the **XStrings** array. These labels will appear below each bar on the horizontal axis. The data for the bars is placed in the **YValues** array. For simplicity, these values are restricted to integers. Finally, since there are four bars to be drawn, the global **NumBars** constant is set to four.

The first step in drawing the chart consists of calling the **DisplayChart** procedure which is provided in Listing 4.2. As you can see, this procedure is passed the various values and titles that are to be displayed as well as a value called **NumRules**. This integer value specifies the number of horizontal divisions that are to be used in the chart. In our example, we'll use four horizontal rules. You may want to experiment with this value to produce different charts.

Essentially, **DisplayChart** is responsible for performing four important tasks. First, it calculates the bounds of the chart which are based upon the size of the screen and the pixel boundaries defined by **ScreenBorderX** and **ScreenBorderY**. Second, the title is written across the screen. To accommodate titles of varying lengths, a modified version of the **ScaleText** procedure that we developed in Chapter 3 is used to automatically adjust the text to fit across the top of the chart. This version of **ScaleText** is designed so that it favors stretching the text the same amount in both the x and y directions. This is done to try to avoid having the text stretched too much in one direction and then become unreadable.

The third part of **DisplayChart** consists of a call to the **GetMax** function and a **while** loop which determines the maximum value for the y (vertical) axis. The **GetMax** function returns the maximum value in the array of values contained in **YValues**. This value is saved in **MaxYValue**. The **while** loop increments **MaxYValue** until it reaches a number that is a multiple of the number of horizontal rules that is defined in the call to **DisplayChart**. The **while** loop ensures that the program selects a maximum value for the chart that will produce whole numbers that can be labeled on the y axis at each horizontal rule on the chart.

Finally, **DrawChart** is called. This routine is also provided in Listing 4.2 (**BarUtil.Pas**). It actually draws out a backdrop for the bar graph as well as the labels for the horizontal and vertical axes and the bars themselves. The backdrop is created by a call to **Bar3D**. Note that we are using this procedure instead of **FillPoly** because its parameters are easier to specify. The procedure **Bar** could easily be used in place of **Bar3D**, however, it would not draw a border to the backdrop.

Within **DrawChart**, the four lines following the call to **Bar3D** and the **for** loop are used to draw the horizontal rules across the backdrop and create thick hash marks and labels on the y axis. The distance between the hash marks is calculated and stored in the variable **Offset** which is used within the **for** loop to place the rules across the chart. The two statements immediately following this **for** loop are used to write the label for the 0 value which corresponds to the horizontal axis.

Next, a scale factor is calculated which is later used to determine exactly how high each bar should be drawn. The statement that performs this calculation is:

```
Scale := (Bottom - Top) / MaxYValue;
```

As shown, the scale factor is dependent on the overall height of the chart and the maximum value which was determined in **DisplayChart**. Figure 4.5 shows the scale factor calculation for a bar.

The lines of code following this statement are similar to those discussed previously to create the vertical labels. However, this code now marks out the divisions and labels on the horizontal axis. The **for** loop uses the strings in the **XStrings** array as the labels. Also within the **for** loop is a call to **Bar3D**. This statement actually creates each of the bars. Once again note that these calls to **Bar3D** use a depth of 0 so that the bars are drawn without a depth. As with the backdrop, **Bar3D** is used instead of the simpler **Bar** procedure because it provides borders around each of the bars.

To adapt this chart program to your own data you will need to provide your own values in **XValues, YValues,** and **Title** as well as change the number represented by **NumBars** to correspond to the number of unique data points you have. Finally, you can choose a value for **NumRules** that will affect the number of horizontal rules drawn by the program and consequently the number of labels on the vertical axis.

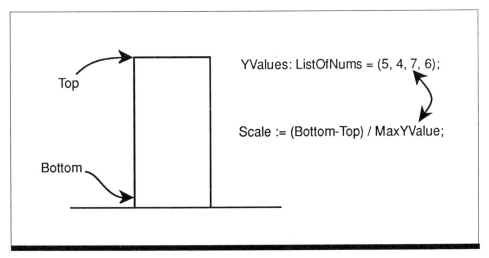

Figure 4.5. Calculating the height of a bar

Some additional things you might try adding are titles for the vertical and horizontal axes. Also you might want to change the program so that it accepts float values along the vertical axes rather than just integers. Of course, there are a great many other alterations you might want to try.

• Listing 4.2

```
program BarUtil;
{ This is a utility program that generates a professional looking bar graph }
uses
   Graph;
type
  ListOfStrings = array[1..4] of string;
  ListOfNums = array[1..4] of integer;
const
  ScreenBorderY: integer = 20;           { 10 pixel border at top and bottom }
  ScreenBorderX: integer = 20;           { 10 pixel border on each side }
  UseRules: integer = 4;                 { Use four rules on the backdrop }
  HashWidth: integer = 8;                { Make hash marks this long }
  NumStrings: integer = 4;               { Four strings on x axis }
  GDriver: integer = Detect;
  YValues: ListOfNums = (5,4,7,6);
  XStrings: ListOfStrings = ('Jan', 'Feb', 'March', 'April');
  Title: string[36] = ' Monthly Sales (in thousands) ';
var
  MaxX, MaxY, GMode: integer;            { Dimensions of graphics screen }
  ch: char;

function IntToStr(n: longint): string;
var
   s: string;
begin
  Str(n, s);
  IntToStr := s;
end;

procedure ScaleText(Left, Top, Right, Bottom: integer; TheString: string);
{ Scale the text so it fits into the specified rectangle. This routine is a
   modification of the ScaleText routine in Chapter 3. It uses setusercharsize to try
   to scale the text so that it looks good. Uses triplex font.
}
```

```
var
   Height: integer;

begin
   SetTextJustify(CenterText, TopText);
   SetUserCharSize(1, 1, 1, 1);
   SetTextStyle(TriplexFont, HorizDir, UserCharSize);
{ In height calculation make room for letters extending below line
  by multiplying TextHeight by 5/4
}
   Height := TextHeight(TheString) * 5 div 4;
   if Height > Bottom-Top then begin
    { Text is too tall so find how. Try scaling down x and y axes by
      same amount in order to keep text well proportioned.
    }
     SetUserCharSize(Bottom-Top, Height, Bottom-Top, Height);
     SetTextStyle(TriplexFont, HorizDir, UserCharSize);
     { Enough room -- so write it }
     if TextWidth(TheString) <= Right - Left then
       OutTextXY((Right+Left) div 2, Top, TheString)
     else begin
       { Doesn't fit with equal scaling - so squash it in!  }
       SetUserCharSize(1, 1, 1, 1);
       SetTextStyle(TriplexFont, HorizDir, UserCharSize);
       SetUserCharSize(Right-Left, TextWidth(TheString), Bottom-Top, Height);
       SetTextStyle(TriplexFont, HorizDir, UserCharSize);
       OutTextXY((Right+Left) div 2, Top, TheString);
     end
   end
   { String is too long - try scaling equally }
   else if TextWidth(TheString) > Right-Left then begin
     SetUserCharSize(Right-Left, TextWidth(TheString),
                     Right-Left, TextWidth(TheString));
     SetTextStyle(TriplexFont, HorizDir, UserCharSize);
     { Enough room -- so write it }
     if TextHeight(TheString)* 5 div 4 <= Bottom-Top then
       OutTextXY((Right+Left) div 2, Top, TheString)
     else begin
       { Doesn't fit with equal scaling - so squash it! }
       SetUserCharSize(1, 1, 1, 1);
```

```
        SetTextStyle(TriplexFont, HorizDir, UserCharSize);
        SetUserCharSize(Right-Left, TextWidth(TheString), Bottom-Top, Height);
        SetTextStyle(TriplexFont, HorizDir, UserCharSize);
        OutTextXY((Right+Left) div 2, Top, TheString);
      end
    end
  else        { Write out text -- enough room }
    OutTextXY((Right+Left) div 2, Top, TheString);
end;


function GetMax(Values: ListOfNums): integer;
{ Find and return the largest value in the array of values }
var
   i, Largest: integer;


begin
  i := 0;  Largest := 1;
  for i := 1 to 4 do
    if Values[i] > Largest then Largest := Values[i];
  GetMax := Largest;
end;


procedure DrawChart(Left, Top, Right, Bottom, NumRules: integer;
   MaxYvalue: integer; XStrings: ListOfStrings; YValues: ListOfNums);
{ Draws the chart's backdrop }
var
  Scale: real;
  i, Height, Incr: integer;
  Buffer: string[10];
  Offset: integer;        { Draw horizontal rules, offset pixels apart }


begin
  { Make a thick border around the backdrop }
  SetLineStyle(SolidLn, 0, ThickWidth);
  SetFillStyle(CloseDotFill, Blue);
  { Use Bar3D with a depth of 0 to draw a bar with a border }
  Bar3D(Left, Top, Right, Bottom, 0, False);
  Offset := (Bottom - Top) div NumRules;
  Incr := MaxYValue div NumRules;
  SetTextJustify(RightText, CenterText);
```

```
SetTextStyle(DefaultFont, HorizDir, 1);
for i := 1 to NumRules do begin
  { Draw rule as thin line }
  SetLineStyle(SolidLn, 0, NormWidth);
  Line(Left, Top+(i-1)*Offset, Right, Top+(i-1)*Offset);
  { Show thick hash mark }
  SetLineStyle(SolidLn, 0, ThickWidth);
  Line(Left-HashWidth, Top+(i-1)*Offset, Left, Top+(i-1)*Offset);
  Buffer := IntToStr(Incr * (NumRules - i + 1));
  OutTextXY(Left-HashWidth-TextWidth(Buffer), Top+(i-1)*Offset, Buffer);
  end;
{ Draw bottom hash mark }
Line(Left-HashWidth, Bottom, Left, Bottom);
OutTextXY(Left-HashWidth-TextWidth(Buffer), Bottom, '0');
{ Write out the values for the horizontal axis }
{ Figure the amount to scale all bars }
Scale := (Bottom - Top) / MaxYvalue;
SetFillStyle(HatchFill, Blue);        { Make all bars Hatch Fill }
Offset := (Right - Left) div (NumStrings + 1);
SetTextJustify(CenterText, TopText);
SetTextStyle(DefaultFont, HorizDir, 1);
for i := 1 to NumStrings do begin
    { Show thick hash mark }
    SetLineStyle(SolidLn, 0, ThickWidth);
    Line(Left+i*Offset, Bottom, Left+i*Offset, Bottom+HashWidth);
    OutTextXY(Left+i*Offset, Bottom+HashWidth+2, XStrings[i]);
{ Draw the bars for the values. Make the total width of one of the bars equal to
  half the distance between two of the hash marks on the horizontal bar.
}
    Height := Round(YValues[i] * Scale);
    Bar3D(Left+i*Offset-Offset div 4, Bottom - Height,
          Left+i*Offset+Offset div 4, Bottom, 0, False);
  end;
end;

procedure DisplayChart(Title: string; XStrings: ListOfStrings;
                  YValues: ListOfNums; NumRules: integer);
var
  MaxYValue, i, Left, Top, Right, Bottom: integer;
```

```
begin
  if NumRules < 0 then
    NumRules := 1;                           { Ensure NumRules is greater than zero }
  { Determine border points of backdrop  }
  Left := ScreenBorderX + MaxX div 8;
  Top := ScreenBorderY;
  Right := MaxX - ScreenBorderX;
  Bottom := MaxY - ScreenBorderY;
  { Display the title at the top. Scale it to fit. }
  ScaleText(Left, 0, Right, Top, Title);
{ Determine a maximum value for the chart scale. It should be at least as large as the
  largest list of values and a multiple of the number of rules that the user desires.
  NumRules should not be greater than MaxYValue.
}
  MaxYValue := GetMax(YValues);             { Get the largest y value }
  while (MaxYValue mod NumRules) <> 0 do
    Inc(MaxYValue);
  { Draw the backdrop }
  DrawChart(Left, Top, Right, Bottom, NumRules, MaxYValue, XStrings, YValues);
end;

begin
  InitGraph(GDriver, GMode, '');
  MaxX := GetMaxX;  MaxY := GetMaxY;
  DisplayChart(Title, XStrings, YValues, UseRules);
  Readln;                                    { Press Enter to quit program }
  CloseGraph;
end.
```

Three-Dimensional Bar Graphs

In the last section we learned how to develop a bar graph utility that can create two-dimensional bar graphs. Next, we'll show you how to modify the program so that it can draw three-dimensional bar graphs. In fact, since **Bar3D** is already used to draw the bars, all we really have to do is change the depth parameter passed to **Bar3D** in the procedure **DrawChart** to get a three-dimensional bar chart.

Generally, if you set the depth of the bar chart to one fourth the height of the highest bar you will get very pleasing results. Therefore an updated statement for **Bar3D** is:

```
Bar3D(Left+i*Offset-Offset div 4, Bottom-Height,
      Left+i*Offset+Offset div 4, Bottom, HeightOfHighestBar div 4, 0);
```

You can easily change the depth of the bars by altering the second to the last parameter in **Bar3D**. If the depth is too large, the bars may begin to merge. If this happens, you will have to place more spacing between the bars or use a smaller value for the depth.

Coin Graphs

Another modification you might try making to the **BarUtil.Pas** program shown in Listing 4.2 is to alter it so that it can create coin graphs like the one shown in Figure 4.6. This coin graph represents the sales of computer monitors for four computer sales people. In order to make the chart interesting, small pictures of the monitors are stacked on top of each other like coins in order to represent the sales totals.

Probably the most challenging task of making a good coin graph is coming up with the right picture to use. Unless you are blessed with an abundance of artistic

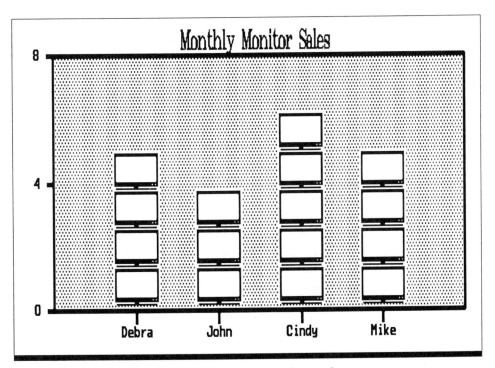

Figure 4.6. A sample coin graph

talent, the best approach is to experiment with different images until you come up with something that looks good.

In order to create a coin chart, the basic idea is to draw a small picture, capture its image with **GetImage**, and then redraw it as necessary using **PutImage**. The coin chart in Figure 4.6 was created from the **BarUtil.Pas** program with only a few minor modifications. Rather than show the entire code once again and risk the possibility of obscuring these changes, let's simply outline them one at a time.

First, we'll need to declare a few new variables. We'll use two constants to define the pixel dimensions of one of the monitors—the image for the coin chart. In addition, we'll need an array to hold the image of the monitor. Therefore, the following lines must be added to the top of **BarUtil.Pas**:

```
const
   PictHeight = 24;
   PictWidth = 32;
var
   Picture: pointer;
```

In addition, the program was modified to use the following values and titles in generating the chart:

```
YValues: array[1..4] of integer = (5,4,7,6);
XStrings: array[1..4] of string = ('Debra', 'John', 'Cindy', 'Mike');
Title: string[23] = ' Monthly Monitor Sales ';
```

The next change to make involves creating an image of the monitor. The monitor image used in Figure 4.6 was created from the following statements which were added to the mainline immediately after the graphics initialization.

```
{ The following lines create the picture of the monitor }
Bar(2,2,PictWidth-2,PictHeight-2);
SetFillStyle(SolidFill, 0);
Bar(4,4,PictWidth-4,PictHeight-5);
SetColor(0);
Line(PictWidth-4,PictHeight-3,PictWidth-5,PictHeight-3);
Line(PictWidth-8,PictHeight-3,PictWidth-9,PictHeight-3);
SetColor(GetMaxColor);
SetFillStyle(SolidFill,GetMaxColor);
Bar(PictWidth div 2-2,PictHeight,PictWidth div 2+2,PictHeight);
Line(4,PictHeight,PictWidth-4,PictHeight);
```

Once the picture of the object is drawn, its image is copied and saved into the array **picture** that we declared earlier. Here are the statements for this task:

```
GetMem(Picture,ImageSize(0,0,PictWidth,PictHeight));
GetImage(0,0,PictWidth,PictHeight,Picture^);
PutImage(0,0,Picture^,XorPut);
```

Note also that we must erase the original picture on the screen before we go on. This is accomplished by using the **XorPut** option as shown earlier. Now that we have an image to work with we are ready to call our chart program to create our coin graph.

This leads us to our next change. Within the **DrawChart** procedure, we need to replace the call to **Bar3D** that draws the bars with the code to draw a stack of the coin images. This can be done by replacing the call to **Bar3D** with a **for** loop which stacks images of **Picture** according to the height that represents the chart value. Here is the new **for** loop:

```
NumImages := (Height - PictHeight) div PictHeight;
for j := 1 to NumImages do
   PutImage(Left + i * Offset - PictWidth div 2,
            Bottom - (j * PictHeight) - 4, Picture^, CopyPut);
```

Note that this statement draws only whole copies of the coin image. It does not draw fractional images. If you need this additional capability you might try overwriting the percentage of the image you don't need by the background or backdrop color.

Animated Graphs

Graphs and charts do not have to be static and lifeless. One way to make a graph more interesting is by adding animation. This section discusses a way of animating bar graphs by using a technique called *inbetweening*.

Briefly, inbetweening is a process where an object's initial and final shapes are predefined and the program automatically calculates intermediate states between them. By sequencing through these intermediate states, the object is effectively animated. We'll look at inbetweening and other animation techniques in greater detail in Chapter 6.

For a bar in a bar graph, the initial state is simply a bar of zero height and the final image is the bar displayed at its full height. The intermediate images of the bar simply depict the bar at ever increasing heights. Figure 4.7 presents the final output of the animated bar chart program. The smoothness of the animation usually

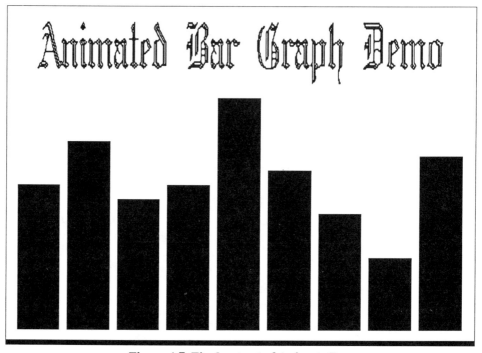

Figure 4.7. Final output of Animate.Pas

depends on the amount of change between the intermediate states of the object, that is, the smoothness depends on the number of intermediate states that are used in the animation.

Shown in Listing 4.3 is a program that demonstrates the concept of inbetweening as it can be applied to bar charts. The code merely demonstrates the concept. If you want to experiment with it further you might try integrating it in with the **BarUtil.Pas** program created earlier.

• Listing 4.3

```
program Animate;
{ Demonstrates how an animated bar graph can be created }
uses
   Graph;
const
   NumSteps: integer = 10;          { Controls the "growth" rate of the }
                                    { bars as they are animated }
```

```
   Title: string[23] = 'Animated Bar Graph Demo';
   GDriver: integer = Detect;
var
   GMode: integer;
   Col: integer;

procedure AnimatedBar(Left, Top, Right, Bottom: integer);
var
   i: integer;
   inc: integer;

begin
   inc := (Bottom - Top) div NumSteps;
   for i := 0 to NumSteps - 1 do
      Bar(Left, Bottom-inc*i, Right, Bottom);
end;

begin
   InitGraph(GDriver, GMode, '');
   { Write a header to the graph }
   SetTextJustify(LeftText, TopText);
   SetTextStyle(GothicFont, HorizDir, 5);
   { Center the title on the first row of the screen }
   OutTextXY((GetMaxX - TextWidth(Title)) div 2, 0, Title);
   SetFillStyle(SolidFill, Magenta);

   { Draw and animate the bars one at a time }
   AnimatedBar(50, 100, 100, 200);
   AnimatedBar(110, 70, 160, 200);
   AnimatedBar(170, 110, 220, 200);
   AnimatedBar(230, 100, 280, 200);
   AnimatedBar(290, 40, 340, 200);
   AnimatedBar(350, 90, 400, 200);
   AnimatedBar(410, 120, 460, 200);
   AnimatedBar(470, 150, 520, 200);
   AnimatedBar(530, 80, 580, 200);

   Readln;
   CloseGraph;
 end.
```

5

Graphics Techniques in Two Dimensions

In this chapter we'll lay the foundation for developing two-dimensional graphics programs. We'll begin by exploring the relationship between screen coordinates and world coordinates and we'll present techniques for mapping between these coordinates. In addition, we'll introduce the concept of transformations, which we'll use to describe how objects can be manipulated in two dimensions. As part of our exploration, we'll develop a package called **Matrix.Pas** that applies many of the concepts presented. Finally, we'll examine object-oriented programming. Again, we'll develop a programming toolkit called **Object.Pas** which we'll use to add object-oriented capabilities to our graphics applications.

Screen Coordinates

As we've seen earlier, the BGI supports various graphics adapters and modes each with its own range of colors, resolution, and number of memory pages. Unfortunately, this flexibility introduces compatibility problems for the graphics programs that we develop. After all, how can we write a program so that it works equally well under the various graphics modes? One problem that we have already encountered is the issue of screen resolution. Not only must we consider the resolutions of the various modes, but we must also adjust for the aspect ratio of a screen in the various modes. Let's examine how this is done.

Working with Aspect Ratios

Each graphics mode has an aspect ratio associated with it. The aspect ratio is based on the ratio between the width and height of each pixel. This ratio is critical when we try to draw a figure of a particular size and shape on the screen. For instance, if we use the CGA 320 by 200 mode, each pixel is approximately twice as high as it is wide. Therefore, if we draw a 4 by 4 block of pixels we won't get a square on the screen. To actually draw a square we must adjust for the aspect ratio of the mode as shown in Figure 5.1.

Fortunately, the BGI provides the **GetAspectRatio** routine that we can use to determine the aspect ratio of the current mode. It is defined in the unit **Graph** as:

```
procedure GetAspectRatio(var Xasp, Yasp: word);
```

The parameters **Xasp** and **Yasp** can be divided together to calculate the aspect ratio of the screen. In most modes, the pixels are taller than they are wide, therefore the BGI normalizes the **Yasp** value to 10,000 and returns some value less than 10,000 in **Xasp**. The aspect ratio of the screen, therefore, can be calculated as:

```
AspectRatio := Xasp/Yasp;
```

This value can then be multiplied against each y dimension in order to draw an object correctly proportioned and positioned. For instance, in Figure 5.1, the height of the 4 by 4 square shown becomes:

```
ScreenHeight := 4 * AspectRatio
```

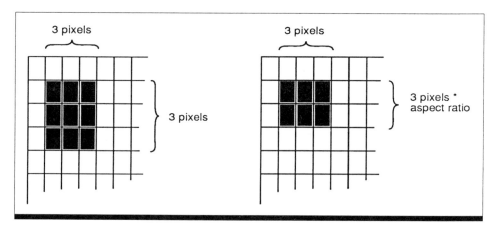

Figure 5.1. Adjusting for the screen's aspect ratio

Since **Xasp** is generally smaller than **Yasp**, **AspectRatio** is set to some fractional value and **ScreenHeight** is calculated as a value less than 4. This produces a correctly proportioned square as shown in Figure 5.1.

Screen and World Coordinates

In the last section we learned how to adjust for the difference between the x and y dimensions that exist in most of the graphics modes. Similarly, we must make adjustments to graphics objects so they retain their size when displayed in graphics modes with different screen resolutions. To achieve this, we'll use a standard coordinate system called *world coordinates*.

Up until now, we have been working only with screen coordinates. This approach can lead to problems when we work with graphics modes with different resolutions. For instance, a 10 by 10 square in a 320 by 200 mode appears quite different in a 640 by 200 mode. In addition, if we define an object to be located at (500, 150) it would not even appear in the 320 by 200 mode. What we need is the ability to map objects so that they are displayed proportionally and correctly positioned. We'll do this by expressing objects in *world coordinates* (such as in inches, feet, meters, etc.), and then map them to *screen coordinates* so that they fit properly on the screen before they are drawn.

Mapping Between Coordinate Systems

In general, we want to be able to map between world coordinates and screen coordinates as shown in Figure 5.2. To do this we can use the relations shown in Figure 5.3. The equations:

$$x' = a * x + b$$
$$y' = c * y + d$$

define how a point (x, y) in world coordinates can be mapped to a screen coordinate (x', y'). The values **L1**, **T1**, **R1**, and **B1** represent the range of values that we are considering in the world coordinates and similarly **L2**, **T2**, **R2**, and **B2** define the size of the screen area that the object is to be mapped into. Now let's put these equations into our unit **Matrix.Pas**. The code for this file is shown later in this chapter.

First, we need two routines that can set the ranges of the world and screen coordinates. These procedures are called **Set_Window** and **Set_ViewPort**. Each is

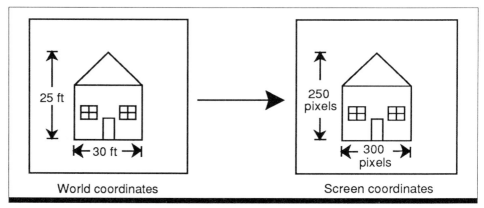

Figure 5.2. Mapping objects from world to screen coordinates

called with the left, top, right, and bottom bounds of its region, and internally sets an appropriate group of global variables within **Matrix.Pas** to these ranges. In addition, **Set_ViewPort** calculates the ratios shown in Figure 5.3. For example, the two statements:

```
Set_Window(0.0, 0.0, 3.0, 3.0);
Set_ViewPort(0, 0, GetMaxX, GetMaxY);
```

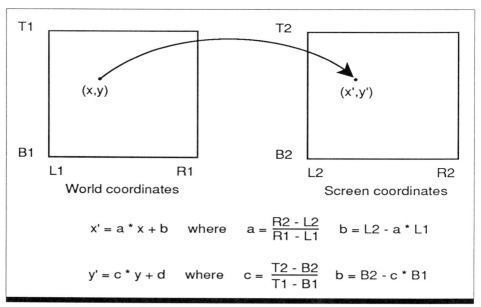

Figure 5.3. Equations for mapping from world to screen coordinates

set the range of values in the world and screen coordinates so that all objects between (0.0, 0.0) and (3.0, 3.0) in world coordinates are mapped to the full screen. Objects outside this range are clipped and not displayed.

As another example, you could use the same world coordinate settings but define the viewport on the screen to be:

```
Set_ViewPort(0, 0, GetMaxX div 2, GetMaxY div 2);
```

In this case, the same objects that would appear above would now appear in only the top-left half of the screen. Similarly, you can effectively zoom in on the objects displayed by decreasing the size of the region passed to **Set_Window**. Note that, as written, you must match each call to **Set_Window** with a succeeding call to **Set_ViewPort** in order to make changes take effect.

The routines in **Matrix.Pas** that actually map between the coordinate systems are called **WorldToPC** and **PCtoWorld**. Each routine maps one point from one of the coordinate systems to the other. For example, **WorldToPC** maps a world coordinate to a screen coordinate by using the code:

```
procedure WorldToPC(xw, yw: real; var xpc, ypc: integer);
begin
   xpc := Round(a * xw + b);
   ypc := Round(c * yw + d);
end;
```

The parameters **xw** and **yw** are the world coordinates to be mapped to the screen coordinates **xpc** and **ypc**. You should compare these statements to the equations shown in Figure 5.3. Similarly, **PCToWorld** maps a screen coordinate to world coordinates by the statements:

```
procedure PCToWorld(xpc, ypc: integer; var xw, yw: real);
begin
   xw := (xpc - b) / a;
   yw := (ypc - d) / c;
end;
```

We'll be using these routines in the CAD program that we will develop in Chapter 12 to define how and where objects are displayed.

Transformations

In the last section, we learned how to map objects represented in world coordinates to the screen. Now let's explore ways to manipulate these objects so that they can be drawn at different locations, orientations, and scales. We'll use transformations to produce these effects.

Transformations are a basic mathematical operation in graphics programming. Quite literally, a *transform* is a function (or equation) that defines how one set of data is to be changed or transformed into another. For example, let's say that we have a picture of a wheel on the screen that we want to rotate. We can use a rotation transformation to determine how the wheel is supposed to be affected as it is moved.

The most common transformations are translation, rotation, and scaling. In this section we'll explore each of these transformations in detail and add routines to **Matrix.Pas** to perform these operations. A list of the transformation routines that will be added to **Matrix.Pas** is shown in Table 5.1.

Table 5.1. Two-dimensional transformations supported in Matrix.Pas

Routine	Description
PCTranslatePoly	Translates a polygon in screen coordinates
PCScalePoly	Scales a polygon in screen coordinates
PCRotatePoly	Rotates a polygon in screen coordinates
PCShearPoly	Shears a polygon in screen coordinates
WorldTranslatePoly	Translates a polygon in world coordinates
WorldScalePoly	Scales a polygon in world coordinates
WorldRotatePoly	Rotates a polygon in world coordinates

The CAD program which we'll develop in Chapter 12 uses the **Matrix.Pas** unit to translate and rotate objects. When we explore three-dimensional graphics in Chapter 13 we'll rely upon transforms to generate perspective views of three-dimensional objects. For now, however, we will only be concerned with objects in two dimensions.

Translation

One of the simplest transforms produces a translation. Essentially, a translation defines how a point is supposed to be moved from one location in space to another.

For example, if we have a box drawn on the left-hand side of the screen and we want to move it to the right, we can use a translation transformation to specify how each point must be moved.

For instance, translating a pixel on the screen can be done by adding an appropriate value to each of the x and y coordinates that the point is to be moved. This can be written in Pascal as:

```
NewX := x + TranslateX;
NewY := y + TranslateY;
```

The values **TranslateX** and **TranslateY** can be either positive or negative and define how much the point (x, y) should be translated in the x and y directions, respectively.

Translating an object, like a polygon, is only a matter of translating each of the points that make up the polygon as illustrated in Figure 5.4. A routine in **Matrix.Pas** that does this is called **PCTranslatePoly**.

```
procedure PCTranslatePoly(NumPoints: integer; var Poly: PCArray;
                          tx, ty: integer);
{ Translates a two-dimensional polygon by tx and ty. The polygon
  should be in screen coordinates.
}
var
   i: integer;

begin
   for i := 1 to NumPoints do begin
     Poly[i].x := Poly[i].x + tx;
```

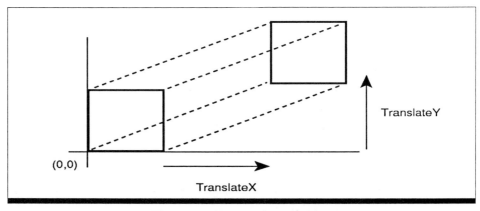

Figure 5.4. Translating an object

```
      Poly[i].y := Poly[i].y + ty;
   end
end;
```

It is designed to work in screen coordinates since the translation amounts are specified as integers. A similar routine, **WorldTranslatePoly**, is included in **Matrix.Pas** that is designed to translate a polygon specified in world coordinates. Because of this, **Tx**, **Ty**, and the array **Poly** are defined as using real values.

Scaling a Two-Dimensional Polygon

Scaling a two-dimensional polygon can be accomplished by multiplying each of the coordinates of the original polygon by a scale factor. For example, assume we want to scale the box shown in Figure 5.5 by 2 in the x direction and by one half in the y direction. This can be done by applying the following equations to each of the coordinates of the box:

```
ScaleDx := x * ScaleX;
ScaleDy := y * ScaleY;
```

A routine in **Matrix.Pas** that performs this operation for a polygon in screen coordinates is called **PCScalePoly.**

```
procedure PCScalePoly(NumPoints: integer; var Poly: PCArray;
                      sx, sy: real);
{ Scales a polygon by sx in the x dimension and sy in the y
  dimension. The polygon should be in screen coordinates.
}
var i: integer;

begin
   for i := 1 to NumPoints do begin
     Poly[i].x := Round(Poly[i].x * sx);
     Poly[i].y := Round(Poly[i].y * sy);
   end;
end;
```

A similar routine exists for polygons specified in world coordinates. It is called **WorldScalePoly**.

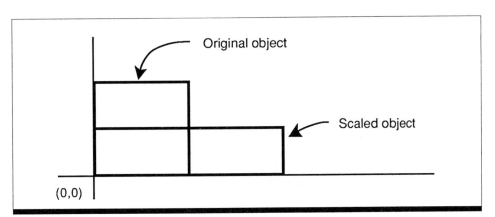

Figure 5.5. Scaling an object by two in x and one half in y

Merely calling **PCScalePoly** to scale an object does not always produce the results expected, however. Since each coordinate in the object is multiplied by a scale factor, the object may be moved as well as scaled as shown in Figure 5.6. That is, unless one of the coordinates is (0, 0). This coordinate would stay the same. Therefore, if you want to scale an object, yet keep one of its points stationary so that the object doesn't move, two additional steps must be taken. First, the object must be translated so that the point you want to scale about (keep fixed) moves to the origin. Second, after applying the scaling transformation, the object must be translated back by the amount that it was earlier translated. The net effect is that the object is scaled, but the point that is translated to the origin and back remains

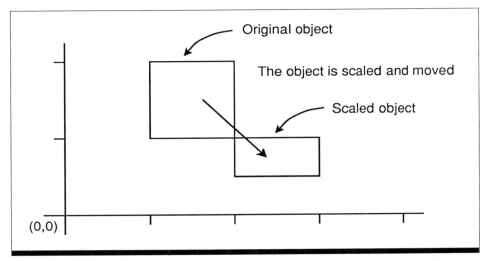

Figure 5.6. Scaling an object not at the origin changes its size and location

stationary. This scaling sequence, as illustrated in Figure 5.7, is actually more useful than the first.

For example, the following code doubles the size of the polygon in the array **Poly** by translating it so that its first point is at the origin, scaling it, and then translating the polygon back.

```
px := Poly[1].x;
py := poly[1].y;
PCTranslatePoly(NumPoints, Poly, -px, -py);
PCScalePoly(NumPoints, Poly, 2.0, 2.0);
PCTranslatePoly(NumPoints, Poly, px, py);
```

Rotating a Two-Dimensional Polygon

Another useful transformation rotates an object about a point. The equations to perform the rotation are:

```
RotatedX := x * Cos(Angle) - y * Sin(Angle);
RotatedY := x * Sin(Angle) + y * Cos(Angle);
```

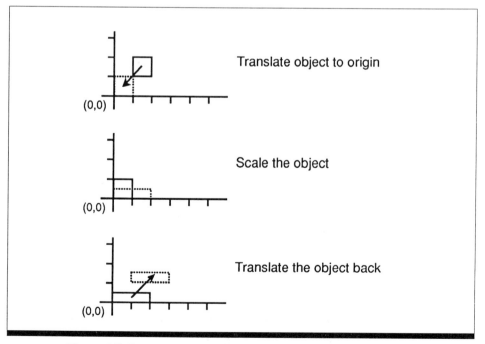

Translate object to origin

Scale the object

Translate the object back

Figure 5.7. Process to properly scale an object not at the origin

Rather than go into the geometry that derives these equations, let's look at them from a user's standpoint. The **x** and **y** variables on the right side of the equation represent the point being rotated and the **Angle** variable specifies the angle on which the point is to be rotated. In Turbo Pascal this value needs to be expressed in radians. Since degrees are more natural for us to specify angles, we'll use the function **ToRadians** to convert angles in degrees to radians.

Actually, to rotate an object successfully we need to pick a point about which the object is to be rotated, translate it to the origin, rotate the polygon, and then translate the object back. The routine in **Matrix.Pas** that performs the rotation operation is called **PCRotatePoly** and can be used to rotate a polygon as shown in Figure 5.8.

```
procedure PCRotatePoly(NumPoints: integer; var Poly: PCArray;
                       Angle: real);
{ Rotates a polygon by the number of degrees specified in angle.
  The polygon should be in screen coordinates.
}
var
   i: integer;
   x, y, Radians, CosTheta, SinTheta: real;

begin
   Radians := ToRadians(Angle);
   CosTheta := cos(Radians);
```

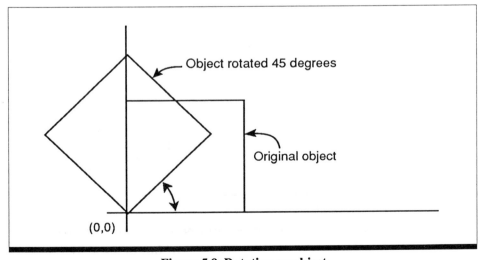

Figure 5.8. Rotating an object

```
    SinTheta := sin(Radians);
    for i := 1 to NumPoints do begin
    x := Poly[i].x;
    y := Poly[i].y;
    Poly[i].x := Round(x*CosTheta-y*SinTheta/AspectRatio);
    Poly[i].y := Round(x*SinTheta*Aspectratio+y*CosTheta);
    end
end;
```

Note that the **y** values in the equations are adjusted by **AspectRatio**. This is required because this routine is operating with screen coordinates. The procedure **WorldRotatePoly** has similar code, except that since it is designed to work with world coordinates, it does not need these adjustments.

The Shear Transform

Some transformations produce some rather interesting effects. One of the more common transformations that falls into this category shears objects to which it is applied as shown in Figure 5.9. It involves multiplying each of the coordinates of the object by a scale factor and adding an offset. A pair of equations that produces the shear effect are:

```
ShearedX := x + c * y;
ShearedY := d * x + y;
```

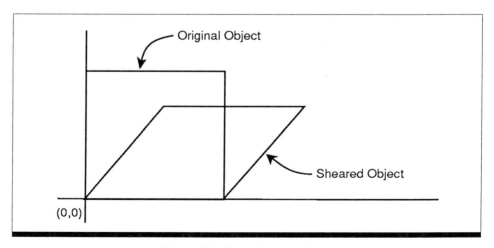

Figure 5.9. Shearing an object

As with rotations, we want to shear the polygon about a point, so we must translate the polygon to the origin, apply the shear transform, and then translate the object back. In addition, if we transform pixels on the screen we will need to compensate for the monitor's aspect ratio. The routine that can be used to shear a polygon situated at the origin is **PCShearPoly**. You should refer to **Matrix.Pas** for a complete listing of this routine.

• Listing 5.1

```
unit Matrix;
{ The following set of matrix operations are used in the two-dimensional graphics
  programs
}
interface
uses
   Graph;
const
   MaxPoint = 5;
type
   PCArray = array[1..MaxPoint] of PointType;
   WorldType = record
     x, y: real;
   end;
   WorldArray = array[1..MaxPoint] of WorldType;
var
   AspectRatio: real;         { Define the aspect ratio }
   XAsp, YAsp: word;

{ These are the procedures that Matrix.Pas provides }
function ToRadians(Degrees: real): real;
procedure PCTranslatePoly(NumPoints: integer; var Poly: PCArray; tx, ty: integer);
procedure PCScalePoly(NumPoints: integer; var Poly: PCArray; sx, sy: real);
procedure PCRotatePoly(NumPoints: integer; var Poly: PCArray; Angle: real);
procedure PCShearPoly(NumPoints: integer; var Poly: PCArray; c, d: real);
procedure CopyPoly(NumPoints: integer; var PolyFrom, PolyTo: PCArray);
procedure WorldTranslatePoly(NumPoints: integer; var Poly: WorldArray; tx, ty: real);
procedure WorldScalePoly(NumPoints: integer; var Poly: WorldArray; sx, sy: real);
procedure WorldRotatePoly(NumPoints: integer; var Poly: WorldArray; Angle: real);
procedure CopyWorldPoly(NumPoints: integer; var PolyFrom, PolyTo: WorldArray);
```

```pascal
procedure WorldToPC(xw, yw: real; var xpc, ypc: integer);
procedure PCToWorld(xpc, ypc: integer; var xw, yw: real);
procedure Set_Window(xmin, xmax, ymin, ymax: real);
procedure Set_ViewPort(xmin, xmax, ymin, ymax: integer);
procedure PCPolyToWorldPoly(NumPoints: integer;
                           var PCPoly: PCArray; var WorldPoly: WorldArray);
procedure WorldPolyToPCPoly(NumPoints: integer;
                           var WorldPoly: WorldArray; var PCPoly: PCArray);
implementation
var
  a, b, c, d: real;              { Internal values set by  }
  xvl, xvr, yvt, yvb: integer;   { set window and viewport }
  xwl, xwr, ywt, ywb: real;      { to map to screen coords }

function ToRadians(Degrees: real): real;
{ Convert degrees to Radians }
begin
  ToRadians :=  Pi * Degrees / 180.0;
end;


procedure PCTranslatePoly(NumPoints: integer; var Poly: PCArray; tx, ty: integer);
{ Translates a two-dimensional polygon by tx and ty. The polygon should be in
  screen coordinates.
}
var
  i: integer;


begin
  for i := 1 to NumPoints do begin
    Poly[i].x := Poly[i].x + tx;
    Poly[i].y := Poly[i].y + ty;
  end
end;


procedure PCScalePoly(NumPoints: integer; var Poly: PCArray; sx, sy: real);
{ Scales a polygon by sx in the x dimension and sy in the y
  dimension. The polygon should be in screen coordinates.
}
var
  i: integer;
```

```
begin
   for i := 1 to NumPoints do begin
      Poly[i].x := Round(Poly[i].x * sx);
      Poly[i].y := Round(Poly[i].y * sy);
   end;
end;

procedure PCRotatePoly(NumPoints: integer; var Poly: PCArray; Angle: real);
{ Rotates a polygon by the number of degrees specified in angle.
  The polygon should be in screen coordinates.
}
var
   i: integer;
   x, y, Radians, CosTheta, SinTheta: real;

begin
   Radians := ToRadians(Angle);
   CosTheta := cos(Radians);
   SinTheta := sin(Radians);
   for i := 1 to NumPoints do begin
      x := Poly[i].x;
      y := Poly[i].y;
      Poly[i].x := Round(x * CosTheta - y * SinTheta / AspectRatio);
      Poly[i].y := Round(x * SinTheta * Aspectratio + y * CosTheta);
   end
end;

procedure PCShearPoly(NumPoints: integer; var Poly: PCArray; c, d: real);
{ Shears a polygon by applying c to the x dimension and d to
  the y dimension. The polygon should be in screen coordinates.
}
var
   i: integer;
   x, y: real;

begin
   for i := 1 to NumPoints do begin
      x := Poly[i].x;
      y := Poly[i].y;
      Poly[i].x := Round(x + c * y / AspectRatio);
```

```pascal
         Poly[i].y := Round(d * x * AspectRatio + y);
      end
end;


procedure CopyPoly(NumPoints: integer; var PolyFrom, PolyTo: PCArray);
{ Copies from one integer polygon to another }
var
   i: integer;

begin
   for i := 1 to NumPoints do begin
      PolyTo[i].x := PolyFrom[i].x;
      PolyTo[i].y := PolyFrom[i].y;
   end
end;


procedure WorldTranslatePoly(NumPoints: integer; var Poly: WorldArray;
                             tx, ty: real);
{ Translates a polygon in world coordinates }
var
   i: integer;

begin
   for i := 1 to NumPoints do begin
      Poly[i].x := Poly[i].x + tx;
      Poly[i].y := Poly[i].y + ty;
   end
end;


procedure WorldScalePoly(NumPoints: integer; var Poly: WorldArray;
                         sx, sy: real);
{ Scales a polygon in world coordinates by sx and sy }
var
   i: integer;

begin
   for i := 0 to NumPoints do begin
      Poly[i].x := Poly[i].x * sx;
      Poly[i].y := Poly[i].y * sy;
   end
end;
```

```
procedure WorldRotatePoly(NumPoints: integer;
                          var Poly: WorldArray; Angle: real);
{ Rotates a polygon in world coordinates }
var
  i: integer;
  Rad: real;
  CosTheta, SinTheta: real;
  x, y: real;

begin
  Rad := ToRadians(Angle);
  CosTheta := cos(Rad);
  SinTheta := sin(Rad);
  for i := 1 to NumPoints do begin
    x := Poly[i].x;
    y := Poly[i].y;
    Poly[i].x := x * CosTheta - y * SinTheta;
    Poly[i].y := x * SinTheta + y * CosTheta;
  end
end;


procedure CopyWorldPoly(NumPoints: integer; var PolyFrom, PolyTo: WorldArray);
{ Copies one polygon in world coordinates to another }
var
  i: integer;

begin
  for i := 1 to NumPoints do begin
    PolyTo[i].x := PolyFrom[i].x;
    PolyTo[i].y := PolyFrom[i].y;
  end
end;


procedure WorldToPC(xw, yw: real; var xpc, ypc: integer);
{ Converts a world coordinate to a screen coordinate }
begin
  xpc := Round(a * xw + b);
  ypc := Round(c * yw + d);
end;
```

```pascal
procedure PCToWorld(xpc, ypc: integer; var xw, yw: real);
{ Converts a screen coordinate to a world coordinate }
begin
  xw := (xpc - b) / a;
  yw := (ypc - d) / c;
end;

procedure Set_Window(xmin, xmax, ymin, ymax: real);
{ Defines the window used in real world coordinates }
begin
  xwl := xmin;    xwr := xmax;
  ywb := ymin;    ywt := ymax;
end;

procedure Set_ViewPort(xmin, xmax, ymin, ymax: integer);
{ Defines the region on the screen that world objects are mapped to }
begin
  xvl := xmin;    xvr := xmax;
  yvb := ymin;    yvt := ymax;
  a := (xvr - xvl) / (xwr - xwl);    b := xvl - a * xwl;
  c := (yvt - yvb) / (ywt - ywb);    d := yvb - c * ywb;
end;

procedure PCPolyToWorldPoly(NumPoints: integer; var PCPoly: PCArray;
                            var WorldPoly: WorldArray);
{ Convert a list of polygon points from screen coordinates to world coordinates }
var
  i: integer;

begin
  for i := 1 to NumPoints do
    PCToWorld(PCPoly[i].x, PCPoly[i].y, WorldPoly[i].x, WorldPoly[i].y);
end;

procedure WorldPolyToPCPoly(NumPoints: integer; var WorldPoly: WorldArray;
                            var PCPoly: PCArray);
{ Convert a list of polygon points from world coordinates to screen coordinates }
var
  i: integer;
```

```
begin
    for i := 1 to NumPoints do
        WorldToPC(WorldPoly[i].x, WorldPoly[i].y,
            PCPoly[i].x, PCPoly[i].y);
end;


end.
```

A Matrix Demo

Listing 5.2 presents a short program that you can use to test the matrix operations included in **Matrix.Pas**. It applies several of the transformations developed in **Matrix.Pas** to the polygon in the array **Points**. After displaying the result of each of the transforms, you must press a key to proceed to the next one.

• Listing 5.2

```
program MtxtTest;
{ This program tests the transforms defined in the Matrix.Pas unit }
uses
    Graph, Matrix, Crt;
const
    GDriver: integer = Detect;
    NumPoints = 5;
    Points: PCArray = ((x:150; y:80), (x:400; y:80), (x:400; y:150),
                        (x:150; y:150), (x:150; y:80));
var
    PolyCopy: PCArray;
    GMode, px, py, i: integer;
    ch: char;

begin
    InitGraph(GDriver, GMode, '');
    GetAspectRatio(XAsp, YAsp);
    AspectRatio := XAsp / YAsp;
    Rectangle(0, 0, GetMaxX, GetMaxY);
    { Test translate polygon }
    DrawPoly(NumPoints, Points);
    CopyPoly(NumPoints, Points, PolyCopy);
```

```
  px := PolyCopy[1].x;
  py := PolyCopy[1].y;
  PCTranslatePoly(NumPoints, PolyCopy, -px, -py);
  DrawPoly(NumPoints, PolyCopy);
  ch := ReadKey;

  { Scale the polygon about the point (px, py) }
  CopyPoly(NumPoints, Points, PolyCopy);
  PCTranslatePoly(NumPoints, PolyCopy, -px, -py);
  PCScalePoly(NumPoints, PolyCopy, 1.5, 1.5);
  PCTranslatePoly(NumPoints, PolyCopy, px, py);
  DrawPoly(NumPoints, PolyCopy);
  ch := ReadKey;

  { Rotate the object about the point (px, py) }
  CopyPoly(NumPoints, Points, PolyCopy);
  PCTranslatePoly(NumPoints, PolyCopy, -px, -py);
  PCRotatePoly(NumPoints, PolyCopy, 45.0);
  PCTranslatePoly(NumPoints, PolyCopy, px, py);
  DrawPoly(NumPoints, PolyCopy);
  ch := ReadKey;

  { Shear the object about the point (px, py) }
  ClearViewPort;
  DrawPoly(NumPoints, Points);
  CopyPoly(NumPoints, Points, PolyCopy);
  PCTranslatePoly(NumPoints, PolyCopy, -px, -py);
  PCShearPoly(NumPoints, PolyCopy, 0, 1);
  PCTranslatePoly(NumPoints, PolyCopy, px, py);
  DrawPoly(NumPoints, PolyCopy);
  ch := ReadKey;
  CloseGraph;    { Exit graphics mode }
end.
```

Object-Oriented Programming

Object-oriented programming (OOP) is a simple but powerful concept. Although the specifics of an object-oriented application can vary greatly, there are several general principles that all OOP systems have in common.

The main principle in OOP is that information is grouped as entities called objects. Each object usually has a special routine associated with it. Also, objects communicate with each other by passing messages. The distinguishing factor in OOP, however, is that actions are accessed through the objects. This contrasts with traditional programming methods where procedures and functions are used to access data and perform actions.

There are many advantages to OOP. First, it can be used to hide any special processing that a set of data requires so that all objects effectively look the same from a higher level. In addition, OOP can make your programs more readable and easier to maintain and modify. These are the two main reasons that we'll be using an OOP style in our graphics environments.

Working with OOP

In an interactive graphics environment icons, text, menus, and graphical figures can all be manipulated as objects. Each of these objects usually has a routine associated with it that is executed when its object is selected. Objects are selected by using a pointing device such as a mouse. (When a mouse is used, an object is selected by clicking a mouse button on the object.)

Internally, objects are maintained in a list. Whenever a region of the screen is selected with a pointing device, the list is checked to see if an object is located at the position selected. If so, that object's routine is executed. For instance, if we click a mouse button on a line icon, the line routine is invoked. Figure 5.10 provides a graphical view of this process.

An Object-Oriented Utility

To complete this chapter, we'll develop an OOP utility that we'll use in several application programs later in the book. The utility is shown in the source file **Object.Pas** presented in Listing 5.3. It uses some of the mouse utilities that we will develop in Chapter 7; however, these routines are not critical in order to understand the majority of **Object.Pas**. We'll focus on the various components of this short utility in the following sections.

The Internal Object List

As mentioned previously, in our OOP environment all objects are maintained in an internal list. The objects consist of icons, text, and eventually various graphical

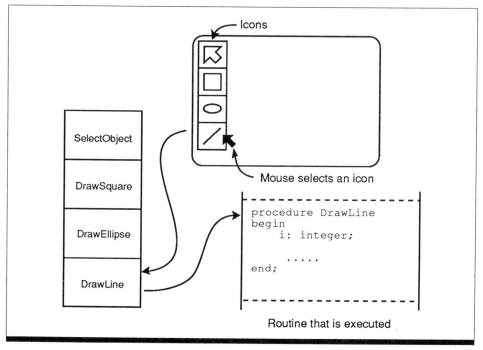

Figure 5.10. Executing a function by selecting an object from an object list

figures. For simplicity we will use an array of objects which is limited to **MaxObjects** in size. This is a constant set to 50. The array is actually a collection of **ObjectRec** records and is declared as:

```
ObjList: array[1..MaxObjects] of ObjectRec;
```

The **ObjectRec** record contains the relevant information about each object that is needed in order to determine if it has been selected. In addition, it provides a pointer to a routine which is to be invoked if the object is chosen. The record **ObjectRec** is:

```
type
  ProcType = procedure;

  ObjectRec = record
    ObjType: word;                    { Type of object }
    Code: char;                       { Quick access code value }
    Left, Top: integer;               { Screen bounds of object }
```

```
    Right, Bottom: integer;
    Proc: ProcType;          { Routine to execute if selected }
  end;
```

The first part of this record includes a number which specifies the type of object stored (**IconObj**, **TextObj**, etc.). The next field, **Code**, is included in the **ObjectRec** to provide a unique code that can be used to select the object. It provides a way of selecting an object through the keyboard rather than by pointing to it with a mouse. The next four record fields define the pixel boundaries of the object on the screen. The last line of the record is a pointer to a procedure of type **ProcType**, which is simply a procedure with no parameters, that is to be executed whenever the object is selected. We will write these routines in Chapters 10, 11, and 12.

Adding an Object

Application programs that exploit our OOP utility will always begin by building up a list of objects that they will use. Each object is added to the object list through the routine **AddObject** which is included in **Object.Pas**.

The **AddObject** routine assigns the various fields of the **ObjectRec** record for the object being added, and increments a pointer, **ObjNum**, to the next available **ObjectRec** record in the list of objects.

Several parameters are passed to **AddObject**. Let's take a look at these one at a time. The left-most parameter is a numeric value which represents the type of object being added. For now, we'll support two types of objects—**IconObj** and **TextObj**. Both of these are constants defined at the top of **Object.Pas**. The **Code** is the next parameter in the list. Typically, this should be a single letter that you can type to quickly access the icon rather than having to point and click on it with a mouse. The access code is followed by two coordinate pairs which locate the top-left and bottom-right pixel boundaries of the object. When you click on an object, such as an icon, these pixel boundaries are tested to see which object the mouse is pointing to, if any. The last parameter is a pointer to the routine that is to be executed when the object is selected.

A test is made at the beginning of **AddObject** to see if the array of objects is full. If it is, the routine immediately returns with no action taken. Otherwise, the next available location in the object array, indexed by **ObjNum**, is loaded with the object information passed to **AddObject**. Once the **ObjectRec** record is set to its proper values, **ObjNum** is incremented to the next location in the array and the routine terminates.

By way of example, suppose we want to add an icon to save the current state of our program to disk. Let's say the icon is bounded by the coordinate locations (0,48) and (16,64). The routine that is invoked to perform the action is called **SaveState** and is defined at the top of our file as:

```
procedure SaveState;
```

In addition, we want our routine to be accessible if the user types the letter s. The statement that adds such an object to the object list is:

```
AddObject(IconObj, 's', 0, 48, 16, 64, SaveState);
```

Selecting an Object

Typically, we'll be selecting an object from the screen by pressing a mouse button while the mouse is pointing to it or by typing the appropriate access code. In either case, the routine **AnyToProcess** is used to decide which object has been selected, if any. Although this routine calls several mouse routines that will be developed in Chapter 7, let's take a look at how it works.

First, note that **AnyToProcess** takes one integer parameter called **c**. This parameter tells **AnyToProcess** which **Code** has been selected or if a mouse button has been pressed. These two meanings are distinguished by the outer **if** statement in **AnyToProcess** which test whether **c** is positive or negative. If **c** is less than zero, it is assumed that a mouse button has been pressed and the code executes the **else** part of the routine. This block of code calls a mouse routine to determine the mouse position and then checks these coordinates with the boundaries of objects to see if any overlap. If so, the overlapping object is executed. We'll look at how an object routine is invoked by showing what happens if **c** is positive.

When **c** is positive, the top of the **if** statement is executed. The routine is designed so that if **AnyToProcess** is called with a value greater than zero, then **c** is potentially one of the access codes. Therefore a **for** loop searches through the list of objects in **ObjList** by testing whether any of the objects have a **Code** field in their **ObjectRec** records that is equal to **c**. If so, the routine corresponding to the object with the matching **Code** is executed by the statement:

```
ObjList[i].Proc;
```

For instance, in our example previously described, this single line would invoke the routine **SaveState**. After the object's routine terminates, **AnyToProcess** returns.

You may have noticed that the statement that invokes the object's routine is surrounded by two **if** statements. These statements test whether the object type is an

IconObj. If so, **ReverseIcon** is called to highlight the icon and then later called again to restore it to its original state. The routine **ReverseIcon** performs this operation by inverting the image of the icon by copying it from the screen using **GetImage** and then overwriting it with **PutImage** using the **NotPut** option. Therefore, the first time **ReverseIcon** is called it inverts the image of the icon and when it is called again, it restores the icon image to its original form.

• Listing 5.3

```
unit Object;
{ An object oriented programming tool }
interface
uses
   Graph, MousePac;
const
   MaxObjects = 50;        { Maximum number of objects at one time }
   IconObj: integer = 1;   { An icon object }
   FillObj: integer = 2;   { A Fill pattern object (used in Paint and CAD) }
   TextObj: integer = 3;   { A text object }
type
   ProcType = procedure;
   ObjectRec = record
     ObjType: word;
     Code: char;
     Left, Top: integer;
     Right, Bottom: integer;
     Proc: ProcType;
   end;
var
   ObjList: array[1..MaxObjects] of ObjectRec;
   ObjNum: integer;

procedure AddObject(ObjType: integer; Code: char; Left, Top,
                    Right, Bottom: integer; Proc: ProcType);
procedure AnyToProcess(c: integer);

implementation
procedure AddObject(ObjType: integer; Code: char; Left, Top,
        Right, Bottom: integer; Proc: ProcType);
```

```
{ This routine adds objects to the object list }
begin
  if ObjNum <= MaxObjects then begin
    ObjList[ObjNum].ObjType := ObjType;
    ObjList[ObjNum].Code := Code;
    ObjList[ObjNum].Left := Left;
    ObjList[ObjNum].Top := Top;
    ObjList[ObjNum].Right := Right;
    ObjList[ObjNum].Bottom := Bottom;
    ObjList[ObjNum].Proc := Proc;
    Inc(ObjNum);
  end
end;


procedure ReverseIcon(Left, Top, Right, Bottom: integer);
var
  IconBuff: pointer;
  Size: word;

begin
  Size := ImageSize(Left, Top, Right, Bottom);
  GetMem(IconBuff, Size);
  if IconBuff <> Nil then begin
    HideMouse;
    GetImage(Left, Top, Right, Bottom, IconBuff^);
    PutImage(Left, Top, IconBuff^, NotPut);
    ShowMouse;
    FreeMem(IconBuff, Size);
  end
end;


procedure AnyToProcess(c: integer);
var
  ch: char;
  i, x, y: integer;

begin
  if c > 0 then begin
    for i := 1 to ObjNum do begin
      if Ord(ObjList[i].Code) = c then begin
```

```
              if ObjList[i].Objtype = IconObj then
                 ReverseIcon(ObjList[i].Left, ObjList[i].Top,
              ObjList[i].Right, ObjList[i].Bottom);
              ObjList[i].Proc;
              if ObjList[i].ObjType = IconObj then
                 ReverseIcon(ObjList[i].Left, ObjList[i].Top,
                    ObjList[i].Right, ObjList[i].Bottom);
              Exit;
           end;
        end
     end
  else if c < 0 then begin
     GetMouseCoords(x, y);
     for i := 1 to ObjNum do begin
        if MouseInBox(ObjList[i].Left, ObjList[i].Top,
           ObjList[i].Right, ObjList[i].Bottom, x, y) then begin
           if ObjList[i].ObjType = IconObj then
              ReverseIcon(ObjList[i].Left, ObjList[i].Top,
                          ObjList[i].Right, ObjList[i].Bottom);
           ObjList[i].Proc;
           if ObjList[i].ObjType = IconObj then
              ReverseIcon(ObjList[i].Left, ObjList[i].Top,
                          ObjList[i].Right, ObjList[i].Bottom);
           Exit;
        end;
     end
  end
end;


begin
  ObjNum := 1;      { Initialize object list index }
end.
```

6

Animation

Animation is an attractive graphics feature for several reasons. It can help draw attention to a portion of a display, demonstrate how something works, lay the foundation for interactive programs, or simply make a program visually more interesting. In this chapter we'll explore some of the various animation techniques that you can experiment with in your own graphics programs. Some of the techniques we'll present include inbetweening, moving objects by using **GetImage** and **PutImage**, animating objects by changing palette colors, and using multiple screen pages to create motion.

A Closer Look at Inbetweening

In Chapter 4 we briefly explored inbetweening by using it to animate a bar graph. Now we'll take a closer look at it to see how it can be used to produce more general animation effects.

The inbetweening technique is a simple one. The basic idea is to define the start and stop coordinates of an object and then calculate and display the object as it progresses from its initial state to its final one. Let's take a simple case. Suppose we want to animate a single point by moving it from one location to another. All we need to know is where the point starts, stops, and the number of intermediate steps it should take. For example, if our point starts at $(0, 0)$ and we want it to move to $(150, 150)$ in 15 steps, we must move the point in 10 pixel increments.

The next step is to write a program that can calculate and plot the intermediate steps of our animated point. The calculation is merely a linear interpolation between the start and stop positions of the point. In our case, we want to plot the point 15 times, by moving it 10 pixels each time in the x and y directions. Therefore, the code that can perform this is:

```
NumberOfSteps := 15;
StepSize := (StopX - StartX) / NumberOfSteps;
for j := 0 to NumberOfSteps - 1 do begin
   IncAmount := Round(StepSize * j);
   PutPixel(StartX + IncAmount, StartY + IncAmount, White);
   PutPixel(StartX + IncAmount, StartY + IncAmount, Black);
end;
PutPixel(x + IncAmount, y + IncAmount, White);
```

The variable **StepSize** determines the distance the point should be moved between each state. It is dependent on the number of intermediate states that are desired, (in this case 15), and the total distance to travel. The **for** loop steps through each of the intermediate steps of the animation, plots the pixel by a call to **PutPixel** and then erases it by another call to **PutPixel**. The location of the pixel is determined by **IncAmount** which continually moves the point closer to the final state as **j** increases toward 15. In this example, the x and y directions are incremented equally, but we can easily modify the code so that the x and y directions change by different amounts.

This example shows us how to move a point across the screen, but what about animating an object? The transition is simple. If we have an object that is drawn as a series of line segments, for instance, all we need to do is run our inbetweening algorithm on each of the endpoints of the line segments and draw the lines between the points at each step in the process. The following section looks at animating objects using this technique.

Animating a Line

Before we proceed with animating an object drawn from line segments, we need to re-examine the way we to draw lines. In order to animate an object we must draw the object, remove it from the screen, draw it in its new position, erase it, draw it at the next location, and so on. However, if we remove the line segments from the screen by overwriting them with the background color, the screen may quickly become a mess if there are other objects on the screen that the animated object crosses over. Clearly, this is not what we want.

In Chapter 2, we learned that an object could be moved *cleanly* by using the **XorPut** option of the **PutImage** procedure. Although we won't use **PutImage** to animate a line segment, we can still use the same **XorPut** option to *cleanly* move a line across the screen.

The BGI allows us to set the line drawing routines so that they draw exclusive-OR lines. Because of the exclusive ORing, we'll be able to remove any line from the screen by simply drawing it again. In order to turn the exclusive-OR capability of the line drawer on, we must use the **SetWriteMode** routine. It is defined in **Graph** as:

```
procedure SetWriteMode(Mode: integer);
```

The **Mode** parameter can be set to **CopyPut** or **XorPut**. By default the BGI uses **CopyPut**. This means that lines are drawn by setting each pixel along the line segment to the current drawing color. If the **XorPut** option is used, each pixel in the line segment is exclusive-ORed with the screen image. Therefore, if a line routine is called twice with the same coordinates when the **XorPut** option is used, the line will be drawn and then erased, without the original screen being effected. Note, the **SetWriteMode** procedure only works with **Line, LineRel, LineTo, Rectangle,** and **DrawPoly**.

Working with Inbetweening

Now let's apply **SetWriteMode** to inbetweening so that we can animate a set of line segments. The code shown next, for instance, will move a rectangle across the screen as shown in Figure 6.1.

The starting coordinates of the rectangle are defined in the array **StartPoints**, where the array contains a series of x and y coordinates. The final location of the rectangle is stored in the array **StopPoints**. Since **DrawPoly** is used to draw the lines, the arrays are declared so that their first and last coordinates are the same. An additional array, **Inbetween**, is also declared to be the same size as **StartPoints** and **StopPoints** so that it can hold and display each intermediate state of the animated rectangle. The constant **NumSteps** defines the number of intermediate steps used in the animation. In this example, **NumSteps** is set to a value of 100. Other than the use of these variables, the inbetweening procedure, **InBetweenPoints** is similar to the one presented earlier. Here is the complete program:

```
program InBetwn;
{ Demonstrates the animation technique called inbetweening }
uses
   Graph, Crt;
```

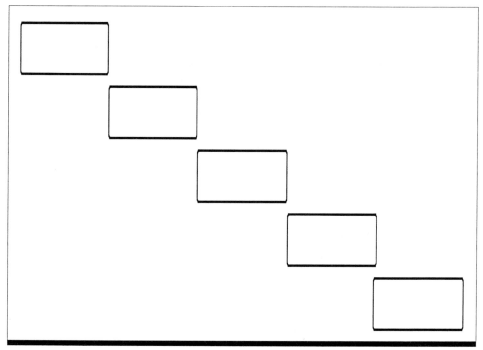

Figure 6.1. Time-lapsed output of InBetwn.Pas

```
const
   Length = 5;                    { Number of coordinate pairs in arrays }
   NumSteps: integer = 100;   { Number of steps from start to end }
                                  { Also controls speed of movement }
   StartPoints: array[1..Length] of PointType = ((x:0;    y:0),
                      (x:100; y:0), (x:100; y:20),
                      (x:0;    y:20), (x:0;    y:0));
   StopPoints: array[1..Length] of PointType =  ((x:400; y:100),
                      (x:500; y:100), (x:500; y:120),
                      (x:400; y:120), (x:400; y:100));
   GDriver: integer = Detect;
var
   InBetween: array[1..Length] of PointType;
   GMode, i: integer;


procedure InBetweenPoints;
var
   StepSize, IncAmount: real;
   i, j: integer;
```

```
begin
   StepSize := 1.0 / (NumSteps - 1.0);
   for i := 1 to NumSteps do begin
      IncAmount := (i-1) * StepSize;
      for j := 1 to Length do begin
         InBetween[j].x := StartPoints[j].x + Round(IncAmount *
                           (StopPoints[j].x - StartPoints[j].x));
         InBetween[j].y := StartPoints[j].y + Round(IncAmount *
                           (StopPoints[j].y - StartPoints[j].y));
      end;
      DrawPoly(Length, InBetween);    { Draw lines }
      Delay(100);                     { Wait so line doesn't flicker }
      DrawPoly(Length, InBetween);    { Erase line }
   end;
   DrawPoly(Length, InBetween);       { Redraw the final lines }
end;

begin
   InitGraph(GDriver, GMode, '');
   SetWriteMode(XorPut);
   InBetweenPoints;
   Readln;
   CloseGraph;
end.
```

One intriguing thing about inbetweening is that the first and last images of the object being animated do not have to be the same. Figure 6.2 shows the previous code modified so that the rectangle is turned into a triangle. The only restriction here is that the number of line segments in the start and final states must be the same. Actually, we can break this rule by adding various figures to the final version of the animated object to produce interesting results. As an exercise you might try turning a square into a face for instance. Of course, the difficulty here is coming up with the proper coordinates that can draw the shapes.

The following are two array declarations for **StartPoints** and **StopPoints** that you can use to replace the ones shown in the previous example. The coordinates in these two arrays will produce a picture of a rectangle turning into a triangle as described previously. Since the number of line segments must be the same in the start and stop states, but clearly the rectangle and triangle have a different number of vertices, we have declared **StopPoints** so that the first and last coordinate is specified three times. In other words, one of the line segments in the rectangle

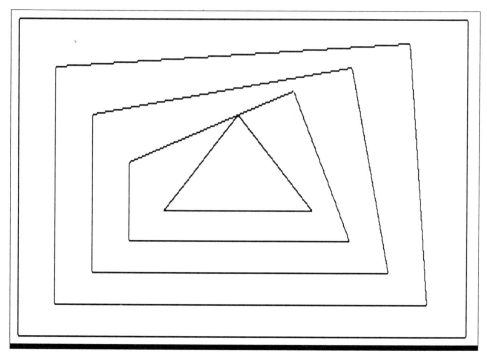

Figure 6.2. Using inbetweening to convert a rectangle into a triangle

shrinks to a line of zero length. Therefore, although there will be the same number of line segments declared in the arrays, it appears that the triangle has one less line.

```
StartPoints: array[1..Length] of PointType = ((x:0;    y:0),
      (x:639; y:0), (x:639; y:199), (x:0;    y:199), (x:0;    y:0));
StopPoints: array[1..Length] of PointType = ((x:210; y:120),
      (x:315; y:60), (x:420; y:120), (x:210; y:120), (x:210; y:120)));
```

Working with GetImage and PutImage

One of the drawbacks to using inbetweening is that the animated object must be redrawn at each step along the way. For complex objects this process can be slow. An alternative method is to draw the image once and then move it across the screen using the **GetImage** and **PutImage** routines.

Chapter 2 introduced the **GetImage** and **PutImage** procedures and described the various placement options that are available with **PutImage**. In this section we'll focus on using them, rather than understanding how they operate. (See Chapter 2 for more specific details on these routines and how they function.)

Our first animation example using **GetImage** and **PutImage** shows a bicycle moving across the screen (see Figure 6.3). The code for this example is listed here.

```
program Bike;
{ This program demonstrates animation using BGI's GetImage and PutImage
  procedures. The program draws a bicycle on the screen and then copies
  the image of the bicycle across the screen using the XorPut option of
  PutImage.
}
uses
   Graph;
const
   Step: integer = 5;       { Number of pixels to move bicycle each time }
   GDriver: integer = CGA;    { Use CGA high-resolution mode }
   GMode: integer = CGAHI;
var
   BikePtr: pointer;            { Points to the image of the bicycle }
```

Figure 6.3. Time-lapsed output of Bike.Pas

```
procedure DrawBike;
{ Draw a bicycle using calls to Circle and Line. Then capture
  the image of the bicycle with GetImage.
}
begin
  Circle(50, 100, 25);        { Draw the wheels }
  Circle(150, 100, 25);
  Line(50, 100, 80, 85);      { Draw part of the frame }
  Line(80, 85, 134, 85);
  Line(77, 82, 95, 100);
  Line(130, 80, 150, 100);
  Line(128, 80, 113, 82);     { Handlebars }
  Line(128, 80, 116, 78);
  Line(72, 81, 89, 81);       { Seat }
  Line(73, 82, 90, 82);
  Circle(95, 100, 5);         { Draw the pedals }
  Line(92, 105, 98, 95);
  Line(91, 105, 93, 105);
  Line(97, 95, 99, 95);
  Line(95, 100, 136, 87);
  GetMem(BikePtr,ImageSize(25, 75, 175, 125));   { Allocate image }
  GetImage(25, 75, 175, 125, BikePtr^);          { Capture image of }
end;                                             { the bicycle }

procedure MoveBike;
{ Move bicycle across the screen in increments of Step }
var
  i, Times: integer;

begin
  times := (GetMaxX-180) div Step;
  for i := 0 to Times do begin
    PutImage(25+i*Step, 75, BikePtr^, XorPut);      { Erase bicycle }
    PutImage(25+(i+1)*Step, 75, BikePtr^, XorPut);  { Display bicycle }
  end
end;

begin
  InitGraph(GDriver, GMode, '');
  DrawBike;
```

```
   MoveBike;
   Readln;
   CloseGraph;
end.
```

The original image of the bicycle is created by a series of calls to **Line** and **Circle** in the routine **DrawBike**. Next, memory space is allocated to the pointer **BikePtr** to hold the screen image of the bicycle and then the image is retrieved by a call to **GetImage**. Here are the two statements that perform these operations:

```
GetMem(BikePtr,ImageSize(25, 75, 175, 125));
GetImage(25, 75, 175, 125, BikePtr^);
```

Next, the routine **MoveBike** is called to move the bicycle image in **BikePtr** across the screen. In this example, the image is moved from the coordinate (25, 75) to (GetMaxX-180, 75) in steps of 5 pixels. The movement is accomplished by the **for** loop in **MoveBike** which is:

```
times := (GetMaxX-180) div Step;
for i := 0 to Times do begin
   PutImage(25+i*Step, 75, BikePtr^, XorPut);     { Erase bicycle }
   PutImage(25+(i+1)*Step, 75, BikePtr^, XorPut); { Display bicycle }
end;
```

As you can see, the **for** loop calls **PutImage** twice. The first erases the current image of the bicycle image by exclusive ORing **BikePtr** to the screen. The second displays the bicycle image at its next location using the **XorPut** option.

We can improve our example by rotating the bicycle's pedals as it moves. The basic idea is to create several images of the pedals at different orientations and then sequence through them to make it look like the pedals are turning. There are two ways of accomplishing this. For instance, we could make several images of the whole bicycle with the pedals at different orientations and then sequence through them or we could have one complete image of the bicycle and a series of smaller images that just show the pedals at various positions. With the second technique, we must overlay the pedal images with the bicycle image to create the motion.

You may be wondering why we would want to have two sets of images, one for the bicycle and one for animating the pedals. One important reason, which isn't critical for this example, is that for large pictures we can speed up the animation process and save memory by only swapping images of the regions that must be changed. In addition, several images of the whole bicycle can consume a lot more memory than a single image of the bicycle and a companion set of smaller images. For example, in high-resolution graphics modes, it is very easy to consume an excessive amount of memory.

Now let's return to the task of animating the bicycle pedals. The following program animates the bicycle by moving it across the screen as well as rotating its pedals. The program accomplishes this by creating four different images of the bicycle, each with different pedal orientations and sequencing through them.

```pascal
program Bike2;
{ This program demonstrates animation using BGI's GetImage and PutImage
  procedures. The program creates four images of a bike -- each with
  the pedals in a different orientation -- so that when the images are
  played back it looks like the pedals are moving as the bicycle is
  moved across the screen.
}
uses
   Graph, Crt;
const
   Step: integer = 5;                  { Amount to move bicycle }
   GDriver: integer = CGA;             { Use CGA high-resolution mode }
   GMode: integer = CGAHI;
var
   BikePtr1, BikePtr2,                 { The images of the bicycle }
   BikePtr3, BikePtr4: pointer;

procedure DrawBike;
{ Create four images of the bicycle. Each one will have a different
  pedal orientation so that when they are shown in sequence it
  appears as if the pedals are turning.
}
var
   Pedals: pointer;                    { Temporary image used to }
   Size: word;                         { draw bicycle }

begin
   Circle(50, 100, 25);               { Draw wheels }
   Circle(150, 100, 25);
   Line(50, 100, 80, 85);             { Draw part of frame }
   Line(80, 85, 134, 85);
   Line(77, 82, 95, 100);
```

```
      Line(130, 80, 150, 100);
      Line(128, 80, 113, 82);                      { Handlebars }
      Line(128, 80, 116, 78);
      Line(72, 81, 89, 81);                        { Seat }
      Line(73, 82, 90, 82);
      GetMem(BikePtr1,ImageSize(25, 75, 175, 125));
      GetMem(BikePtr2,ImageSize(25, 75, 175, 125));
      GetMem(BikePtr3,ImageSize(25, 75, 175, 125));
      GetMem(BikePtr4,ImageSize(25, 75, 175, 125));
      Size := ImageSize(85, 90, 110, 110);
      GetMem(Pedals,Size);
      Circle(95, 100, 5);                          { Draw base of pedals }
      Line(95, 100, 136, 87);
      GetImage(85, 90, 110, 110, Pedals^);         { Save screen of pedals}
      Line(86, 100, 104, 100);                     { Draw pedals in }
      Line(85, 100, 87, 100);                      { first position }
      Line(103, 100, 105, 100);
      GetImage(25, 75, 175, 125, BikePtr1^);
      PutImage(85, 90, Pedals^, CopyPut);          { Restore pedal area }
      Line(88, 96, 102, 104);                      { Draw pedals in second }
      Line(87, 96, 89, 96);                        { position }
      Line(101, 104, 103, 104);
      GetImage(25, 75, 175, 125, BikePtr2^);
      PutImage(85, 90, Pedals^, CopyPut);          { Restore pedal area }
      Line(95, 95, 95, 105);                       { Draw pedals in third }
      Line(94, 95, 96, 95);                        { position }
      Line(94, 105, 96, 105);
      GetImage(25, 75, 175, 125, BikePtr3^);
      PutImage(85, 90, Pedals^, CopyPut);          { Restore pedal area }
      Line(102, 96, 88, 104);                      { Draw pedals in forth }
      Line(101, 96, 103, 96);                      { position }
      Line(87, 104, 89, 104);
      GetImage(25, 75, 175, 125, BikePtr4^);
      FreeMem(Pedals,Size);
    end;

  procedure MoveBikeAndPedals;
  { Sequences through the four images of the bicycle in order to move
    the bicycle across the screen
  }
```

```
var
   i, Times: integer;

begin
   Times := (GetMaxX-175) div Step;
   for i := 0 to Times-1 do begin
     case i mod 4 of
        0 :  begin
          PutImage(25+i*Step, 75, BikePtr4^, XorPut);
          PutImage(25+(i+1)*Step, 75, BikePtr1^, XorPut);
          end;
         1 :  begin
          PutImage(25+i*Step, 75, BikePtr1^, XorPut);
          PutImage(25+(i+1)*Step, 75, BikePtr2^, XorPut);
          end;
         2 :  begin
          PutImage(25+i*Step, 75, BikePtr2^, XorPut);
          PutImage(25+(i+1)*Step, 75, BikePtr3^, XorPut);
          end;
         3 :  begin
          PutImage(25+i*Step, 75, BikePtr3^, XorPut);
          PutImage(25+(i+1)*Step, 75, BikePtr4^, XorPut);
          end;
      end;
      Delay(10);                 { Delay controls the speed of the bicycle }
   end
end;

begin
   InitGraph(GDriver, GMode, '');
   DrawBike;
   MoveBikeAndPedals;
   Readln;
   CloseGraph;
end.
```

Animating Objects On a Backdrop

Thus far we have only used **GetImage** and **PutImage** to move objects across a plain background. Unfortunately, this does not represent the typical situation. In most animation programs, you'll probably want to place several objects in the background to make the screen more interesting. For example, we could use a country scene as the backdrop of our bicycle animation program. Unfortunately, if we put objects on the screen that our bicycle must cross over, the bicycle might change its color as the two objects overlap. The reason is that the animated object and the screen are exclusive-ORed together. Therefore, wherever the image being animated contains a bit value of 1, copying the image to the screen will change its corresponding pixel color if the screen is also a 1 at that location. Fortunately, there is a way around this problem. The solution is to use two slightly different images for the animated object. These two special masks will be combined so that the animated object will not change color as it passes over the background.

The method uses one mask that is ANDed with the screen and a second mask that is XORed over the first. When these two masks are combined in this manner, the object will appear on the screen in its normal colors. To remove the object, we'll need to save the screen image beneath the region where it is to be displayed so that we can later restore the screen by copying back the saved screen to the display. Table 6.1 shows how the bits in the AND and the XOR mask can be combined to select particular colors on the screen. By chosing appropriate values in each of the masks you can set each screen bit to 0, 1, keep it the same value, or invert it.

Table 6.1. Using an AND and XOR mask

AND Mask Value	XOR Mask Value	Resulting Screen Bit
0	0	0
0	1	1
1	0	Unchanged
1	1	Inverted

Unfortunately, this technique of animation can be slow. The problem is that there are several screen images that we must deal with. First, we must save the screen, then AND an image, followed by XORing an image, and finally restore the screen to its original state by copying back the saved screen image. This can take a great deal of time—especially when the size of the object being animated is large. In fact, the bicycle image that we have been working with is too large to effectively animate with this approach.

Therefore, the next example program will only move a small ball across the screen which has a backdrop as shown in Figure 6.4. The ball is drawn to the screen using two masks as outlined earlier. Actually, the ball is made from two small circles

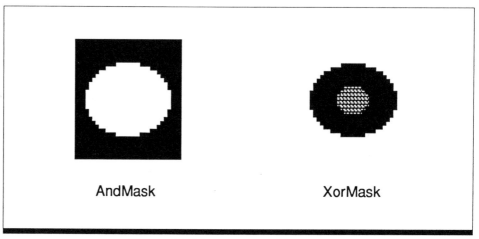

Figure 6.4. The masks used in Ball.Pas

filled with different colors. This should give you a good idea of how the dual-mask approach works.

The two masks that are combined to make up the ball are shown in Figure 6.5. In the program, these two masks are accessed through the pointers **AndMask** and **XorMask**. A third pointer, **Covered,** is used to save the portion of the screen that

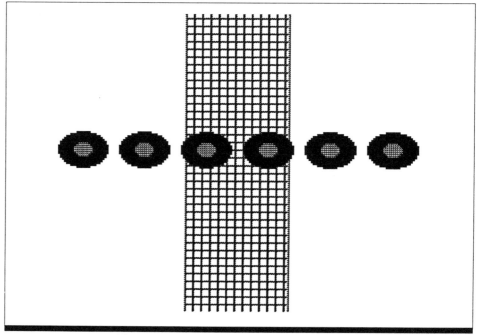

Figure 6.5. Time-lapsed output of Ball.Pas

is covered by the masks at any given time. Therefore, the process of moving the ball across the screen is encapsulated in the following four statements in the procedure **MoveBall**:

```
PutImage(35+Move, 85, Covered^, CopyPut);
GetImage(35+Step+Move, 85, 65+Step+Move, 115, Covered^);
PutImage(35+Step+Move, 85, Andmask^, AndPut);
PutImage(35+Step+Move, 85, XorMask^, XorPut);
```

The first statement overwrites the current position of the ball. The next statement saves the screen where the ball will next appear. And the last two statements write the two masks to the screen and draw the ball.

```
program Ball;
{ This program demonstrates animation using an AND and a XOR mask. It
  has been written to work in CGA medium-resolution mode only.
}
uses
   Graph, Crt;
const
   Step = 2;
   DelayTime = 50;
   GDriver: integer = CGA;                { Written for CGA mode }
   GMode: integer = CGAC3;
var
   XorMask, AndMask, Covered: pointer;

procedure DrawBall;
begin
   GetMem(Covered, ImageSize(35, 85, 65, 115));
   GetMem(XorMask, ImageSize(35, 85, 65, 115));
   GetMem(AndMask, ImageSize(35, 85, 65, 115));
   GetImage(35, 85, 65, 115, Covered^);
   { Create the AND mask first }
   SetFillStyle(SolidFill, GetMaxColor);
   Bar(35, 85, 65, 115);
   SetColor(0);
   SetFillStyle(SolidFill, 0);
   PieSlice(50, 100, 0, 360, 12);
   GetImage(35, 85, 65, 115, AndMask^);
```

```
      { Create the XOR mask }
      PutImage(35, 85, Covered^, CopyPut);
      SetColor(GetMaxColor);
      SetFillStyle(SolidFill, GetMaxColor);
      PieSlice(50, 100, 0, 360, 12);
      SetFillStyle(SolidFill, 1);
      SetColor(1);
      Circle(50, 100, 4);
      FloodFill(50, 100, 1);
      GetImage(35, 85, 65, 115, XorMask^);
      { Erase ball and make the backdrop }
      PutImage(35, 85, Covered^, CopyPut);
      SetFillStyle(HatchFill, 2);
      Bar3D(100, 10, 150, 199, 0, False);
      { Redraw the ball on the screen by saving the screen area to
        be overwritten, using the AND mask and then the XOR mask
      }
      GetImage(35, 85, 65, 115, Covered^);
      PutImage(35, 85, AndMask^, AndPut);
      PutImage(35, 85, XorMask^, XorPut);
   end;

procedure MoveBall;
{ Move the ball across the screen by first overwriting the currently
  displayed ball and then moving it to the next location by using the
  AND and XOR masks
}
var
   i, Move: integer;

begin
   for i := 0 to 150 do begin
      Move := i * Step;
      PutImage(35+Move, 85, Covered^, CopyPut);
      GetImage(35+Step+Move, 85, 65+Step+Move, 115, Covered^);
      PutImage(35+Step+Move, 85, Andmask^, AndPut);
      PutImage(35+Step+Move, 85, XorMask^, XorPut);
      Delay(DelayTime);
   end
end;
```

```
begin
   InitGraph(GDriver, GMode, '');
   DrawBall;
   MoveBall;
   repeat until KeyPressed;
   CloseGraph;
end.
```

Animating Multiple Objects

We can easily extend our program so that it will animate more than one object at a time. The major change that we need to make to the program is to supply more than one image or sequences of images to the screen to be moved. Then by sequencing through the list of animated objects as well as the images, we can easily create a scene with multiple moving objects.

Limitations of GetImage and PutImage

Using **GetImage** and **PutImage** to animate objects has several limitations that may restrict their usefulness. First, they can use up a lot of memory—particularly as the size of the image increases. In addition, as the image to save or write gets larger the speed at which **GetImage** and **PutImage** operate deteriorates.

   However, when dealing with animation, one of the biggest drawbacks to using these two routines is that they do not allow for the bitmap image to be scaled or rotated. You could write routines to perform these operations yourself, but the bitmap patterns that the BGI uses are different for many of the modes. Therefore, you would have to write routines to handle each of the modes. This is a tedious task and one that we won't tackle here. Despite these issues, **GetImage** and **PutImage** provide a powerful, yet simple way of moving objects around the graphics screen.

Animation Using the Palette

Typically animation is created by drawing an object as it moves across the screen or copying the image of an object and moving it across the screen. However, an alternative method of animation that is sometimes quite dramatic and simple uses the palette to produce animation. The basic idea is to draw objects on the screen using different colors. Then the colors in the palette are changed. When this is done, all of the objects on the screen immediately change their colors and it appears as if all the objects were redrawn to new locations. By ordering objects so that their colors reflect the series of color changes, animation can be created.

Unfortunately, not all the graphics adapters support palette manipulation equally. In fact, the EGA and VGA are the most powerful in terms of this feature. With either graphics adapter you can use the **SetPalette** procedure to alter the colors in the palette. Only some graphics adapters allow you to change the palette. As mentioned earlier, by switching the colors in the palette, you can make objects appear to move.

A common example of animation using the color palette displays a mountain scene with flowing water. Actually, the water motion is induced by a series of changes to the palette. Since it would take a great deal of time and programming to create a good looking mountain scene, we'll use a simpler programming example.

The program that we'll look at is called **FireWork.Pas** and is listed in this section. The program continually displays a series of fireworklike color bursts on the screen. Three images of random pixels are saved in memory and rapidly drawn to the screen using **PutImage** to create an expanding explosion pattern. The trick in the program is to use changes in the palette in order to achieve a wide variety of burst colors. This saves us from having to save many different burst patterns, each with a different color.

The program is written to operate in the high-resolution mode of CGA; however, it should be a fairly simple process to translate so that it will run on either an EGA or VGA system. You may be wondering how we can use the high-resolution mode of the CGA to produce all these colors—after all it has only two colors (black and white). It's true that it can have only two colors at one time; however, we can use the **SetBkColor** procedure of the BGI to select any of 15 other colors to replace the white color. This palette change will give us the variety of colors we want.

Now let's take a closer look at the code. The fireworks' burst pattern is generated by randomly plotting pixels on the screen. This is accomplished by the **for** loop:

```
for i := 0 to BlastSize * 3 div 2 - 1 do
  PutPixel(Random(BlastSize), Random(YRange), 1);
```

which plots some number of white pixels in a region bounded by (0, 0) and (**BlastSize, YRange**). The bottom-right coordinate pair of this region, is dependent on the **BlastSize**. In this case it is 300 pixels wide. The variable **YRange** is simply **BlastSize** which is scaled by the aspect ration of the screen. After this **for** loop finishes, a square region on the top right of the screen will be filled with randomly placed pixels. Of course, we want a circular, and not square, burst pattern. Therefore, the following statements are used to extract a circle of pixels.

```
Circle(BlastSize div 2, YRange div 2, BlastSize div 2 - 10);
Rectangle(0, 0, BlastSize, YRange);
FloodFill(1, 1, 1);
SetFillStyle(SolidFill, 0);
FloodFill(1, 1, 0);
GetImage(0, 0, BlastSize, YRange, Blast3^);
```

These statements use the **FloodFill** routine to erase all of the pixels between a circle (drawn to the size of the burst pattern desired) and a square encompassing the block of pixels. The first statement draws a circle that will define the burst pattern size. Next, the bounding rectangle is drawn by **Rectangle**. Then **FloodFill** is used to fill the region between the circle and rectangle with white. Note, black is not used because the background already contains it; therefore **FloodFill** would think that it has filled the region after encountering a few of the background pixels. Continuing to the next statement, the code refills the region between the circle and rectangle by another call to **FloodFill**. This time, however, the region is filled with black. Now the only thing remaining on the screen is the circular burst pattern. The final statement, therefore, is a call to **GetImage** to capture the image of the burst pattern. A similar process is performed in order to generate two smaller burst patterns, which are stored in **Blast2** and **Blast1**. Later, by sequencing through these images, it will appear that the burst pattern is expanding.

Of course, a good fireworks display would not be complete without a rocket to launch the fireworks from. The image for such a rocket is created by the next several lines. The rocket is drawn using **Bar**, **PutPixel**, and two calls to **Line**. The image of the rocket is saved to a pointer called **Rocket**.

The **while** loop that follows is used to continually draw a series of firework explosions until a key is pressed. The location of the explosion is randomly calculated by the lines:

```
x := Random(GetMaxX-BlastSize);
y := Random(GetMaxY div 3);
```

The (**x**, **y**) coordinate pair mark the top-left corner of the burst pattern images that will be written to the screen to create the firework effect. The **x** value is kept between 0 and **GetMaxX–BlastSize** so that the burst images will not extend off the edge of the screen and be clipped. The **y** coordinate is restricted to one third of the maximum y range, which you'll later see corresponds to the top portion of the screen.

The rocket is launched by the **for** loop after the two statements listed above. Its starting location and ending coordinates are calculated so that the rocket will steer to the middle of the burst pattern that is to be written to the screen. The call to **SetBkColor** before the **for** loop is to ensure that the rocket is drawn white.

The statements after the **for** loop display the burst patterns in **Blast1**, **Blast2**, and **Blast3**. The burst images are displayed on the screen much like we have discussed in the past, so we will not look at them in detail. The unique part of the code, however, is the calls to the **SetBkColor** routine. These are used to change the color of the fireworks. For instance, the line:

```
SetBkColor(Random(16));
```

randomly changes the palette color to one of the 16 possible colors in the CGA. In order to provide a little variety, the color of the second burst pattern, **Blast2**, is designed so that it may or may not be changed. Depending on whether the **Random** statement in the **if** statement, which follows, returns a 0 value or not (remember **Random** returns a value between 0 and *n*-1):

```
if Random(2) > 0 then SetBkColor(Random(16));
```

Similarly, the **if** statement surrounding the **PutImage** function used to draw **Blast1** is used to randomly restrict when it is drawn. By doing this, the program will generate two different sized fireworks patterns.

You may have noticed a number of calls to the Turbo Pascal **Delay** function in **FireWork.Pas**. Each of these statements are used to give the fireworks program an aesthetic appeal. They control the speed of the rocket as well as how long any fireworks burst is displayed. The values that are needed will depend on the speed of your PC.

The only remaining part of the program involves the pointer **Covered** which is used to save the screen before any of the burst patterns are generated or displayed. It is used to remove the fireworks from the screen and restore it to its original state.

```
program FireWork;
{ This program simulates a fireworks display by using the GetImage/
  PutImage functions as well as palette animation. The program is
  designed to run under CGA hires mode, but it can easily be ported to
  run under EGA or VGA.
}
uses
   Graph, Crt;
const
   BlastSize: integer = 300;         { Size of fireworks in pixels }
   RocketHeight: integer = 7;        { Rocket is 7 pixels tall }
   RocketWidth: integer = 4;         { and 4 pixels wide }
```

```
      RocketStep: integer = 2;    { Rocket moves 2 pixels at a time }
      GDriver: integer = CGA;
      GMode: integer = CGAHI;     { Use CGA high-resolution mode }
  var
    x, y: integer;
    i: integer;
    StepTimes: integer;
    XAsp, YAsp: word;
    YRange: integer;
    Color: integer;
    ry: integer;
    AspectRatio: real;
    Covered: pointer;             { Holds screen under fire burst }
    Blast1, Blast2, Blast3: pointer;   { Three burst patterns }
    Rocket: pointer;                   { The fire rocket }
    Size: word;

  begin
    InitGraph(GDriver, GMode, '');
    Randomize;
    GetAspectRatio(XAsp, YAsp);
    AspectRatio := XAsp / YAsp;
    YRange := Round(BlastSize * AspectRatio);
    Size := ImageSize(0, 0, BlastSize, YRange);
    GetMem(Blast1, Size);
    GetMem(Blast2, Size);
    GetMem(Blast3, Size);
    GetMem(Covered, Size);
    GetImage(0, 0, BlastSize, YRange, Covered^);
    { Make the burst pattern by randomly filling a square with pixels }
    for i := 0 to BlastSize * 3 div 2 do
      PutPixel(Random(BlastSize), Random(YRange), 1);
        { Then convert the square pixel pattern into a circle by erasing
          all of the pixels outside of a circle. Use a floodfill to
          perform this operation. Repeat this process three times, each
          with a smaller circle and after each capture the circular
          burst pattern in burst1, burst2, or burst3.
        }
      Circle(BlastSize div 2, YRange div 2, BlastSize div 2 - 10);
      Rectangle(0, 0, BlastSize, YRange);
```

```
FloodFill(1, 1, 1);
SetFillStyle(SolidFill, 0);
FloodFill(1, 1, 0);
GetImage(0, 0, BlastSize, YRange, Blast3^);   { Capture the large  }
                                              { burst pattern }
SetFillStyle(SolidFill, 1);                       { Make smaller pattern }
Circle(BlastSize div 2, YRange div 2, BlastSize div 4 + 10);
Rectangle(0, 0, BlastSize, YRange);
FloodFill(1, 1, 1);
SetFillStyle(SolidFill, 0);
FloodFill(1, 1, 0);
{ Capture the middle burst pattern }
GetImage(0, 0, BlastSize, YRange, Blast2^);
Setfillstyle(SolidFill, 1);                      { Make smallest burst }
Circle(BlastSize div 2, YRange div 2, 20);
Rectangle(0, 0, BlastSize, YRange);
FloodFill(1, 1, 1);
SetFillStyle(SolidFill, 0);
FloodFill(1, 1, 0);
GetImage(0, 0, BlastSize, YRange, Blast1^);   { Get small burst }
PutImage(0, 0, Covered^, CopyPut);               { Erase burst pattern }
{ Create the rocket }
Size := ImageSize(0, 0, RocketWidth, RocketHeight);
GetMem(Rocket, Size);
SetFillStyle(SolidFill, 1);
Bar(1, 2, RocketWidth-1, RocketHeight-1);
PutPixel(2, 1, 1);
Line(0, RocketHeight-2, 0, RocketHeight);
Line(RocketWidth, RocketHeight-2, RocketWidth, RocketHeight);
GetImage(0, 0, RocketWidth, RocketHeight, Rocket^); { Rocket }
PutImage(0, 0, Rocket^, XorPut);                 { Erase rocket image }
{ Draw fireworks until a key is pressed }
while (KeyPressed <> True) do begin
  { Randomly decide where the rocket should explode. Use the upper
    half of the screen and avoid the edges of the screen. (x, y)
    corresponds to the top-left corner of the blast images.
  }
  x := Random(GetMaxX - BlastSize);
  y := Random(GetMaxY div 3);
  SetBkColor(15);                            { Make rocket white }
```

```
      ry := GetMaxY - RocketHeight;
      StepTimes := (ry - YRange) div RocketStep;
      for i := 0 to StepTimes do begin
         Putimage(x+BlastSize div 2, ry-i*RocketStep, Rocket^, XorPut);
         Delay(20);
         Putimage(x+BlastSize div 2, ry-i*RocketStep, Rocket^, XorPut);
      end;
      SetBkColor(Random(16));            { Randomly select burst color }
      GetImage(x, y, x+BlastSize, y+YRange, Covered^);   { Save screen }
      PutImage(x, y, Blast1^, CopyPut); { Draw smallest burst }
      Delay(100);                         { Keep it on screen for a while }
      PutImage(x, y, Blast2^, CopyPut); { Show second burst }
      { Maybe change color }
      if (Random(2) > 0) then SetBkColor(Random(16));
      Delay(100);
      if (Random(2) > 0) then begin       { Randomly decide to }
         PutImage(x, y, Blast3^, CopyPut);    { show third burst }
         if (Random(2) > 0) then SetBkColor(Random(16));
      end;
      Delay(400 + Random(750));          { Wait for a while }
      PutImage(x, y, Covered^, CopyPut);   { Erase burst }
      Delay(Random(3000));               { Wait for next rocket }
   end;
   CloseGraph;
end.
```

A slight variation on the palette animation is to use it to make objects immediately appear on the screen. For instance, we can add a bolt of lightning to our fractal program in Chapter 1 that will immediately appear on the screen, yet is really there all of the time. The trick is to draw the lightning bolt the same color as the background color, however, a different palette index is used. Then to make the lightning appear for a short time, the palette index color is changed to the lightning color and then restored to the background. Swapping the palette colors produces the effect that the lightning bolt is drawn to the screen; however, since it really is already there it saves the drawing time and makes for a very fast animation technique.

Using Multiple Screen Pages

Another animation technique that can produce fast animation effects uses multiple memory pages. This method takes advantage of the graphics hardware which provides several independent sections, or pages, of memory that you can draw in and display. However, like the palette trick, this approach is only possible on some graphics adapters (i.e. Hercules, EGA, and VGA). The basic idea is to have several partial or complete images of the screen ready to be displayed and then swap between them. By doing this animation can be created. The number of pages available depends on the graphics mode being used. For a complete list of the graphics modes and the pages that they have, refer to the *Turbo Pascal Reference Guide*.

The BGI routine **SetActivePage** is used to select where the graphics operations will be written. The procedure **SetActivePage** is defined in the unit **Graph** as:

```
procedure SetActivePage(Page: word);
```

where **Page** is the page number to be used. Note, the active page does not have to be the page currently being displayed. In fact, the visual page is selected by the routine **SetVisualPage**. It is defined as:

```
procedure SetVisualPage(Page: word);
```

Another way to use multiple memory pages is as a scratch pad. The idea is to use one of the nonvisible pages as a working area to combine masks or create images of objects that can later be copied over to the visual page rapidly using **GetImage** and **PutImage**. In this manner, you can avoid having to display everything. For example, in the last program, we needed to create the pixel pattern for fireworks. This was done on the screen; however, if other memory pages had been available, we could have hidden these operations by doing them on a nonvisible page.

7

Creating Mouse Tools

In Chapters 7 through 11 we'll develop an ensemble of powerful interactive graphics tools. Each chapter will focus on a different aspect of programming for interactive graphics environments. The tools that we'll build will become the heart of several application programs that we'll be writing in Chapters 11 and 12.

Our first stop is the mouse which is covered in this chapter, and then we'll proceed to discuss icons (Chapter 8), pop-up windows (Chapter 9), and a handful of interactive drawing routines (Chapter 10).

Starting with the Mouse

Although the keyboard is an invaluable input device, it is not always best suited for interactive graphics programs. Even with useful positioning features such as cursor keys, the keyboard lacks speed and the ability to randomly select locations on the screen. These operations are typically required in an interactive graphics environment. Because of this, the mouse is a much better input device.

The mouse will be our primary means of user interaction while in graphics mode. Although we'll try to support the keyboard as much as possible along the way, we'll design all of our input routines around the mouse.

This chapter will show you how you can access a mouse from within your own graphics programs. We'll develop several mouse related routines to perform such operations as initializing the mouse, determining the status and position of the mouse, and controlling its movement within a program. In addition, we'll provide routines to emulate the mouse with the keyboard if a mouse isn't available. All of these routines will be combined into a stand-alone file called **MousePac.Pas**.

Mouse Overview

Pointing devices are a natural way for a user to interact with a graphics environment. There are a handful of pointing devices from which we can choose. A few of these are the light-pen, the joy-stick, and the mouse. In this chapter we'll be working with the Microsoft compatible mouse which happens to be the most common mouse standard for the PC.

A mouse system actually consists of two essential elements: the mouse mechanism and a memory resident program called a mouse driver. The mouse driver provides all of the low-level support needed to communicate with the mouse. In addition, it is responsible for automatically maintaining the mouse's cursor position and detecting any button presses.

Normally, the mouse driver is loaded into memory at power-up by a statement in your **autoexec.bat** file. Once the driver is loaded, the mouse becomes available to any program that is subsequently executed.

A mouse is surprisingly simple to use in an application program. There are, however, some minor differences between text and graphics programs using the mouse; we'll be focusing on the mouse in graphics mode only.

Accessing the Mouse Driver

We'll access the various features of the mouse and mouse driver through the PC software interrupt 33h. The mouse driver services calls to this interrupt location by redirecting them to its built-in low-level mouse routines. The specific routine which is selected depends on the value in the AX register at the time of the interrupt. Three other registers, BX, CX, and DX are used to pass parameters to the mouse routines. Similarly, the mouse functions use these four registers to return such things to the calling routine as the mouse location and the status of the mouse buttons. Figure 7.1 illustrates how a program uses interrupt 33h to invoke a mouse function.

Interrupt 33h can be invoked by the special Turbo Pascal routine **Intr**. It provides direct access to the interrupt capabilities of the microprocessor and typically is of the form:

```
intr(interrupt_number, registers);
```

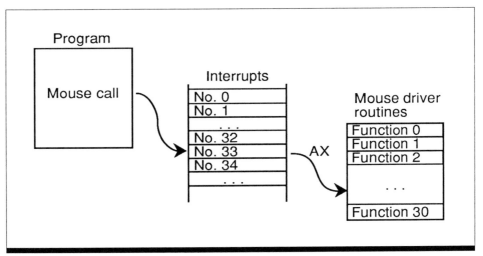

Figure 7.1. Sequence of invoking a mouse function

where the first parameter is the interrupt vector to be used and the second parameter is a record containing several register values. The declaration for this record is defined in the unit **Dos**.

The core mouse routine that we'll use to interact with the mouse driver is built around the **Intr** procedure and is given below. The **Mouse** routine simply loads the various registers with the parameters passed to it, calls the interrupt, and then copies the register values back into the parameters. The values contained in the parameters passed to **Mouse** select the particular mouse function that is executed. Therefore, it is up to the caller of **Mouse** to ensure that the correct parameter values are provided. Throughout our program, we'll refer to the four mouse parameters as **m1, m2, m3,** and **m4**. They correspond to the registers AX, BX, CX, and DX, respectively. The routine for **Mouse** is:

```
procedure Mouse(var m1, m2, m3, m4: word);
var
  Regs: Registers;

begin
  Regs.AX := m1;  Regs.BX := m2;
  Regs.CX := m3;  Regs.DX := m4;
  Intr($33, Regs);
  m1 := Regs.AX;  m2 := Regs.BX;
  m3 := Regs.CX;  m4 := Regs.DX;
end;
```

By setting the parameters **m1, m2, m3**, and **m4** to different values we can easily perform various operations such as initializing the mouse, reading the current position of the mouse, or determining the state of the mouse buttons. In the next section we'll look at several of these operations.

The Mouse Functions

The mouse driver includes more than 20 mouse functions, most of which are listed in Table 7.1. We won't be using all of these functions; they are listed here for your reference. If you are interested in exploring the mouse further, you should refer to the *Microsoft Mouse Programmer's Guide* (available from Microsoft).

Let's take a step-by-step look at how the mouse is actually used so that we can begin to develop our custom toolkit.

Mouse Initialization

Before being able to use the mouse, we must first initialize it. This is done by invoking function number 0 (see Table 7.1). After this function is called, the mouse driver is reset to various default values and returns a −1 in AX if the mouse hardware and driver are detected; otherwise, it returns a 0. Therefore, by using the reset function, function 0, we'll be able to tell whether a mouse is present or not. We can write our own mouse reset function as:

```
function ResetMouse: boolean;
var
   m1, m2, m3, m4: word;

begin
   m1 := MouseReset;
   Mouse(m1, m2, m3, m4);
   if m1 < 0 then ResetMouse := True
      else ResetMouse := False
end;
```

The **MouseReset** term is a constant for function 0 which is defined at the top of **MousePac.Pas**. We'll define similar constants for the other mouse functions that we'll be discussing in later sections.

Table 7.1. Mouse driver functions

Function Number (placed in AX)	Description
0	Resets the mouse and returns its status
1	Shows the mouse cursor on the screen
2	Removes the mouse cursor from the screen
3	Retrieves the current status of the buttons and the mouse position
4	Moves the mouse cursor to virtual location (x,y)
5	Retrieves the number of times a button was pressed since the last call
6	Retrieves the number of times a button was released since the last call
7	Sets the horizontal limits of the cursor
8	Sets the vertical limits of the cursor
9	Defines the cursor used in graphics mode
10	Sets the cursor used in text mode
11	Reads mouse movement counters
12	Sets up an interrupt routine
13	Turns light-pen emulation on
14	Turns light-pen emulation off
15	Sets mickey/pixel ratio which is the ratio of the mouse movement to the cursor movement
16	Hides the mouse if it is within a region
19	Sets the parameters to allow faster mouse movement
20	Swaps interrupt routines
21	Retrieves mouse driver status
22	Saves mouse driver status
23	Restores mouse driver status
29	Sets CRT page number used by mouse cursor
30	Gets CRT page number used by mouse cursor

Notice that our reset function does little more than load **m1** with the function number, make a call to **Mouse** and then return the status flag held in **m1**. The variables **m2**, **m3**, and **m4** are ignored in this case. Most of the other mouse functions will be similar in form.

Although **ResetMouse** provides the basic mouse reset function, we need a higher-level routine to handle the complete task of initializing the mouse. We'll call this routine **InitMouse**. Among other things, it calls **ResetMouse** and sets a global variable, **MouseExists**, to True if **ResetMouse** is successful. Otherwise, **MouseExists** is set to False. Later, we'll see that the variable **MouseExists** is used in all of our mouse routines so that we can avoid making calls to the mouse driver if it hasn't been detected. In fact, when **MouseExists** is False we'll switch to the keyboard for input. We'll explore this feature in a forthcoming section.

Although, we'll need to expand our **InitMouse** routine, an intermediate form of it follows. The primary feature still missing is the one that processes the keyboard input when a mouse is not present. As mentioned, this will be added in a later section.

```
function InitMouse: boolean;
{ Call this routine at the beginning of your program, after the graph-
  ics adapter has been initialized. It will initialize the mouse and
  display the mouse cursor at the top left of the screen, if one
  is present.
}
var
   GMode: integer;

begin
   MouseExists := True;
   if ResetMouse then begin          { If mouse reset okay, assume }
      GMode := GetGraphMode;         { mouse exists. Test if Hercules }
      if GMode = HercMonoHi then     { is used. If so, patch memory }
         Mem[$0040:$0049] := $06;    { location 40h:49h with 6. }
      MoveMouse(0,0);                { Mouse exists and draw the }
      ShowMouse;                     { cursor at (0,0) }
      InitMouse := True;             { Return a success flag }
   end
end;
```

The function **InitMouse** also sets the mouse location to the top-left corner of the screen by a call to the mouse function **MoveMouse** and switches the display of the mouse cursor on by a call to the routine **ShowMouse**. Both **MoveMouse** and **ShowMouse** are part of our mouse toolkit and will be looked at shortly.

One oddity of the **InitMouse** function is the call to the BGI routine **GetGraphMode**. It is used to test whether your program is running on a Hercules card. If it is, you must write a value of 6 to memory location 40h:49h. This is done by the statements:

```
if GMode = HercMonoHi then    { If Hercules card is used patch memory }
  Mem[$0040:$0049] := $06;     { location 40h:49h with 6 }
```

This is a peculiarity of the Hercules board and is not needed for any other graphics adapter.

More Mouse Routines

Thus far we have covered the mouse initialization and reset functions. Now we'll examine the routines that actually put the mouse to use. The complete list of mouse specific functions that we'll include in **MousePac.Pas** are shown in Table 7.2.

Table 7.2. Mouse processing routines in MousePac.Pas

Routine	Description
InitMouse	Initialize the mouse
ResetMouse	Reset the mouse and return its status
MoveMouse	Move the mouse to location (x,y)
ShowMouse	Display the mouse cursor
HideMouse	Remove the mouse cursor from the screen
GetMouseCoords	Get the coordinates of the mouse cursor
GetMouseMovement	Get the amount the mouse cursor has moved since the last call
MouseButtonPressed	Test whether a mouse button has been pressed since the last call
MouseButtonReleased	Test whether a mouse button has been released since the last call
TestButton	Internal routine to test the buttons
MouseInBox	Check whether the mouse cursor is in a region

We'll begin by writing these routines assuming that a mouse is present, but later we'll modify them to support the keyboard when a mouse isn't detected.

The Mouse Cursor

The routines that we'll now look at control the display of the mouse cursor. We saw in **InitMouse** that there is a procedure called **ShowMouse** that turns on the display of the mouse cursor. There is also a complementary routine, called **HideMouse**, that removes the mouse cursor from the screen. One important thing to note here is that both of these routines affect the display of the mouse cursor only. In other words, no matter what the display status of the mouse cursor is, the mouse driver will always update and maintain the cursor's position.

The **ShowMouse** and **HideMouse** routines use mouse functions 1 and 2 respectively. They do not require any parameters or return any values. Both routines are straightforward and are included in **MousePac.Pas** (see Listing 7.1).

It's easy to imagine that there are times when it is necessary to turn the mouse cursor on or off by using **ShowMouse** and **HideMouse**. However, their use is probably more important than first imagined. It turns out that whenever you *read or write anything* to the screen while using the mouse, you must always turn the mouse off first by a call to **HideMouse**. After you are done accessing the screen, you can restore the mouse display by calling **ShowMouse**. Why? The reason is that the mouse cursor image is actually combined into the screen image. Therefore, whenever you access the screen when the mouse cursor is on, you run the risk of accessing the mouse cursor image or at least incorrectly modifying whatever is under the mouse cursor. Only by using **HideMouse** and **ShowMouse** before and after accessing the screen can you guarantee that the mouse will not interfere with what is on the screen.

Caution: You should not call **HideMouse** if the mouse is not already displayed. If you do violate this rule, you must accompany every subsequent call to **Hide-Mouse** with a companion call to **ShowMouse**. This is required because of the way that the mouse driver internally determines when to display the mouse cursor.

The Default Mouse Cursor

In graphics mode, the default mouse cursor is displayed as an arrow symbol as shown in Figure 7.2. Although it is possible to change the type of cursor displayed

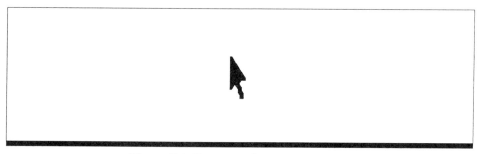

Figure 7.2. The graphics mouse cursor

by calling function 9, we won't take advantage of this feature in the mouse driver. You should refer to the *Microsoft Mouse Programmer's Reference Guide* if you would like to explore this further.

Mouse Position

In the previous sections we learned how the mouse driver controls the display of the mouse cursor's image. Now let's see how we can access and control the position of the mouse cursor through the driver.

Part of the responsibility of the mouse driver is to maintain the position of the mouse cursor. In addition, we can query the mouse driver to return the coordinates of the mouse by calling function 3. Our mouse program includes a procedure called **GetMouseCoords** that performs this operation.

Function 3 does not expect any parameters to be passed to it and it returns the x and y coordinates of the mouse in **m3** and **m4**. Actually, mouse function 3 does more than just return the mouse coordinates. It also returns the current status of the buttons in **m2**; however, we'll be ignoring this aspect of the routine.

The coordinates that function 3 returns will, in most cases, correspond to the screen coordinates of the mouse. Note, however, that we say "in most cases." It turns out that the mouse driver refers to all mouse coordinates in a virtual coordinate system and not in screen coordinates. Usually these two coordinate systems are identical in graphics mode. However, whenever the screen is in a mode with 320 columns, the virtual coordinates in the x direction are not identical. However, the adjustment is fairly simple. In these situations, the real screen coordinates are always one half the virtual coordinates. Therefore the coordinates to the mouse driver need only be divided by two whenever the current graphics mode has 320 columns. Figure 7.3 shows the relationship between the coordinate systems for a 320 column graphics mode. For now our **GetMouseCoords** routine becomes:

```
procedure GetMouseCoords(var x, y: integer);
{ Get the current location of the mouse cursor }
var
   m1, m2, m3, m4: word;

begin
   if MouseExists then begin
     m1 := GetMouseStatus;
     m3 := x;   m4 := y;
     Mouse(m1, m2, m3, m4);
```

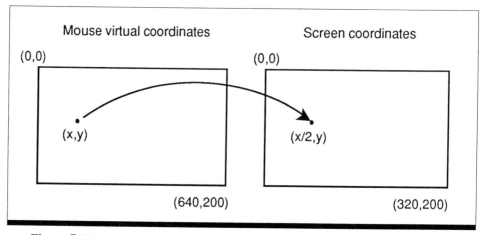

Figure 7.3. Mapping between mouse and CGA 320 by 200 mode coordinates

```
    x := m3;   y := m4;
    if GetMaxX = 319 then
        x := x div 2;   { Adjust for virtual coordinates of mouse }
  end
end;
```

Mouse Buttons

The Microsoft mouse also provides two buttons that can be accessed through the mouse driver. Note that although other mice may have more buttons, usually these can be handled as a superset of the Microsoft mouse.

There are three ways to test the mouse buttons. For each button you can check its current state, whether it has been pressed, and whether it has been released. We'll use the last two methods of testing buttons in our programs and avoid testing the current status of the buttons, since it is possible that with it we may not be fast enough to catch all of the button presses.

The mouse functions 5 and 6 are used to determine the number of times that one of the mouse buttons has been pressed or released since the last check or mouse initialization. Both functions can test either of the buttons. Which particular button is tested depends on the value in parameter **m2** at the time of the function call. If **m2** is 0, then the left button is checked; if **m2** is 1, then the right button is tested. The number of button actions (number of button presses for function 5, for instance) is returned in **m2**. In addition, these functions return the location of the last button action in **m3** and **m4** (**m3** is the x coordinate and **m4** is the y coordinate). Note that the left and right buttons status information is maintained separately.

Our mouse package uses functions 5 and 6 in the routines **MouseButton-Pressed** and **MouseButtonReleased** to test the status of the mouse buttons. Both are boolean functions that accept a single parameter that specifies which button is to be tested. This parameter can take on one of three values which are defined in **MousePac** as **LeftButton**, **RightButton**, and **EitherButton**. In the case of **Mouse-ButtonPressed**, the function returns True if the button indicated has been pressed since the last call to **MouseButtonPressed**. Otherwise, the function returns False. Similarly, **MouseButtonReleased** only returns True if the button specified in its parameter list has been released since the last time **MouseButtonReleased** was invoked.

Therefore, we can write the following loop which waits until either of the buttons is pressed:

```
while not MouseButtonPressed(EitherButton) do ;
```

Actually, the low-level mouse functions do not allow us to ask whether either button has been pressed. We have to test the left and right buttons individually. But this is easy to do.

Since there is a lot of similarity between the button pressed and button released functions, we have combined their code into a function called **TestButton**. This function also returns a boolean value; however, it takes two parameters. They are the action to test for (whether it is a button press or release) and which button to check. The function is:

```
function TestButton(TestType, WhichButton: integer): boolean;
var
  m1, m2, m3, m4: word;
  FoundAction: boolean;

begin
  TestButton := False;
  FoundAction := False;
  if (WhichButton = LeftButton) or (WhichButton = EitherButton)
    then begin
    m1 := TestType;
    m2 := LeftButton;
    Mouse(m1, m2, m3, m4);
    if m2 > 0 then begin      { Return True if action occurred }
      TestButton := True;
      FoundAction := True;
    end
```

```
    end;
    if not FoundAction and ((WhichButton = RightButton) or
        (WhichButton = EitherButton)) then begin
      m1 := TestType;
      m2 := RightButton;
      Mouse(m1, m2, m3, m4);
      if m2 > 0
        then TestButton := True;        { Return True if action occurred }
    end;
  end;
```

Note that the mouse function number, which is loaded into **m1**, is passed as the parameter **TestType**. In addition, the mouse variable **m2** is loaded from the parameter **WhichButton** in order to select between the left and right buttons. Remember, this variable can take on one of the values: **LeftButton**, **RightButton**, or **EitherButton**. Note, however, that if the user specifies **EitherButton** that both buttons must be individually checked.

After **TestButton** calls the mouse driver via **Mouse**, **m2** contains the number of button actions for the button specified in **WhichButton**. Since we are concerned only with whether the button has been pressed or released, not how many times it has occurred, **TestButton** simply returns True if **m2** indicates that there was one or more button presses. Otherwise, **TestButton** returns False.

The function **TestButton** ignores two pieces of information that you may find valuable. First, it throws away the number of button actions that have taken place since the last test. You may find this useful; although it is very rare that you'd be able to click fast enough to register more than one button press or release.

Also, both function 5 and 6 return the coordinates of the last button action in **m3** and **m4**. We'll ignore these and instead use **GetMouseCoords** to retrieve the location of the mouse after a button action; however, the delay between the button detection and the call to **GetMouseCoords** can be significant. Therefore, you may want to try to integrate the coordinates returned in **m3** and **m4** into your code to avoid this situation.

Mouse in a Box

When using the mouse, we'll often want to be able to test whether the mouse cursor is within a particular region on the screen. In order to accomplish this, the **MouseInBox** function is included in the **MousePac** utilities. **MouseInBox** checks to see whether the mouse cursor coordinates provided it are within a rectangular region bounded by a pair of screen coordinates as shown in Figure 7.4. The screen coordinates correspond to the upper-left and lower-right corners of the region being checked. If the mouse is in the rectangle, **MouseInBox** will return True; otherwise it will return False. The function is:

```
function MouseInBox(Left, Top, Right, Bottom, x, y: integer): boolean;
begin
   MouseInBox := ((x >= Left) and (x <= Right) and
                  (y >= Top) and (y <= Bottom));
end;
```

More Mouse Control

Our mouse control routines are rounded out by the procedures **GetMouseMovement** and **MoveMouse**. Each of these routines is fairly simple to understand and is shown in the listing of **MousePac.Pas** later in this chapter.

The routine **MoveMouse** uses mouse function 4 to move the mouse cursor to a particular (x, y) screen location. Note in **MoveMouse** that the screen coordinates passed to it must be adjusted into virtual coordinates when the graphics adapter is in a 320 column mode. This is done by the line:

```
if GetMaxX = 319 then x := x * 2;
```

The **GetMouseMovement** routine, however, returns the amount that the mouse has moved in the x and y directions since the last call to it. The routine, using mouse function 11, returns the change in cursor location in its two parameters, x and y. Note

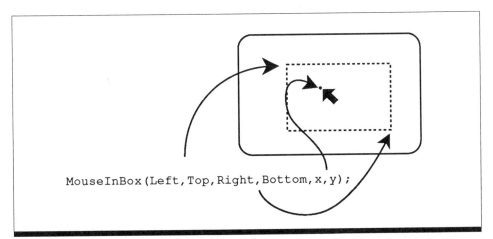

MouseInBox(Left,Top,Right,Bottom,x,y);

Figure 7.4. Locating the mouse within a region is done with MouseInBox

that these values are converted from virtual coordinates to screen coordinates before they are returned to the caller by the line:

```
if GetMaxX = 319 then x := x / 2;
```

Adding Keyboard Input

Although the mouse is an excellent input device in the graphics world, it is sometimes useful to be able to use the keyboard. For instance, there are times when it's easier for the user to select a function by typing a quick-key combination rather than using the mouse. Therefore, we have added two functions that can capture any keyboard input yet also support the mouse. These routines are shown in Table 7.3.

Table 7.3. Keyboard input functions

Function	Description
GetInput	Check if a mouse button has been pressed and released or whether a key has been pressed
WaitForInput	Loop until a button has been pressed or until a key has been pressed

Both the **GetInput** and **WaitForInput** functions are designed to work with the keyboard and the mouse. They are written so that they first check the keyboard buffer to see if any keys have been pressed. If so, they immediately return the first character in the keyboard buffer. Otherwise, the functions test the appropriate mouse buttons to see if they have been pressed or released. Actually, **WaitForInput** does nothing more than call **GetInput** in a loop until a button has been pressed or the user has typed a character.

The keyboard buffer is checked by the Turbo Pascal function **KeyPressed**. If it returns False, no key has been pressed, and **GetInput** proceeds to test if the mouse buttons have been pressed. If they have been pressed, then **GetInput** returns a –1. Otherwise, if a key has been pressed, **GetInput** returns the value of the key pressed.

Emulating a Mouse

Thus far we have been talking about using the mouse almost exclusively. However, not everyone has a mouse and the reality of the situation is that a good program must accommodate nonmouse systems. Although you could use **GetInput** and **WaitForInput** to help support both the keyboard and the mouse, you would have to integrate the keyboard support into your application programs. This can get very messy. Instead, we'll modify our mouse routines so that they will use the keyboard to control an emulated mouse. In other words, we'll be able to use our new mouse routines whether or not there is actually a mouse connected. We'll use the cursor keys to move the emulated mouse cursor around the screen and the INS and DEL keys to simulate the mouse buttons.

In order to select between the mouse code and the emulated mouse support, the global variable **MouseExists**, which is set in **InitMouse**, is checked upon entering every mouse routine. If **MouseExists** is False, then the currently executed routine is redirected to the emulated mouse routines. Otherwise it proceeds through the code using the mouse.

Emulating the mouse requires several new variables and routines to be added to **MousePac.Pas**. In fact, a good portion of **MousePac** now becomes dedicated to the mouse emulation feature. So if you have a mouse, and don't want to bother with this latest feature, you could omit all the code that refers to the emulated mouse. These are the variables and functions that begin with underscores.

The Emulated Mouse Cursor

Now let's look at how we can emulate the mouse cursor. The basic idea is to use **GetImage** and **PutImage** to move the image of an emulated mouse cursor about the screen. We'll create the simulated cursor image in a new routine called _InitCursor. A global pointer, called _Cursor, will point to the cursor image which we'll actually draw in the procedure _DrawCursor. The space for the cursor image is allocated in _InitCursor. In addition, memory is allocated in _InitCursor, so that another global pointer, called _UnderCursor, can be used to save the portion of the screen that is currently covered by the emulated mouse cursor. Moving the emulated cursor on the screen then becomes a three-step process:

1. Remove the current cursor image from the screen by overwriting it with the previously saved image in _UnderCursor
2. Use **GetImage** to save the screen region in _UnderCursor where the cursor is to appear next
3. Use **PutImage** to draw the cursor at its new location

Creating the original cursor image in _InitCursor follows this same process. First, the screen area where the cursor image is to be created is saved in _UnderCursor. Then an arrow-shaped cursor is drawn by the procedure _DrawCursor using a series of calls to **Line**. Next, the cursor image is saved in **_Cursor** by a call to **GetImage** so that it can later be copied to the screen. Finally, the screen is restored to its original state, by overwriting the cursor with the image in **_UnderCursor**. This removes the cursor image and restores the screen to its original state.

If you'd like to experiment with the type of cursor used in the emulated mode you need only change the procedure **_DrawCursor**. Note, the size of the cursor is declared by the constants **CursHeight** and **CursWidth** to be 8 pixels high and wide.

Emulated Mouse Position

The position of the emulated mouse cursor is maintained in the variables **_CX** and **_CY**. Consequently, a call to **GetMouseCoords** does nothing more than return these values when the emulated cursor is used. The variables **_CX** and **_CY** are updated whenever the program calls **GetInput** and the user has pressed one of the arrow keys on the keypad. This latter change involves an extensive portion of code in a new function called **_GetKbInteraction**. Essentially, it checks to see if any keyboard action has taken place. If so, it calls **_GetKb** to retrieve the input (which may be an extended scan code). Next, the input is matched against a list of arrow key definitions. If one of the arrow keys was pressed the function updates **_CX**, **_CY**, **_CDeltaX**, and **_CDeltaY**. The variables **_CDeltaX** and **_CDeltaY** are used to keep track of the amount that the mouse has moved between calls to **GetMouseMovement**. Note that the emulated cursor position is also clipped to the coordinates **_CMinX**, **_CMinY**, **_CMaxX**, and **_CMaxY**. Although we do not use these clipping parameters, they can be used to mimic mouse functions 7 and 8, which can be used to restrict the movement of the mouse cursor to a rectangular region on the screen. Finally, note that **_GetKbInteraction** returns zero whenever it adjusts the position of the emulated cursor. This is equivalent to telling the calling function that no action need be taken, in other words, no key or emulated button was pressed.

Emulated Mouse Buttons

The mouse buttons are emulated by the INS and DEL keys on the keypad. In the case statement in **_GetKbInteraction**, the user input is tested to see if it corresponds to the INS or DEL keys. If it does, a corresponding flag is set. These flags are **_LButtonPress** and **_RButtonPress**, corresponding to the left and right buttons, respectively. In addition, **_NumLPressed** and **_NumRPressed** are two counters that are incremented each time there is a button press. Finally, if the button specified by **WhichButton** corresponds to the button actually pressed, a −1 is returned to the caller.

Detecting button presses is easy using this technique. However, emulating button releases is another matter. To solve this problem we'll count the second key press of one of the emulated buttons as a button release. Therefore, whenever **_LButtonPress** or **_RButtonPress** is True and a button action occurs (the INS or DEL keys are pressed), it is considered a button release and the button release counters, **_NumLReleased** and **_NumRReleased** are incremented and the corresponding button press flag is set False.

• Listing 7.1

```
unit MousePac;
{ Routines to support a Microsoft compatible mouse. These routines also provide
  keyboard emulation of a mouse, if one does not exist. This package assumes that you
  are running under graphics mode. To move the emulated cursor use the arrow keys on
  the keyboard and the INS and DEL keys as the left and right mouse buttons,
  respectively. The gray + and - keys can be used to change the amount the
  emulated mouse cursor is moved by.
}
interface
{ These constants are available to your programs }
const
    LeftButton: integer = 0;          { Use left mouse button }
    RightButton: integer = 1;         { Use right mouse button }
    EitherButton: integer = 2;        { Use either mouse button }
{ These procedures and functions are visible to programs that use the MousePac unit }
procedure Mouse(var m1, m2, m3, m4: word);
procedure HideMouse;
procedure ShowMouse;
procedure MoveMouse(x, y: integer);
function InitMouse: boolean;
procedure GetMouseCoords(var x, y: integer);
procedure GetMouseMovement(var x, y: integer);
function MouseButtonReleased(WhichButton: integer): boolean;
function MouseButtonPressed(WhichButton: integer): boolean;
function MouseInBox(Left, Top, Right, Bottom, x, y: integer): boolean;
function GetInput(WhichButton: integer): integer;
function WaitForInput(WhichButton: integer): integer;
implementation
uses
    Graph, Crt, Dos;
```

```pascal
const
{ The following is a list of constants that correspond to the
  mouse routines supported in MousePac.Pas
}
  MouseReset = 0;
  MouseShow = 1;
  MouseHide = 2;
  GetMouseStatus = 3;
  SetMouseCoord = 4;
  CheckButtonPress = 5;
  CheckButtonRelease = 6;
  SetMouseHorizRange = 7;     { Not used }
  SetMouseVertRange = 8;      { Not used }
  SetGraphicsCursor = 9;      { Not used }
  MouseMovement = 11;
  SetMickeyRatio = 15;        { Not used }
  CursWidth = 8;              { The emulated cursor is 8 by 8 pixels }
  CursHeight = 8;
  _MaxInc: integer = 32;      { Largest increment amount of emulated mouse cursor }
var
  MouseExists: boolean;       { Internal variable set true if a mouse driver is }
                              { detected during initialization. This variable is used }
                              { to select between the mouse code (if a mouse exists) }
                              { and the keyboard's emulated mouse. }
  { All of the variables and functions that begin with an under-
    score are used to simulate a mouse when one is not present.
  }
  _Cx, _Cy: integer;          { Internal variables used to maintain the cursor }
                              { location when the mouse is not used }
  _Cinc: integer;             { Internal variable used for increment }
                              { amount of the nonmouse cursor }
  _Cursor: pointer;           { Points to the image of the emulated mouse cursor }
  _UnderCursor: pointer;      { Area saved under the internally maintained cursor }
  _CursorOn: boolean;         { True if cursor currently visible }
  _CMinX, _CMaxX: integer;    { Minimum, maximum x coordinates for internal cursor }
  _CMinY, _CMaxY: integer;    { Minimum, maximum y coordinates for internal cursor }
  _LButtonPress: boolean;     { True if simulated left or right }
  _RButtonPress: boolean;     { button was pressed. These are }
  _NumLPress: integer;        { reset after button pressed again is }
  _NumRPress: integer;        { used to simulate button release }
  _NumLRelease: integer;      { and button press count. }
```

```
  _NumRRelease: integer;
  _CDeltaX, _CDeltaY: integer;        { Keeps track of the emulated mouse's movements }

procedure Mouse(var m1, m2, m3, m4: word);
{ This routine provides the communication between the mouse driver and an application
  program. There are several predefined mouse functions supported by the Microsoft
  mouse (see accompanying text). Parameters are sent back and forth to
  the mouse driver through the AX, BX, CX, and DX registers.
}
var
  Regs: Registers;

begin
  Regs.AX := m1;   Regs.BX := m2;
  Regs.CX := m3;   Regs.DX := m4;
  Intr($33, Regs);
  m1 := Regs.AX;   m2 := Regs.BX;
  m3 := Regs.CX;   m4 := Regs.DX;
end;


procedure _ToggleCursor;
{ Used by the simulated mouse to turn the mouse cursor on and off. The viewport
  settings may have changed so temporarily reset them to the full screen while the
  cursor image is displayed or erased.
}
var
  VP: ViewPortType;
  OldX, OldY: integer;

begin
  GetViewSettings(VP);                              { Save view settings }
  OldX := GetX;   OldY := GetY;                     { and current position }
  SetViewPort(0, 0, GetMaxX, GetMaxy, True);
  if _CursorOn then begin                           { To erase the cursor, }
    PutImage(_Cx,_Cy,_UnderCursor^,CopyPut);        { overwrite it with }
    _CursorOn := False;                             { the saved image of }
  end                                               { the screen }
  else begin                                        { To draw the cursor first }
    GetImage(_Cx,_Cy,_Cx+CursWidth,_Cy+CursHeight,_UnderCursor^);
    PutImage(_Cx,_Cy,_Cursor^,CopyPut);             { save the area where the cursor }
```

```pascal
    _CursorOn := True;                    { will be and then display the cursor }
  end;
  SetViewPort(VP.x1, VP.y1, VP.x2, VP.y2, True);   { Reset the viewport settings }
  MoveTo(OldX, OldY);
end;

procedure _DrawCursor(x, y: integer);
{ This routine draws a cursor if a mouse does not exist. It draws a small arrow. If
  you want a different cursor, just change this routine. CursWidth and CursHeight
  define the dimensions of the cursor.
}
begin
  SetColor(GetMaxColor);
  Line(x+1, y+1, x+CursWidth-1, y+CursHeight-1);
  Line(x+2, y+1, x+CursWidth-1, y+CursHeight-2);
  Line(x+1, y+2, x+CursWidth-2, y+CursHeight-1);
  Line(x+2, y+1, x+2, y+5);  Line(x+1, y+1, x+1, y+5);
  Line(x+1, y+1, x+5, y+1);  Line(x+1, y+2, x+5, y+2);
end;


procedure _InitCursor;
{ Creates the image of the simulated mouse. It calls DrawCursor which is a routine
  that you must supply to actually draw the cursor.
}
begin
{ Allocate space for the emulated mouse cursor and for the space
  below it. If not enough memory, quit the program.
}
  GetMem(_Cursor,ImageSize(0, 0, CursWidth, CursHeight));
  GetMem(_UnderCursor,ImageSize(0, 0, CursWidth, CursHeight));
  if (_Cursor = Nil) or (_UnderCursor = Nil) then begin
    CloseGraph;
    writeln('Not enough memory for program.');
    halt(1);
  end;
  { Save the image of the screen where the cursor image will be
    created. Clear this space and call DrawCursor to draw cursor.
  }
  GetImage(_Cx,_Cy,_Cx+CursWidth,_Cy+CursHeight,_UnderCursor^);
  SetLineStyle(SolidLn, 0, 0);
  SetFillStyle(SolidFill, 0);
```

```
    Bar(_Cx, _Cy, _Cx+CursWidth, _Cy+CursHeight);
    _DrawCursor(_Cx, _Cy);
    { Save the image of the cursor and overwrite the screen area
      where the cursor is with the original screen image.
    }
    GetImage(_Cx, _Cy, _Cx+CursWidth, _Cy+CursHeight, _Cursor^);
    PutImage(_Cx, _Cy, _UnderCursor^, CopyPut);
end;


function _GetKb: integer;
{ Low-level keyboard input routine that retrieves some of the extended codes produced
  by the arrow and gray keys. It does not support all the extended key codes.
}
var
    ch1, ch2: integer;

begin
    ch1 := Ord(ReadKey);
    if ch1 = 0 then begin          { Arrow keys have two character sequences }
        ch2 := Ord(ReadKey);       { where the first character is a zero }
        ch2 := ch2 shl 8;          { Combine these two characters into one }
        ch2 := ch2 or ch1;         { and return the value }
        _GetKb := ch2;
    end
    else _GetKb := ch1;
end;


procedure HideMouse;
{ Removes the mouse cursor from the screen. Call this procedure before you write or
  draw anything to the screen. It is also a good idea to turn off the mouse at the end
  of a program. Use ShowMouse to restore the mouse on the screen. The mouse movement
  will be maintained while the mouse is not visible. Due to a peculiarity of the mouse
  driver, make sure you don't call HideMouse if the mouse is not already visible (see
  text discussion).
}
var
    m1, m2, m3, m4: word;


begin
    if not MouseExists then         { Mouse doesn't exist, so turn }
        _ToggleCursor               { off the emulated cursor }
```

```
    else begin
      m1 := MouseHide;                          { Invoke hide mouse function }
      Mouse(m1, m2, m3, m4);
    end
end;

procedure ShowMouse;
{ Display the mouse cursor. Normally, you should not call this routine if the mouse
  is already visible. The keyboard mouse is clipped to the min and max ranges
  in this routine.
}
var
  m1, m2, m3, m4: word;

begin
  if not MouseExists then _ToggleCursor       { If the mouse doesn't exist, use }
  else begin                                  { the emulated mouse cursor }
    m1 := MouseShow;
    Mouse(m1, m2, m3, m4);                     { Display the mouse cursor }
  end
end;

function _GetKbInteraction(WhichButton: integer): integer;
{ This routine is used only if the mouse does not exist. It updates the location of
  the cursor whenever an arrow key is pressed or will set the button pressed or
  released flags if a button key is pressed. In addition, it will change the cursor
  increment amount if the plus or minus keys are pressed. If the "button" specified is
  pressed or was already pressed, the function returns -1. If an arrow key is pressed
  then a zero is returned, which means that the caller does not have to perform any
  action. Finally, if some other key is pressed, then its value is returned.
}
var
  c: integer;

begin
  if KeyPressed then begin
    c := _GetKb;
    HideMouse;
    case(c) of
      $5200 : begin  { Emulated left mouse button press -- INS Key}
        if not _LButtonPress then _LButtonPress := True
```

```
        else _LButtonPress := False;
   ShowMouse;
   if ((WhichButton = LeftButton) or (WhichButton = EitherButton)) then
      _GetKbInteraction := -1              { Return mouse button click signal }
   else begin
      _GetKbInteraction := 0;              { Wrong mouse "button" pressed, }
      if _LButtonPress then Inc(_NumLPress) { but remember it }
         else Inc(_NumLRelease);
      end;
   exit;
   end;
$5300 : begin                          { Emulated right mouse button -- DEL Key }
   ShowMouse;
   if not _RButtonPress then _RButtonPress := True
      else _RButtonPress := False;
   if (WhichButton = RightButton) or (WhichButton = EitherButton) then
      _GetKbInteraction := -1              { Return mouse button signal }
   else begin
      _GetKbInteraction := 0;              { Wrong mouse "button" released, }
                 if _RButtonPress then Inc(_NumRPress)   { but remember it }
         else Inc(_NumRRelease);
      end;
   exit;
   end;
$002b : begin          { Gray plus key. Increase the mouse movement amount. }
   if _Cinc < _MaxInc then Inc(_Cinc,6)
      else _Cinc := _MaxInc;
   end;
$002d : begin          { Gray minus key. Decrease the mouse movement amount. }
   if _Cinc > 1 + 6 then _Cinc := _Cinc - 6
      else _Cinc := 1;
   end;
$4800 :  begin      { Up key. Move the cursor up by the increment amount. }
   Dec(_Cy,_Cinc);                        { Make sure the cursor does }
   if _Cy < _CMinY then _Cy := _CMinY;    { not go too far. Also decrement }
   Dec(_CDeltaY,_Cinc);                   { the mouse movement amount. }
   end;
$4B00 : begin                             { Left key }
   Dec(_Cx,_Cinc);
   if _Cx < _CMinX then _Cx := _CMinX;
```

```
      Dec(_CDeltaX,_Cinc);
    end;
 $4D00 :begin                              { Right key }
    Inc(_Cx,_Cinc);
    if _Cx > _CMaxX then _Cx := _CMaxX;
    Inc(_CDeltaX,_Cinc);
    end;
 $4700 : begin                             { Home key }
    Dec(_Cy,_Cinc);  Dec(_Cx,_Cinc);
    if _Cy < _CMinY then _Cy := _CMinY;
    if _Cx < _CMinX then _Cx := _CMinX;
    Dec(_CDeltaX,_Cinc);  Dec(_CDeltaY,_Cinc);
    end;
 $4900 : begin                             { PgUp Key }
    Dec(_Cy,_Cinc);  Inc(_Cx,_Cinc);
    if _Cy < _CMinY then _Cy := _CMinY;
    if _Cx > _CMaxX then _Cx := _CMaxX;
    Inc(_CDeltaX,_Cinc);  Dec(_CDeltaY,_Cinc);
    end;
 $4F00 : begin                             { End Key }
    Inc(_Cy,_Cinc);  Dec(_Cx,_Cinc);
    if _Cy > _CMaxY then _Cy := _CMaxY;
    if _Cx < _CMinX then _Cx := _CMinX;
    Dec(_CDeltaX,_Cinc);  Inc(_CDeltaY,_Cinc);
    end;
 $5000 : begin                             { Down key }
    Inc(_Cy,_Cinc);
    if _Cy > _CMaxY then _Cy := _CMaxY;
    Inc(_CDeltaY,_Cinc);
    end;
 $5100 : begin                             { PgDn key }
    Inc(_Cy,_Cinc);  Inc(_Cx,_Cinc);
    if _Cy > _CMaxY then _Cy := _CMaxY;
    if _Cx > _CMaxX then _Cx := _CMaxX;
    Inc(_CDeltaX,_Cinc);  Inc(_CDeltaY,_Cinc);
    end;
 else begin
    ShowMouse;
    _GetKbInteraction := c;
    exit;
    end;
```

```
      end;
      _GetKbInteraction := 0;
      ShowMouse;
    end
    else
      _GetKbInteraction := 0;
end;

function TestButton(TestType, WhichButton: integer): boolean;
{ Called by MouseButtonPressed and MouseButtonReleased to explicitly test the mouse
  button states, the function returns True if the specified mouse button (in
  WhichButton) performed the specified action (as indicated by TestType). Otherwise
  the function returns False which means that the action tested for did not occur.
}
var
  m1, m2, m3, m4: word;
  FoundAction: boolean;

begin
  TestButton := False;
  FoundAction := False;
  if (WhichButton = LeftButton) or (WhichButton = EitherButton) then begin
    m1 := TestType;   m2 := LeftButton;
    Mouse(m1, m2, m3, m4);
    if m2 > 0 then begin                    { Return True if action occurred }
      TestButton := True;
      FoundAction := True;
    end
  end;
  if not FoundAction and ((WhichButton = RightButton) or
                          (WhichButton = EitherButton)) then begin
    m1 := TestType;   m2 := RightButton;
    Mouse(m1, m2, m3, m4);
    if m2 > 0 then TestButton := True;      { Return True if action occurred }
  end;
end;

function _SimulatedButtonPressed(WhichButton: integer): boolean;
{ This routine returns True if the specified simulated mouse
  button has been pressed
}
```

```
begin
  if (((WhichButton = LeftButton) or
      (WhichButton = EitherButton)) and (_NumLPress > 0)) then begin
    Dec(_NumLPress);
    _SimulatedButtonPressed := True;
  end
  else if (((WhichButton = RightButton) or
      (WhichButton = EitherButton)) and (_NumRPress > 0)) then begin
    Dec(_NumRPress);
    _SimulatedButtonPressed := True;
  end
  { If there isn't already a button pressed, check and see if
    the user just pressed one, and if so repeat the earlier tests.
  }
  else if _GetKbInteraction(WhichButton) < 0 then begin
    if ((WhichButton = LeftButton) or (WhichButton = EitherButton)) then begin
      Dec(_NumLPress);
      _SimulatedButtonPressed := True;
    end
    else if ((WhichButton = RightButton) or (WhichButton = EitherButton)) then begin
      Dec(_NumRPress);
      _SimulatedButtonPressed := True;
    end
  end
  else _SimulatedButtonPressed := False;
end;


function _SimulatedButtonReleased(WhichButton: integer): boolean;
{ Returns True if the specified simulated mouse button has been released }
begin
  if (((WhichButton = LeftButton) or
      (WhichButton = EitherButton)) and (_NumLRelease > 0)) then begin
    Dec(_NumLRelease);
    _SimulatedButtonReleased := True;
  end
  else if (((WhichButton = RightButton) or
      (WhichButton = EitherButton)) and (_NumRRelease > 0)) then begin
    Dec(_NumRrelease);
    _SimulatedButtonReleased := True;
  end
```

```
  { If there isn't already a button released, check and see if
    the user just released one, and if so repeat the earlier tests
  }
  else if _GetKbInteraction(WhichButton) < 0 then begin
    if ((WhichButton = LeftButton) or (WhichButton = EitherButton)) then begin
      Dec(_NumLRelease);
      _SimulatedButtonReleased := True;
    end
    else if ((WhichButton = RightButton) or (WhichButton = EitherButton)) then begin
      Dec(_NumRRelease);
      _SimulatedButtonReleased := True;
    end
  end
  else _SimulatedButtonReleased := False;
end;

function ResetMouse: boolean;
{ Resets the mouse cursor to: screen center, mouse hidden, using arrow cursor with
  minimum and maximum ranges set to full virtual screen dimensions. If a mouse driver
  exists, this function returns True otherwise it returns False.
}
var
   m1, m2, m3, m4: word;

begin
   m1 := MouseReset;
   Mouse(m1, m2, m3, m4);
   if m1 < 0 then ResetMouse := True
      else ResetMouse := False
end;

procedure MoveMouse(x, y: integer);
{ Moves the mouse to the location (x,y) }
var
   m1, m2, m3, m4: word;

begin
   if not MouseExists then begin
      HideMouse;                     { Erase the current mouse cursor }
      _Cx := x;    _Cy := y;         { Update mouse cursor's location }
      ShowMouse;                     { Display mouse at new location }
```

```
      _CDeltaX := 0;  _CDeltaY := 0;   { Reset mouse movement variables }
    end
    else begin
      m1 := SetMouseCoord;
      { Adjust between virtual and actual coords if needed }
      if GetMaxX = 319 then x := x * 2;
      m3 := x;  m4 := y;
      Mouse(m1, m2, m3, m4);
      x := m3;  y := m4;
    end
end;


function InitMouse: boolean;
{ Call this routine at the beginning of your program, after the graphics adapter has
  been initialized. It will initialize the mouse and display the mouse cursor at the
  top left of the screen, if one is present. Otherwise it will cause the emulated
  mouse to appear and the keyboard will be used to move the "mouse" cursor.
}
var
    GMode: integer;


begin
    MouseExists := True;
    if ResetMouse then begin        { If mouse reset okay, assume mouse exists}
      GMode := GetGraphMode;        { Test if Hercules graphics card is used }
      if GMode = HercMonoHi then    { If so, patch memory }
        Mem[$0040:$0049] := $06;    { location 40h:49h with 6 }
      MoveMouse(0,0);               { Mouse exists and draw the cursor at (0,0) }
      ShowMouse;
      InitMouse := True;            { Return a success flag }
    end
    else begin                      { No mouse was found -- emulate a }
      MouseExists := False;         { mouse using the keyboard }
      _Cx := 0;                     { To do this, maintain a cursor on }
      _Cy := 0;                     { the screen using these }
      _Cinc := 1;                   { internal variables }
      _CMinX := 0;                  { The functionality of the emulated }
      _CMaxX := GetMaxX - 1;        { mouse is the same as the real thing }
      _CMinY := 0;                  { Therefore, to begin with, }
      _CMaxY := GetMaxY - 1;        { set the internal cursor }
      _CDeltaX := 0;                { to the top left of the screen, }
```

```
    _CDeltaY := 0;                          { set its bounds to the size of the }
    _RButtonPress := False;                 { full screen, initialize its movement }
    _LButtonPress := False;                 { counters, initialize button states }
    _NumLPress := 0;                        { to False, and set button counters }
    _NumRPress := 0;                        { to zero }
    _NumLRelease := 0;
    _NumRRelease := 0;
    _InitCursor;                            { Create cursor image }
    _CursorOn := False;
    ShowMouse;                              { Call ShowMouse to display it }
    InitMouse := False;                     { Return a flag indicating mouse }
  end                                       { doesn't exist }
end;


procedure GetMouseCoords(var x, y: integer);
{ Get the current location of the mouse cursor }
var
  m1, m2, m3, m4: word;


begin
  if not MouseExists then begin
    x := _Cx;   y := _Cy;                   { The position of the emulated }
  end                                       { mouse is given by _Cx and _Cy }
  else begin
    m1 := GetMouseStatus;
    m3 := x;   m4 := y;
    Mouse(m1, m2, m3, m4);
    x := m3;   y := m4;
    if GetMaxX = 319 then x := x div 2;     { Adjust for virtual coordinates of mouse }
  end
end;


procedure GetMouseMovement(var x, y: integer);
{ Find out how far the mouse has moved since the last call to this function }
var
  m1, m2, m3, m4: word;


begin
  if not MouseExists then begin            { If mouse does not exist, use emulated }
    x := _CDeltaX;   y := _CDeltaY;         { mouse movement variables _CDeltaX and }
```

```
      _CDeltaX := 0;    _CDeltaY := 0;          { _CDeltaY. Reset counters for next call }
    end                                         { to GetMouseMovement. }
    else begin
      m1 := MouseMovement;   m3 := x;   m4 := y;
      Mouse(m1, m2, m3, m4);
      x := m3;   y := m4;
      if GetMaxX = 319 then x := x div 2;      { Adjust for virtual coordinates }
    end
end;


function MouseButtonReleased(WhichButton: integer): boolean;
{ Test if a button has been released since the last call to this function. If so,
  return True, otherwise return False. In the keyboard mode, button release is
  simulated by striking on the button key again.
}
var
  Button: integer;

begin
  if not MouseExists then MouseButtonReleased := _SimulatedButtonReleased(WhichButton)
    else MouseButtonReleased := TestButton(CheckButtonRelease, WhichButton);
end;


function MouseButtonPressed(WhichButton: integer): boolean;
{ Return True if the mouse button specified has been pressed since the last check with
  this function. If the button has not been pressed, return False.
}
var
  Button: integer;

begin
  if not MouseExists then MouseButtonPressed := _SimulatedButtonPressed(WhichButton)
    else MouseButtonPressed := TestButton(CheckButtonPress, WhichButton);
end;


function MouseInBox(Left, Top, Right, Bottom, x, y: integer): boolean;
{ Returns True if the mouse cursor is within the box specified }
begin
  MouseInBox := ((x >= Left) and (x <= Right) and (y >= Top) and (y <= Bottom));
end;
```

```
function GetInput(WhichButton: integer): integer;
{ Returns a character if a key has been pressed, -1 if a mouse button has been
  pressed, or a zero if none of the above. If a mouse exists, this routine favors
  any keyboard action.
}
begin
   if not MouseExists then GetInput := _GetKbInteraction(WhichButton)
   else begin                                      { Check if a key has been pressed }
     if KeyPressed then GetInput := Ord(ReadKey)   { Return the character }
     else begin
        if MouseButtonPressed(WhichButton) then begin
           while not MouseButtonReleased(WhichButton) do ;
           GetInput := -1;
        end
        else if MouseButtonReleased(WhichButton) then GetInput := -1
           else GetInput := 0;
     end
   end
end;

function WaitForInput(WhichButton: integer): integer;
{ Continue to call GetInput until button or key is pressed }
var c: integer;

begin
  repeat
     c := GetInput(WhichButton);
  until c <> 0;
  WaitForInput := c;
end;
end.
```

Putting Your Mouse to the Test

Listing 7.2 presents a program that will partially test your mouse code. The program does nothing more than set your system into graphics mode and then initialize the mouse. If a mouse is detected, it is displayed and you can move the mouse cursor around. The program will continue until you press one of the buttons on the mouse.

If a mouse is not detected, the emulated mouse will appear. You can move it around the screen using the arrow keys. Use the gray + and - keys to change the amount that the emulated mouse cursor is moved. The program will continue until you press either the INS or DEL key. Remember these are the emulated mouse buttons.

• Listing 7.2

```pascal
program MouseTst;
{ This program partially tests MousePac.Pas. It will display a mouse cursor and let
  you move it around the screen until a mouse button is pressed. If no mouse is
  detected, the keyboard emulated mouse is used. Use the arrow keys to move this mouse
  and the INS or DEL keys as the mouse buttons in order to quit the program.
}
uses
   Graph, MousePac;
const
   GDriver: integer = Detect;              { Use auto-detect }
var
   GMode, c, x, y: integer;

begin
   InitGraph(GDriver, GMode, '');          { Initialize the screen }
   if not InitMouse then begin
     HideMouse;                            { Always turn off the mouse cursor }
     OutTextXY(0,0,'No mouse detected');   { before writing to the screen }
     OutTextXY(0,20,'Press INS or DEL key to quit');
     ShowMouse;                            { When done display mouse }
   end
   else begin
     HideMouse;
     OutTextXY(0,10,'Press a mouse button to quit');
     ShowMouse;
   end;                                    { Wait until the mouse routine }
   repeat                                  { returns a negative value. This }
     c := WaitForInput(EitherButton);      { indicates a button was pressed. }
   until c < 0;
   { It's generally a good idea to turn the mouse off when done }
   HideMouse;
   CloseGraph;                             { Exit graphics mode }
end.
```

8

Working with Icons

In Chapter 7 we learned how to use the mouse in a graphics environment. Part of its attraction is that a mouse can play an integral role in building extremely intuitive user interfaces. For instance, in later chapters we'll see how the mouse can be used to easily draw figures on the screen. However, another way to use the mouse is as a pointing device for selecting commands from the screen. Icons are one popular means of representing commands while in graphics mode. If you've ever used a PC graphics application, such as a painting program, you should already be aware of the benefits icons provide.

In this chapter, we'll take a close look at icons and expand our set of graphics programming tools as we develop a stand-alone icon editor that we'll use to create, save, and edit icons. In addition, we'll present several sample icon patterns that we'll use in developing several custom graphics programs in Chapters 11 and 12.

Why Icons?

Icons are used in many graphics-based applications, such as CAD and paint programs, because they can represent complex commands as symbols or pictures. As a result, extremely intuitive and easy to use graphics interfaces can be designed around them. Instead of having to type a command or select one from a list of often ambiguous menus, the mouse can be used to point and click on an icon to invoke the command.

Our goal here is to develop a program that allows us to create icons interactively. Although we could design our icons by hand, the interactive nature of this program simplifies the process of drawing and editing icons. The program can also be used as a tool to help us experiment with different icon designs.

The **IconEd** program (see Listing 8.1) closely resembles the fill pattern editor that we created in Chapter 2. The key difference is that the fill pattern program has been altered so that it can edit icons. In addition, we'll be using the mouse utilities that we developed in Chapter 7 to improve the user interface. In this respect, you'll be able to see how the tools that we have been developing in earlier chapters can be applied to enhance other programs. The first part of this chapter is devoted to developing the icon editor, and the second part presents several icon patterns that we'll be using in programs in Chapters 11 and 12.

Representing Icons

Icons can be represented in various ways. Our primary concern here is to develop icons that look good when displayed with the different graphics modes supported by the BGI. An icon drawn in one of the modes may appear quite different in another mode because of the different screen resolutions that are possible as well as the different screen aspect ratios. In general, it is impossible to create one icon pattern that looks the same in all graphics modes.

We'll standardize our icons so that they are all 16 by 16 pixels. This size seems to work well in most cases (at least in the graphics modes that we'll be using). Nevertheless, we'll need to compensate for the aspect ratio of the screens in order to make the icons look proportionally correct when displayed with different graphics modes. However, we won't be compensating for the size of the icons, so the icons will appear in different sizes and slightly different shapes in each of the graphics modes.

Internally, an icon pattern is represented in our icon editor as a two-dimensional array of bytes. Here's the declaration for this array:

```
const
   IconHeight = 16;
   IconWidth  = 16;
var
   Icon: array[1..IconHeight,1..IconWidth] of byte;
```

The constants **IconHeight** and **IconWidth** specify the height and width of the icon respectively, and are defined as the value 16. Consequently, each location in the icon array represents one pixel in the icon pattern. We'll be using only black and white icons, so these byte locations will take on only a 1 or 0 value. If the value is 1, the corresponding icon pixel is drawn in white; otherwise, it is left as the background color. If you desire, you can add color to your icons; however, keep in mind that not all of the graphic modes can produce the same colors.

Saving Icons

To simplify our application programs and make our icons easier to maintain, we'll save each icon pattern in its own file. In addition, we'll store the icons in text format so that they can be easily inspected.

The format of the icon files consists of two major parts—a header and a body. The header is located at the top of the file and is a single line that specifies the icon's width and height. Since all of our icons are 16 by 16 pixels, the first line will always start with these two numbers. The rest of the file contains the icon pattern that is organized so that each row of the icon is on a separate line. Therefore a 16 by 16 pixel icon has 16 numbers per line where each pixel of the icon image is represented by either a 0 or a 1. Figure 8.1 shows a sample icon and the file that is used to store this icon. If you compare the two, you'll see that there is a one-to-one correspondence between each pixel set in the icon and each value of 1 in the file.

While we are discussing the format of an icon file, let's look at the **SaveIcon** routine, which is used to write an icon pattern to disk. To simplify the user input, **SaveIcon** assumes that it is called while the program is in text mode. It first prompts you to enter the file name of the icon file to be written. It then calls **Assign** and **Rewrite** to open the file and prepare for reading. If the file cannot be opened or

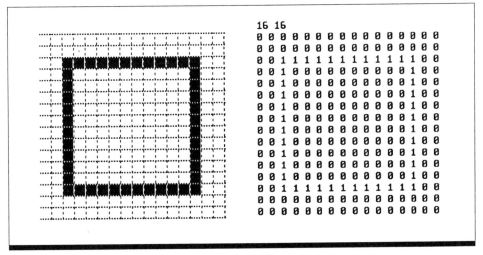

Figure 8.1. An icon and the file that represents it

created the Turbo Pascal error flag, **IOResult**, is nonzero and the routine immediately returns without performing any other actions. However, if the file is opened, **SaveIcon** writes the icon pattern stored in the array **Icon** to the file using the following statements:

```
writeln(IconFile, IconWidth, ' ', IconHeight);   { Write header }
for j := 1 to IconHeight do begin               { Write icon pattern }
  for i := 1 to IconWidth do                    { to file one row at a }
    write(IconFile, Icon[j][i], ' ');           { time }
  writeln(IconFile);
end;
Close(IconFile);
```

The first **writeln** in this code segment writes the header data containing the width and height of the icon to the file. The nested **for** loops that follow copy the icon pattern to the file by writing each row of the icon pattern on a separate line. After the icon pattern is completely written, the file is closed with a call to **Close**.

Reading an Icon File

The process of reading an icon file into the icon editor is similar to that of writing a file and is performed by the routine **ReadIcon**. Like **SaveIcon**, this routine is designed to run in text mode in order to simplify the text input.

The routine begins by initializing an icon pattern so that it contains all zeros as shown:

```
for j := 1 to IconHeight do begin   { Initialize the icon }
  for i := 1 to IconWidth do        { array to all blanks }
    Icon[j][i] := 0;
end;
```

This technique ensures that the icon pattern starts as a completely black icon. The **ReadIcon** routine then continues by displaying a program banner and asking you if you wish to edit an existing icon file. If your response is *yes* (any character but the letter n), **ReadIcon** assumes you want to edit an existing icon and asks you for the name of the file where it is stored. Remember that during this process, the data entry operations are performed in text mode in order to simplify the code. You can, however, try to integrate the **GText.Pas** text processing utilities developed in Chapter 3 in the routine, in order to avoid having to switch between graphics and text modes.

Once the file name is determined, **ReadIcon** attempts to open it for reading. If this operation is successful, the first line of the file, which contains the header, is read. As long as this line consists of two values equivalent to **IconWidth** and **IconHeight**, **ReadIcon** continues. If any other numbers are found, then the file is invalid and **ReadIcon** terminates.

The icon pattern is read from the file into the array **Icon** by two **for** loops like those used in **SaveIcon** to write the icon data to a file. The difference is that here the **Readln** routine is used to read the icon pattern from the file. Once the icon pattern has been read into the array **Icon**, we can display it. We'll look at how this is done later in this chapter in the section "Displaying the Original Icon."

The Interactive Editor

Now that we know how to read and write icon files, we're ready to look at the icon editor itself. Figure 8.2 shows the icon editor while it is being used to edit an icon. Notice that there are two primary regions in the display. On the left side of the screen is an enlarged representation of the icon being edited. All editing is actually performed within this window. On the right side of the screen is the current state of the icon pattern shown in its actual size.

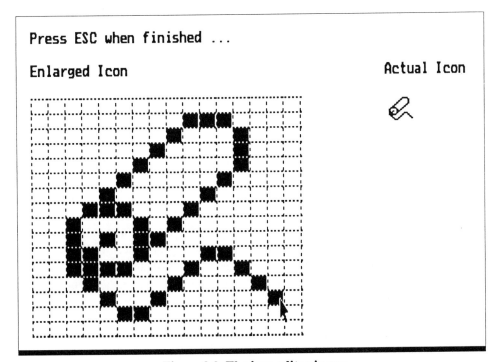

Figure 8.2. The icon editor in use

You can edit an icon by clicking the mouse on any of the big icon bits of the enlarged icon pattern. Each time you click the mouse while it is over one of these big pixels, the pixel's state is toggled from white to black or black to white. In addition, after every mouse action, the current state of the icon is updated on the right side of the screen.

You can use the icon editor by toggling the various pixels that you want to change in the enlarged icon pattern until you are satisfied with how the normal sized icon looks. To exit the editing process, you select the *ESC* key. Once this is done, the screen is cleared and you are asked if you want to save the icon pattern currently in the editor to a file of your choice. If so, you will be prompted to enter the file name and then the program will save the icon pattern and terminate. Otherwise, the program simply ends. Let's next examine the different components of the icon editor program.

Creating the Screen

The first 10 statements in the **IconEd** program initialize various aspects of the icon editor. The process begins by reading an icon file, if necessary, initializing the graphics mode, initializing the mouse, generating the enlarged icon pattern, and displaying the initial state of the icon pattern. The routine calls used are as follows:

```
ReadIcon;
InitGraphics;
InitMouse;
DrawEnlargedIcon;
ShowIcon;
```

These statements must be called in this order. In particular, we want to keep the **ReadIcon** routine in text mode (before graphics initialization), in order to simplify the user interaction. In addition, the mouse initialization must always come after the graphics initialization. The ordering of the last two statements is probably a little more obvious. We'll look at these two routines later in this section.

The next five statements are used to print a series of banners to the screen by calling the **OutTextXY** routine. Note that a pair of **HideMouse** and **ShowMouse** routine calls surround the screen output statements. They are needed to ensure that the mouse cursor is turned off while the screen is being updated with the displayed messages.

Creating an Enlarged Icon

The routine **DrawEnlargedIcon** generates a grid on the left side of the screen in which the enlarged icon pattern is edited. The grid consists of 17 horizontal and vertical dotted lines which mark out a 16 by 16 grid for the icon pattern as shown in Figure 8.3. These are drawn by the following two **for** loops:

```
HideMouse;                        { Draw vertical and horizontal dashed }
for i := 0 to IconHeight do    { lines to make a big icon pattern }
  Line(BigIconLeft, BigIconTop+i*(BigBitSize+NormWidth), Right,
       BigIconTop+i*(BigBitSize+NormWidth));
for i := 0 to IconWidth do
  Line(BigIconLeft+2*(i*(BigBitSize+NormWidth)), BigIconTop,
       BigIconLeft+2*(i*(BigBitSize+NormWidth)), Bottom);
ShowMouse;
```

Once again, note that before anything is written to the screen, the mouse is first turned off by a call to **HideMouse** and later restored by a call to **ShowMouse**.

You have probably noticed by now that **DrawEnlargedIcon** relies on numerous constants. A list of these constants along with a description of their meanings are shown in Table 8.1. You may want to refer to this table to help you understand the **DrawEnlargedIcon** routine.

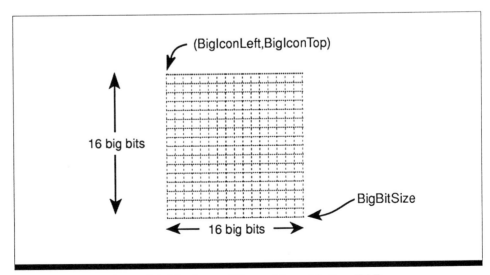

Figure 8.3. The icon editing grid used in IconEd.Pas

Table 8.1. Constants used in drawing the enlarged icon pattern

Constant	Description
BigIconLeft	The column where the big icon pattern begins
BigIconTop	The top row of the big icon pattern
BigBitSize	Size of the big pixels in the enlarged icon pattern
IconWidth	Width of an icon
IconHeight	Height of an icon
DottedLn	From Graph, specifies the line type
NormWidth	From Graph, pixel width of lines

The last line in **DrawEnlargedIcon** is a call to the routine **InitBigBit** which creates an image of an enlarged icon pixel. To toggle the icon pixels in the enlarged icon pattern, we'll exclusive OR the image created by **InitBigBit** to the rectangular regions within the enlarged icon pattern. Let's now look at this routine.

The image of one of the enlarged bits is created at the beginning of **InitBigBit** by the following nested **for** loops:

```
for j := bby+1 to bby+BigBitSize do begin   { Draw a big bit }
   for i := bbx+1 to bbx+2*BigBitSize do     { one pixel at a time }
     PutPixel(i, j, GetMaxColor);
end;
```

These two loops paint a block of pixels in the top-left corner of the enlarged icon pattern the size of **BigBitSize**. Actually, note that the width of the enlarged icon is drawn as twice the width of **BigBitSize**. We do this to adjust for the aspect ratio of many of the graphics modes that we'll be using.

Once the enlarged icon pixel image is created, it is copied into **BigBit**. First, however, space for this image must be allocated by a call to **GetMem**. After storage is allocated, **GetImage** is called to copy the image of the big pixel as shown here:

```
GetMem(BigBit,ImageSize(bbx, bby, bbx+2*BigBitSize, bby+BigBitSize));
GetImage(bbx+1, bby+1, bbx+2*BigBitSize, bby+BigBitSize, BigBit^);
```

Later, when we want to toggle one of the enlarged icon pixels while editing, we'll need only to exclusive OR an image of this pixel pattern, stored in **BigBit**, over the appropriate location in the grid. Of course, now we have a big pixel in the top-left corner of the enlarged icon pixel that we must remove. We do this by a call to **PutImage** using the **XorPut** replacement as shown:

```
PutImage(bbx+1, bby+1, BigBit^, XorPut);
```

After accomplishing these operations, the mouse cursor is finally restored by a call to **ShowMouse** and **InitBigBit** ends.

Displaying the Original Icon

The next step in the screen initialization process consists of displaying the icon pattern that was read in at the beginning of the program. Remember, if an icon file is not read in, then the icon array is initialized to all zeros in **ReadIcon**. The routine **ShowIcon** is used to display the current state of the icon pattern. This routine consists of two nested **for** loops which sequence through the array **Icon**. For each byte location that stores a 1, a corresponding big bit is toggled in the enlarged icon and the small icon pattern is updated as well. Setting one of the big icon pixels is a matter of exclusive-ORing the image of the big icon pixel (discussed in the previous section), at the appropriate locations. The **PutImage** routine located within the inner **for** loop performs this step.

The call to **ToggleIconsBit** is required in order to turn on the appropriate pixel in the small icon pattern. The routine accepts as parameters the logical indexes of a pixel in the **Icon** array, and checks the pixel corresponding to the **Icon** array indexes by testing whether it is equal to the background color. Depending on its current value, the small icon's pixels are toggled. The small icon is displayed at the column indicated by **IconLeft**. Its top row coincides with **BigIconTop**. You will notice that although the icon is represented as a 16 by 16 pattern, the small icon is displayed in a 32 by 16 format. That is, each column of pixels is displayed twice and that's why the multiplication factor of 2 in the x coordinate calculation is required. This technique is used to adjust for the aspect ratio for most of the graphics modes we'll be using. If you use other modes or discover that the icons are not proportionally correct, you should change these factors.

Interacting with the User

After the screen is initialized, the icon editor is ready for business. While editing an icon, there are two types of input that are acceptable:

1. Pressing the left mouse button which toggles the current icon pixel that is pointed at, if there is one
2. Pressing ESC, which exits the program

The **while** loop in the mainline supports this user interaction and is:

```
c := WaitForInput (LeftButton);        { Get input from mouse/keyboard }
while c <> 27 do begin                  { If input is ESC, quit program }
   if c < 0 then begin                  { if input less than zero then a }
      GetMouseCoords (x, y);            { mouse button has been pressed; }
      ToggleBigBit (x, y);             { get current coordinates and }
   end;                                 { toggle big bit }
   c := WaitForInput (LeftButton);
end;                                    { Loop until person types ESC }
```

The loop centers around the use of the mouse routine **WaitForInput,** which we developed in Chapter 7. This routine returns a negative value if the button specified, in this case the left mouse button, is pressed, or it returns the value of a key pressed. The **while** loop is written so that the program will continue until the ESC key is pressed. If the left mouse button is pressed, the routine will progress to the **if** statement. At this point, **GetMouseCoords** retrieves the current location of the mouse cursor and passes it along to the routine **ToggleBigBit** which changes the setting of the icon pixel that the mouse is pointing to.

Toggling an Icon Pixel

Toggling a pixel in an icon that is being edited involves the following three operations:

1. The pixel's value in the icon array must be changed
2. The big pixel image in the enlarged icon pattern must be toggled
3. The icon's pixel in the small icon pattern must be updated

Each of these actions is set in motion by a call to **ToggleBigBit**. This routine takes two parameters that correspond to the screen coordinates of the enlarged icon bit that is to be changed. This screen coordinate is determined from the location of the mouse cursor at the time of the button press. The mouse coordinates come from our mouse routine **GetMouseCoords**.

The bulk of **ToggleBigBit**, which follows, is involved in determining which icon bit should be toggled, if any.

```
for j := 1 to IconHeight do begin
   Line1 := BigIconTop+(j-1)*(BigBitSize+NormWidth);
```

```
    Line2 := BigIconTop+j*(BigBitSize+NormWidth);
    if (Line1 <= y) and (y < Line2) then begin
       for i := 1 to IconWidth do begin
          Col1 := BigIconLeft+2*((i-1)*(BigBitSize+NormWidth));
          Col2 := BigIconLeft+2*(i*(BigBitSize+NormWidth));
          if (Col1 <= x) and (x < col2) then begin
             HideMouse;                          { Toggle the big bit using }
             PutImage(Col1+1, Line1+1, BigBit^, XorPut); { the XOR }
             ShowMouse;                          { feature of putimage }
             { Toggle the corresponding  pixel in the small icon }
             ToggleIconsBit(i, j);
          end
       end
    end
end
```

This is accomplished by the two **for** loops in the routine. They sequence through the locations of the big icon pattern and test whether the coordinates passed to **ToggleBigBit** fall within any of the rows or columns in the big icon pattern. If so, the **PutImage** routine is used to exclusive OR an image of the **BigBit** image made earlier over the current location in the icon pattern. This takes care of toggling the icon pixel in the large icon pattern. Now we need to change the corresponding bit in the small icon pattern. Fortunately, the routine is designed so that the line number and column number determined by the **for** loops will correspond to the indexes that can access the same bit in the icon array. These values, stored in the variables **i** and **j**, are passed to the **ToggleIconsBit** routine to actually change the **Icon** array value and update the small icon on the screen. This routine was presented earlier in this chapter.

Exiting the Icon Editor

The **while** loop discussed earlier which controls the user interaction continues until the ESC key is pressed. Once this is done, the mouse cursor is disabled, the screen is returned to text mode, and you are prompted to save the icon currently in the icon editor. If you respond with anything other than the letter n, the program enters the **SaveIcon** routine and you will be prompted for the file name in which to store the icon. The **SaveIcon** routine was also discussed earlier in this chapter.

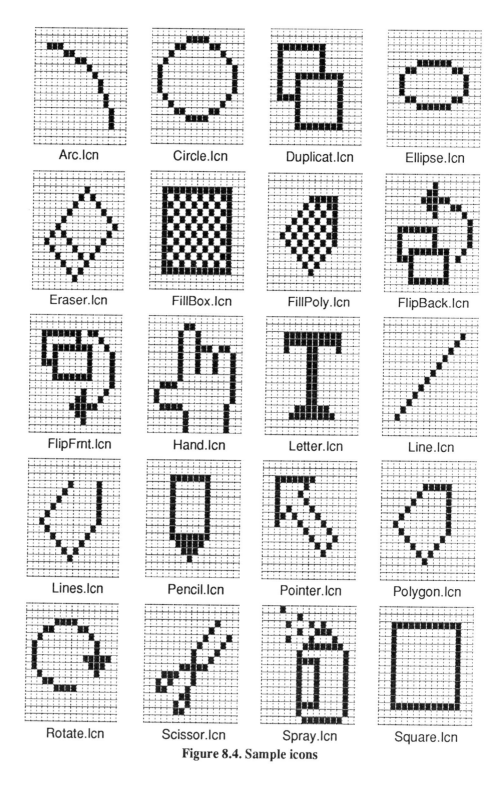

Figure 8.4. Sample icons

Sample Icons

The icons in Figure 8.4 were all developed with the icon editor in this chapter. We will be using many of these icon patterns in later programs in this book. To minimize any confusion, we have provided specific file names for these icons that you should also use. This should guarantee the greatest compatibility with any code we will be developing later.

• Listing 8.1

```pascal
program IconEd;
{ This program will enable you to interactively create icons that can be used in a
  graphics program. It enables you to create an icon, edit an existing one, or
  save an icon pattern to a file. The program supports both keyboard and
  mouse interaction. The icon files are of the form:
      IconWidth IconHeight
      one row of icon pattern
      next row of icon pattern
         .  .  .
      last row of icon pattern

}
uses
  Graph, Crt, MousePac;
const
  BigIconLeft = 20;        { Left side of the big icon pattern }
  BigIconTop = 50;         { Top side of the big icon pattern }
  BigBitSize = 8;          { Big bits are 8 pixels in size }
  IconWidth = 16;          { An icon is a 16 by 16 pattern }
  IconHeight = 16;
  IconLeft = 400;          { Small icon pattern is located here }
var
  BigBit: pointer;         { Points to image of a big bit }
  { Holds the 16x16 icon pattern }
  Icon: array[1..IconHeight,1..IconWidth] of byte;
  x, y, i, j, c: integer;
  ch: char;
  t: boolean;
```

```pascal
procedure InitBigBit;
{ Create the image of a single big bit. This image will be used to toggle the big
  bits later in the program whenever the user clicks on the big icon pattern.
}
var
   bbx, bby, i, j: integer;

begin
   bbx := BigIconLeft;                 { Create the big bit image at the top-left }
   bby := BigIconTop;                  { corner of the big icon already drawn }

   HideMouse;                          { Hide mouse before drawing to screen  }
   for j := bby+1 to bby+BigBitSize do begin      { Draw big bit }
   for i := bbx+1 to bbx+2*BigBitSize do          { one pixel at a }
     PutPixel(i, j, GetMaxColor);                 { time }
   end;
   { Set aside enough memory for the big bit image and then use
     GetImage to capture its image.
   }
   GetMem(BigBit,ImageSize(bbx, bby, bbx+2*BigBitSize,
          bby+BigBitSize));
   GetImage(bbx+1, bby+1, bbx+2*BigBitSize, bby+BigBitSize,
          BigBit^);
   { Erase the big bit by exclusive-ORing it with itself }
   PutImage(bbx+1, bby+1, BigBit^, XorPut);
   ShowMouse;                                     { Turn mouse back on }
end;

procedure DrawEnlargedIcon;
{ This routine draws an enlarged view of the icon pattern being edited. Click on the
  big bits in this pattern to toggle the corresponding icons on and off in the actual
  icon. The enlarged icon is drawn at BigIconLeft, BigIconTop, to Right, and Bottom.
}
var
   i: integer;
   Right, Bottom: integer;

begin
   SetLineStyle(DottedLn, 0, NormWidth);
   Right := 2 * (BigIconLeft + (IconWidth-1) * (BigBitSize + NormWidth));
   Bottom := BigIconTop + IconHeight * (BigBitSize + NormWidth);
```

```
  HideMouse;                                 { Draw vertical and horizontal dashed }
  for i := 0 to IconHeight do                { lines to make a big icon pattern }
    Line(BigIconLeft, BigIconTop+i*(BigBitSize+NormWidth), Right,
      BigIconTop+i*(BigBitSize+NormWidth));
  for i := 0 to IconWidth do
    Line(BigIconLeft+2*(i*(BigBitSize+NormWidth)), BigIconTop,
      BigIconLeft+2*(i*(BigBitSize+NormWidth)), Bottom);
  ShowMouse;
  InitBigBit;                                { Create the big bit image }
end;

procedure ToggleIconsBit(x, y: integer);
{ This routine toggles a single pixel in the icon pattern. It changes the pixel's
  color and its value in the icon pattern array. The parameters x and y are between 0
  and IconWidth or IconHeight. Plot 2 pixels wide to adjust for the aspect
  ratio of many of the graphics modes. You may want to remove this. The array icon
  saves the icon pattern. If one of its locations is 1, then the corresponding pixel
  in the icon is to be drawn on.
}
begin
  HideMouse;
  if GetPixel(2*x+IconLeft, BigIconTop+y) <> Black then begin
    PutPixel(2*x+IconLeft, BigIconTop+y, Black);
    PutPixel(2*x+1+IconLeft, BigIconTop+y, Black);
    Icon[y][x] := 0;
  end
  else begin
    PutPixel(2*x+IconLeft, BigIconTop+y, GetMaxColor);
    PutPixel(2*x+1+IconLeft, BigIconTop+y, GetMaxColor);
    Icon[y][x] := 1;
  end;
  ShowMouse;
end;

procedure ToggleBigBit(x, y: integer);
{ When the user clicks on the big icon pattern, toggle the appropriate big bit and the
  corresponding pixel in the icon pattern. This routine accepts screen coordinates
  that specify where the mouse button was pressed. The two for loops test to see which
  logical bit in the icon pattern must be toggled. Use putimage to toggle the BigBit.
  Call ToggleIconsBit to toggle the appropriate pixel in the icon pattern.
}
```

```
var
   bbx, bby, i, j: integer;
   Line1, Line2, Col1, Col2: integer;

begin
   for j := 1 to IconHeight do begin
      Line1 := BigIconTop+(j-1)*(BigBitSize+NormWidth);
      Line2 := BigIconTop+j*(BigBitSize+NormWidth);
      if (Line1 <= y) and (y < Line2) then begin
         for i := 1 to IconWidth do begin
            Col1 := BigIconLeft+2*((i-1)*(BigBitSize+NormWidth));
            Col2 := BigIconLeft+2*(i*(BigBitSize+NormWidth));
            if (Col1 <= x) and (x < col2) then begin
               HideMouse;                                   { Toggle the big bit using }
               PutImage(Col1+1, Line1+1, BigBit^, XorPut);  { the Xor }
               ShowMouse;                                   { feature of putimage }
               { Toggle the corresponding  pixel in the small icon }
               ToggleIconsBit(i, j);
            end
         end
      end
   end
end;


procedure SaveIcon;
{ This routine writes the icon pattern to a file. The user is prompted for the file
  name. The format of the file is given at the top of the program.
}
var
   FileName: string;
   IconFile: text;
   i, j: integer;

begin
   writeln;
   write('Enter the name of the file you want to');
   write(' store the icon in: ');
   readln(FileName);
   {$I-} Assign(IconFile,FileName);
   Rewrite(IconFile);  {$I+}
```

```pascal
  if not (IOResult = 0) then begin
    CloseGraph;
    writeln('Cannot open file.');
    halt(1);
  end
  else begin
    writeln(IconFile, IconWidth, ' ', IconHeight);          { Write header }
    for j := 1 to IconHeight do begin                        { Write icon pattern }
      for i := 1 to IconWidth do                             { to file one row at a }
        write(IconFile, Icon[j][i], ' ');                    { time }
      writeln(IconFile);
    end;
    Close(IconFile);
  end;
end;


procedure ReadIcon;
{ This routine reads an icon file into the icon pattern array and calls
  ShowIcon to turn the appropriate pixels on. If the header of the file does
  not match the IconWidth and IconHeight values, then the file is invalid and no icon
  will be read in.
}
var
  FileName: string[80];
  ch: char;
  IconFile: text;
  i, j: integer;
  Width, Height: integer;

begin
  for j := 1 to IconHeight do begin                          { Initialize the icon }
    for i := 1 to IconWidth do                               { array to all blanks }
      Icon[j][i] := 0;
  end;

  writeln;
  writeln;
  writeln('-----------  ICON EDITOR -------------');
  writeln;
  write('Do you want to edit an existing icon? (y) ');
```

```
    ch := ReadKey;
    if ch <> 'n' then begin
      writeln;
      write('Enter the name of the file to read the icon from: ');
      readln(FileName);
      {$I-}  Assign(IconFile,FileName);
      Reset(IconFile); {$I+}
      if not (IOResult = 0) then begin
        CloseGraph;
        writeln('Cannot open file.');
        halt(1);
      end;
      { Read the first line of the icon file. It should contain two
        numbers that are equal to IconWidth and IconHeight.
      }
      Readln(IconFile, Width, Height);
      if (Width <> IconWidth) or (Height <> IconHeight) then begin
        writeln('Incompatible icon file.');
        halt(1);
      end
      else begin
        for j := 1 to IconHeight do
          for i := 1 to IconWidth do
            Read(Iconfile, Icon[j][i]);
        Close(IconFile);
      end
    end
end;

procedure InitGraphics;
const
  GDriver: integer = Detect;
var
  GMode, GError: integer;

begin
  InitGraph(GDriver,GMode,'');
  GError := GraphResult;
  if GError < 0 then begin
    writeln('Failed graphics initialization: GError=',GError);
```

```
      halt(1);
      end
  end;

procedure ShowIcon;
{ Show the icon pattern that is in the icon array }
var
    x, y: integer;

begin
    for y := 1 to IconHeight do
        for x := 1 to IconWidth do
            if Icon[y][x] = 1 then begin         { Display each icon bit in }
                PutImage(BigIconLeft+2*((x-1)*(BigBitSize+NormWidth))+1,
                BigIconTop+(y-1)*(BigBitSize+NormWidth)+1,BigBit^,XorPut);
                ToggleIconsBit(x, y);             { the big and small icons }
        end
end;


begin
    ReadIcon;                           { If a person wants an icon file to }
    InitGraphics;                       { be read, read it, otherwise }
    t := InitMouse;                     { simply initialize the screen with }
    DrawEnlargedIcon;                   { an empty big icon pattern }
    ShowIcon;                           { Draw the icon to start with }
    { When using the mouse, first turn it off before writing anything to the screen }
    HideMouse;
    OutTextXY(BigIconLeft, 10, 'Press ESC when finished ...');
    OutTextXY(BigIconLeft, BigIconTop-20, 'Enlarged Icon');
    OutTextXY(IconLeft, BigIconTop-20, 'Actual Icon');
    ShowMouse;                          { Redraws mouse to the screen }

    c := WaitForInput(LeftButton);      { Get input from mouse/keyboard }
    while c <> 27 do begin              { if input is ESC, quit program }
        if c < 0 then begin             { If input is less than zero then a mouse }
            GetMouseCoords(x, y);       { button has been pressed, get current }
            ToggleBigBit(x, y);         { coordinates and toggle big bit }
        end;
        c := WaitForInput(LeftButton);
    end;                                { Loop until person types ESC }
```

```
    HideMouse;                              { Turn mouse off and then get out }
    CloseGraph;                             { of graphics mode to make user }
                                            { input easier }
    write('Do you want to save this icon to a file? (y) ');
    ch := ReadKey;
    if ch <> 'n' then                       { Save the icon to a file if the  }
       SaveIcon;                            { user types anything except "n" }
end.
```

9

Pop-up Windows in Graphics

This chapter presents another useful feature often found in interactive graphics environments—pop-up windows. Like the icons we explored in Chapter 8, pop-up windows have become popular over the last several years. They are attractive because they can be used to tile messages, create pull-down menus, and enhance other forms of program input/output.

Our goal in this chapter is to develop a pop-up window package that we can use in any of the graphics modes supported by the BGI. This window unit, which we'll call **GPopPac.Pas** (see Listing 9.1), allows us to pop-up and remove windows in graphics mode with two simple commands. The window tools that we develop here will be used with the programs in Chapters 11, 12, and 13.

The Basic Approach

With the help of the low-level BGI screen tools, pop-up windows are easy to support in Turbo Pascal. In this section we'll show you the steps involved in both creating and removing a pop-up window.

The process of creating a pop-up window is outlined in Figure 9.1. As this diagram indicates, the basic idea is to save the region of the screen that is to be over-layed by the pop-up window as well as any screen and drawing parameters that might be changed. Later this information can be used to restore the screen to its state before the pop-up window was created. We'll save this information on a stack so that we can build up layers of pop-up windows. Unfortunately, the stack approach limits access to the windows. That is, the windows will have to be removed in reverse order

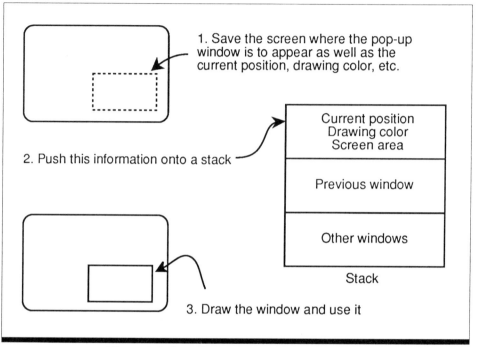

Figure 9.1. Steps in creating a pop-up window

from the way they were created. Therefore, we won't be able to arbitrarily bring a window that is covered by several other windows to the front of the screen. Actually, this feature can be added, but to keep the code simple it is left out.

Similarly, to remove a pop-up window from the screen, all we need do is perform two steps.

1. Overwrite the pop-up window with the stored image of the screen by popping it from the stack.
2. Restore the screen parameters that were saved on the stack.

After this process, the screen will appear as if the pop-up window never existed.

We'll save and restore the screen image using the **GetImage** and **PutImage** routines provided by the BGI. Since these functions work in all graphics modes supported by the BGI, our pop-up windows will also. The screen parameters that we'll save include such attributes as the current drawing position and the drawing colors. We need to save these attributes because the pop-up windows may change them.

Working with a Stack

The main data structure that we'll be using to maintain the pop-up windows is a stack. In order to keep things simple, our stack is implemented as a single-dimensioned array, as shown in Figure 9.2, where each element in the array stores the information discussed earlier for the pop-up windows. Note that the stack pointer is essentially the index of the array and normally points to the next available location on the stack. It is incremented by one each time a new window is pushed on the stack. Therefore, if there are four items on the stack, the stack pointer will point to the fifth element (the array starts at index 1).

Each element is a record of type **GraphicsWindow** which is used to save the viewport settings, the current position, the drawing parameters, and the region of the screen that is below the window. This record is defined in **GPopPac.Pas** as:

```
GraphicsWindow = record                  { Record to save graphics settings }
   VLeft,VTop,VRight,VBottom: integer;        { Parent window boundaries }
   cpx,cpy: integer;               { Current position in parent window }
   SaveArea: pointer;              { Pointer to the saved region }
   DrawColor: word;                { Current drawing color }

   {*** Place other drawing parameters ***}
   {*** that you wish to save here      ***}
end;
```

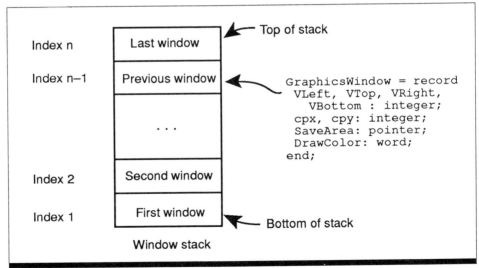

Figure 9.2. The window stack is an array of records

Each record in the stack is used to save anything that may be changed when a window is popped up. These attributes are in turn used to restore the screen settings to their original states when the pop-up window is removed from the screen. Beginning at the top of the record, **VLeft, VTop, VRight,** and **VBbottom** save the current viewport boundaries at the time the pop-up window is created. Similarly, **cpx** and **cpy** save the coordinate of the current position. The **SaveArea** variable is a pointer to the screen area to be saved. The memory storage for saving the screen is allocated just before the window is written. Finally, the drawing color is saved in the record component **DrawColor**. Depending on how you want to use the pop-up window package, you may want to modify **GraphicsWindow** so that it will also save the current line style, fill patterns, and the rest of the BGI drawing parameters.

Our stack, which is an array of records of type **GraphicsWindow**, is defined as:

```
const
    NumGWindows = 10;
var
    WindowStack: array[1..NumGWindows] of GraphicsWindow;
```

Note that we have declared a stack of only 10 records. This means that we'll only be able to have 10 pop-up windows at a time. For most applications, this should be more than enough. If you develop an application program that needs more windows open at once, then you should increase this number appropriately.

The stack pointer, **GWindowPtr,** is an index into this array (we'll see how this pointer is used in the following section). Figure 9.3 shows how the stack changes as a new window is added to the screen.

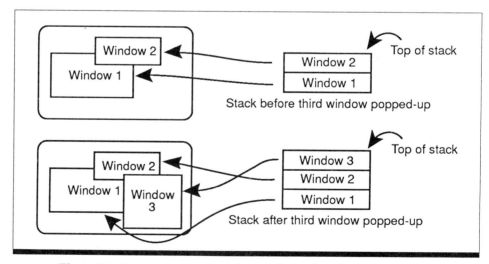

Figure 9.3. The stack changes when a window is added to the screen

Initializing the Windows Package

Like many of the other tools in this book, we need an initialization routine before using any of the pop-up window routines. The window initialization code in **GPopPac.Pas** is built into the initialization section of the unit's file. This nameless routine is responsible for initializing the stack pointer to the first element of the stack array as:

```
GWindowPtr := 1;
```

Although this routine is short, it is important so do not omit it.

The Pop-up Routine

Now let's take a look at the routine **GPopup** which we'll use to pop-up a window. It is declared in the unit **GPopPac.Pas** as:

```
function GPopup(Left, Top, Right, Bottom, BorderType, BorderColor,
                BackFill, FillColor: integer): boolean;
```

As you can see, **GPopup** takes a hefty eight parameters. The first four specify two opposing corners of the pop-up window and must be in full-screen coordinates, not the coordinates of the current window. The other four parameters define the graphics parameters to be used in the pop-up window. These are shown in Table 9.1.

Table 9.1. Drawing parameters used by GPopup

Parameter	Description
BorderType	Defines the line style used to draw the border of the pop-up window
BorderColor	Sets the drawing color to be used to draw the border
BackFill	Defines the fill pattern used to fill the pop-up window
FillColor	Sets the color to be used by the fill pattern

If you want to be able to alter some of the other graphics parameters through a call to **GPopup**, you can easily add them to its list of parameters. For instance, you could add the background color or line style to the list of drawing parameters that are saved by **GPopup**.

Finally, the routine **GPopup** returns True if the window is successfully created; otherwise, it returns False indicating a failure in popping-up the window.

Now let's see how to pop-up a window with **GPopup**. For example, to pop-up a window that stretches from the top left of the screen to its middle, has a solid border, and a solid fill pattern, you can use the line:

```
GPopup(0, 0, GetMaxX div 2, GetMaxY div 2, SolidLn, White,
      SolidFill, White);
```

A Closer Look at GPopup

Now that we have a functional description of the pop-up window routine, let's take a closer look at how it works. In this section, we'll be examining portions of the **GPopup** routine, but for a complete listing of the routine refer to the **GPopPac.Pas** source code listed near the end of this chapter.

The first thing that is done in **GPopup** is to test whether the stack is full. Since we are using an array to implement the stack, this is simply a matter of testing whether or not the stack pointer, **GWindowPtr**, has reached the end of the array **WindowStack**. If it has, then **GPopup** returns False indicating that it cannot pop-up the window. Remember that the stack pointer normally points to the next available location in the stack; therefore, the test for whether the stack is not full is:

```
if GWindowPtr > NumGWindows then GPopup := False;
```

Once we know that there is enough room on the stack for another window, we save the viewport and drawing parameters, because these may be changed when we pop-up the window.

Next we'll save the region of the screen that is to be overwritten by the pop-up window by calling the routine **SaveScreen** (discussed in the next section). However, first the viewport settings are set to the full screen since our pop-up window coordinates are given relative to the full-screen and not the current viewport. This allows us to specify locations for pop-up windows anywhere on the screen, no matter what view settings are currently active. The **if** statement in **GPopup** makes the call to **SaveWindow** which saves the region of the screen to be overwritten. If the **SaveWindow** function returns False, then the operation has failed so the pop-up window should not be created. If this is the case, the viewport settings must be restored (because they were changed before the call to **SaveWindow**). Once this is done the **GPopup** routine reports a failure by returning False. The code that performs these operations is:

```
if not SaveWindow(Left, Top, Right, Bottom) then begin
  { Save screen failed, restore viewport settings and current position
  }
  SetViewPort(OldView.x1, OldView.y1, OldView.x2, OldView.y2, True);
  MoveTo(OldX, OldY);
  GPopup := False;                    { Return failure flag }
end
```

We'll look at what happens if **SaveWindow** succeeds in a short while, but first let's take a close look at what the **SaveWindow** routine does.

Saving the Screen

The routine **SaveWindow** is called to save the region of the screen that is to be overwritten by the pop-up window. We'll use **GetImage** to capture a copy of this screen image; however, first, we must allocate memory space in the window record to store it. This is done with a call to **GetMem** using **ImageSize** to determine the size of the memory.

```
Size := ImageSize(Left, Top, Right, Bottom);
GetMem(WindowStack[GWindowPtr].SaveArea, Size);
```

Once again, there is the possibility that the system might be out of memory and **GetMem** fails. If it does fail, the **SaveArea** pointer will be **Nil** and **SaveWindow** will return immediately with a value of False. Otherwise the routine continues and makes a call to **GetImage** to save the screen and then returns a True value indicating that **SaveWindow** was successful.

```
GetImage(Left, Top, Right, Bottom, WindowStack[GWindowPtr].SaveArea^);
SaveWindow := True;                    { Return a success flag }
```

Caution: when using the pop-up window routine, remember that it will fail if you try to save a window that is too large. Since the memory pointers that we are using are only far pointers, and not huge pointers, the maximum area that they can handle is 64k in size. This may seem like a lot of memory, but the higher-resolution modes on the EGA and VGA can easily surpass this. Generally, as long as you do not allocate windows that are more than about two thirds the size of the screen you should be okay.

Creating the Pop-up Window

Now let's return to our discussion of the **GPopup** routine. We left it at the point where it had just made a call to **SaveWindow** to save the screen image. Next, the drawing parameters that are used to draw the pop-up window are temporarily saved, and then set by calls to **SetColor**, **SetLineStyle**, and **SetFillStyle**. And finally, the pop-up window is drawn by a call to **Bar3D**. This routine is used rather than **Bar** or **Rectangle** because it supports both line styles for its border as well as the full range of fill patterns. As before, we use a depth of zero for **Bar3D** so that it draws a rectangular region.

Next, the current state of the drawing parameters that were previously saved in temporary variables are copied into the current **WindowStack** record. In addition, the fill style, line style, and drawing color are restored to their values before the window was drawn. Then the stack pointer is incremented so that it points to the next location on the stack and **GPopup** returns True as a success flag.

Removing a Pop-up Window

Removing a pop-up window from the screen is handled by the routine **GUnpop**. It is responsible for restoring the original screen image that is overwritten by the pop-up window and for resetting the various screen parameters. The routine is declared in **GPopPac.Pas** as:

```
procedure GUnpop;
```

It does not take any parameters and will only remove an element from the stack if one exists. It does this by checking that **GWindowPtr** is greater than 1.

The next step in the unpop process is to decrement the stack pointer. Since it normally points to the next free location on the stack, decrementing the stack pointer forces it to the top-most window displayed.

Now we have access to the window record that contains the state of the screen before the window was created. First, we'll restore the screen image by using the following call to **PutImage** using **CopyPut**.

```
PutImage(0, 0, WindowStack[GWindowPtr].SaveArea^, CopyPut);
```

Note that the top-left coordinate of the current window is used as the location of the **PutImage**, since it is the window that we are trying to overwrite. The next several lines of the routine reset the viewport, current position, and various drawing parameters before the pop-up window was created. Finally, the memory for the screen image that was allocated in **SaveArea** is freed.

Removing All Windows

Sometimes it is necessary to remove all the pop-up windows at once. This can be done by the Pascal statements:

```
while GWindowPtr > 1 do
    GUnpop;
```

This while loop will continue until **GUnpop** has removed all of the pop-up windows from the screen. For your convenience this line has been included in a routine called **UnpopAllWindows** which is listed in the **GPopPac.Pas** source file.

• Listing 9.1

```
unit GPopPac;
{ This is a set of utilities that provides popup windows in graphics mode. The
  routines use Turbo Pascal's BGI tools to simplify the code. Most of the graphics
  settings are saved before a new window is put up and they are restored when the
  window is closed. This window data is saved on a stack. The stack is implemented
  as an array in order to simplify things.
}
interface
uses
   Graph;
const
   NumGWindows = 10;                        { Allow for 10 pop-up windows }
type
GraphicsWindow = record                    { Record to save graphics settings}
   VLeft,VTop,VRight,VBottom: integer;     { Parent window boundaries }
   cpx,cpy: integer;                       { Current position in parent window }
   SaveArea: pointer;                      { Pointer to the saved region }
   DrawColor: word;                        { Current drawing color }
end;
var
   WindowStack: array [1..NumGWindows] of GraphicsWindow;     { Graphics window stack }
```

```
  { Index to the next available location on the stack to use }
  GWindowPtr: integer;


{ The externally visible routines to this package }
function GPopup(Left, Top, Right, Bottom, BorderType,
          BorderColor, BackFill, FillColor: integer): boolean;
procedure GUnpop;
procedure UnpopAllWindows;


implementation


function SaveWindow(Left, Top, Right, Bottom: integer): boolean;
{ Pushes the graphics window onto the window stack. This is an internal routine that
  saves the area where the window is supposed to appear. This routine will return
  True if successful and False if not. The latter case may occur if there isn't
  enough memory to save the screen area or the stack is full.
}
var
  Size: word;


begin
  Size := ImageSize(Left, Top, Right, Bottom);
  GetMem(WindowStack[GWindowPtr].SaveArea, Size);
  if WindowStack[GWindowPtr].SaveArea = Nil then
    SaveWindow := False                    { Not enough memory to save screen }
  else begin
    { Save the screen image where the window is to appear }
    GetImage(Left, Top, Right, Bottom, WindowStack[GWindowPtr].SaveArea^);
    SaveWindow := True;                    { Return a success flag }
  end
end;


function GPopup(Left, Top, Right, Bottom, BorderType,
        BorderColor, BackFill, FillColor: integer): boolean;
{ Call this routine to pop-up a window in graphics mode. This routine returns True
  if successful and False if not. The routine may not be able to pop-up a window
  if it requires too much memory. This may occur in some high-resolution modes.
}
var
  OldView: ViewPortType;
  OldX, OldY, SaveColor: integer;
```

```
  SaveLine: LineSettingsType;
  SaveFill: FillSettingsType;

begin
  if GWindowPtr > NumGWindows then
    GPopup := False                           { Stack is full }
  else begin
    GetViewSettings(OldView);                 { Save the view settings and }
    OldX := GetX;                             { current position so we can }
    OldY := GetY;                             { temporarily switch viewport to }
    SetViewPort(0, 0, GetMaxX, GetMaxY, True);   { the full screen }
    { Save current drawing parameters before drawing window. This does not support }
    { user-defined line styles or user-defined fill patterns. }
    GetLineSettings(SaveLine);
    SaveColor := GetColor;
    GetFillSettings(SaveFill);
    if not SaveWindow(Left, Top, Right, Bottom) then begin
      { Save screen failed, restore viewport settings and current position }
      SetViewPort(OldView.x1,OldView.y1,
                  OldView.x2,OldView.y2,True);
      MoveTo(OldX,OldY);
      GPopup := False;                        { Return failure flag }
    end
    else begin
      SetColor(BorderColor);                  { Set graphics parameters for }
      SetLineStyle(BorderType,0,NormWidth);   { pop-up window }
      SetFillStyle(BackFill,FillColor);
      Bar3D(Left,Top,Right,Bottom,0,False);
      SetViewPort(Left,Top,Right,Bottom,True);   { Set viewport to window }
      { Save the current state of all settings on the stack }
      WindowStack[GWindowPtr].VLeft := OldView.x1;
      WindowStack[GWindowPtr].VTop := OldView.y1;
      WindowStack[GWindowPtr].VRight := OldView.x2;
      WindowStack[GWindowPtr].VBottom := OldView.y2;
      WindowStack[GWindowPtr].Cpx := OldX;
      WindowStack[GWindowPtr].Cpy := OldY;
      WindowStack[GWindowPtr].DrawColor := SaveColor;
      Inc(GWindowPtr);                        { Increment the stack pointer }
      { Restore drawing parameters }
      SetLineStyle(SaveLine.LineStyle,SaveLine.Pattern,SaveLine.Thickness);
      SetColor(SaveColor);
```

```
        SetFillStyle(SaveFill.Pattern,SaveFill.Color);
        GPopup := True;                          { Return success flag }
      end
    end
end;


procedure GUnpop;
{ Remove the current graphics window from the screen }
begin
  if GWindowPtr > 1 then begin            { Make sure stack not empty }
    Dec(GWindowPtr);                      { Access the most recent window }
    { Restore the screen image }
    PutImage(0,0,WindowStack[GWindowPtr].SaveArea^,CopyPut);
    { Restore the view settings to those before the window was created }
    SetViewPort(WindowStack[GWindowPtr].VLeft,
    WindowStack[GWindowPtr].VTop,WindowStack[GWindowPtr].VRight,
    WindowStack[GWindowPtr].VBottom,True);
    MoveTo(WindowStack[GWindowPtr].cpx,WindowStack[GWindowPtr].cpy);
    SetColor(WindowStack[GWindowPtr].DrawColor);
    { Free stack structure and screen }
    FreeMem(WindowStack[GWindowPtr].SaveArea,
            Sizeof(WindowStack[GWindowPtr].SaveArea));
  end
end;


procedure UnpopAllWindows;
{ Unpop all windows that currently exist. This is a handy routine to clean up the
  screen in certain situations.
}
begin
  while GWindowPtr > 1 do
    GUnpop;
end;


{ This is the initialization code for the window package. It simply sets the window
  stack pointer to the first stack location available.
}
begin
  GWindowPtr := 1;
end.
```

Using the Windows Package

Now that we have dispensed with all of the preliminaries, let's explore how the window package can be used. It is a very simple process. First, you must place the unit **GPopPac** in the list of units being *used* by your application program. Then, whenever you want to pop-up a window, call **GPopup** as discussed earlier in the chapter. Remember that the pop-up window coordinates are specified relative to the whole screen and not the current viewport. This gives you the greatest control over the placement of the pop-up window. To remove the window, make a call to **GUnpop**. You must use one call to **GUnpop** for every window that you have created.

Also, keep in mind that the pop-up windows are maintained on a stack. Therefore, when you call **GUnpop** the most recent window will always be unpopped first.

Once a pop-up window is created, the viewport settings will be changed to reflect the new window. As Figure 9.4 illustrates, the top-left corner of the new pop-up window will correspond to location (0,0), the current position will be set to this point, and clipping will be set on.

Test Program

Before we end this chapter, let's present a test program that will put our graphics window package through its paces. It will also demonstrate how to put the pop-up window package to work. The test program, **PopTest.Pas** (see Listing 9.2), creates three pop-up windows, as shown in Figure 9.5, and then removes them from the

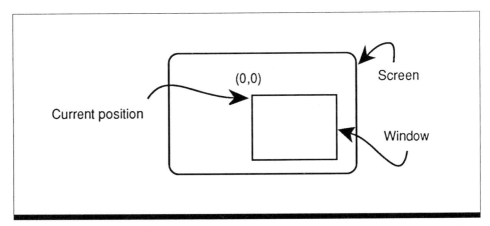

Figure 9.4. Location of the current position in a pop-up window

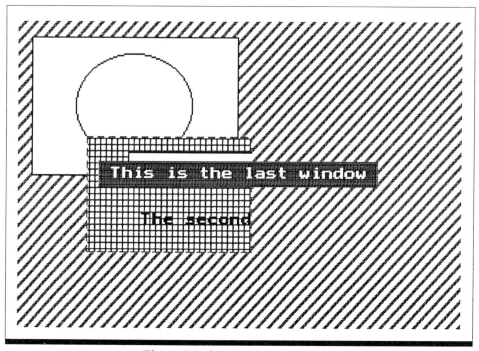

Figure 9.5. Output of PopTest.Pas

screen. After each window is displayed or removed you must press a key in order to proceed with the program.

As written, the program uses one of the CGA modes to provide some color to the program. If you want to try one of the graphics modes, change the values assigned to **GDriver** and **GMode** in the **constant** declarations of the program.

And finally, note how the program accesses the coordinates in each of the windows. For instance, in the first pop-up window a circle is drawn at its center. In order to determine the center point of the window, **GetViewSettings** must be called and then the center of the window is calculated from the view settings. This simply demonstrates that the coordinates in the windows are accessed relative to the current pop-up window.

```
GetViewSettings(View);          { The view settings are now equal }
                                { to the pop-up window boundaries }
                                { Draw a circle in the window }
Circle((View.x2-View.x1) div 2, (View.y2-View.y1) div 2,
       (View.x1+View.x2) div 4);
```

• Listing 9.2

```
program PopTest;
{ Tests the graphics pop-up window routines. This program displays three over-
  lapping pop-up windows on a patterned background. The windows are drawn one at a
  time and then removed one at a time. Press any key to step through the various
  phases of this demonstration. This routine shows how the screen is saved and how to
  use the screen coordinates in a pop-up window. It is best run in a mode with
  several colors. As written, the program forces the screen to CGAC3 mode. You may
  want to change this and the GDriver variable if you have another graphics device.
}
uses
   Graph, Crt, GPopPac;
const
   GDriver: integer = CGA;                { Use a graphics mode with several }
   GMode: integer = CGAC3;                { colors }
   Message: string[25] = ' This is the last window ';
var
   View: ViewPortType;
   HalfWidth, Height: integer;
   ch: char;

procedure WindowError;
begin
   CloseGraph;
   writeln('Failed to open window');
   halt(1);
end;

begin
   InitGraph(GDriver,GMode,'');

   SetFillStyle(SlashFill,Blue);          { Draw a background that  }
   SetLineStyle(DashedLn,0,White);        { covers the entire screen }
   Bar(0,0,GetMaxX,GetMaxY);
{ Pop-up a window in the top-left portion of the screen. Use a solid line border in
  the maximum color and fill the pop-up window with color 0.
}
   if not GPopup(10,10,GetMaxX div 2,100,SolidLn, GetMaxColor,SolidFill,0) then
      WindowError;
```

```
    GetViewSettings(View);                  { The view settings are now equal }
                                            { to the pop-up window boundaries }
    { Draw a circle in the window }
    Circle((View.x2-View.x1) div 2, (View.y2-View.y1) div 2, (View.x1+View.x2) div 4);
    ch := ReadKey;                          { Wait until a key is pressed }
{ Draw a second pop-up window with a dashed border drawn with
  color 1 and the window's background set to color 2
}
    if not GPopup(50,75,GetMaxX div 2+10,150,DashedLn,1,HatchFill,2) then
      WindowError;
    SetFillStyle(WideDotFill,Black);
    Bar3D(30,10,200,20,0,False);            { Draw a box in the window }
    SetColor(GetMaxColor);
    OutTextXY(20,50,'The second window');   { This text might clip }
    ch := ReadKey;                          { Wait for a key to be pressed }
{ The last pop-up window displays a message at the center of the screen. This
  type of pop-up window is good for displaying error messages in graphics mode.
}
    HalfWidth := TextWidth(Message) div 2;  { Calculate the size of the }
    Height := TextHeight(Message);          { window based on the string }
    if not GPopup(GetMaxX div 2-HalfWidth,GetMaxY div 2-Height,
         GetMaxX div 2+HalfWidth,GetMaxY div 2+Height, SolidLn,1,SolidFill,2) then
      WindowError;
    SetColor(0);
    SetTextJustify(CenterText,CenterText);  { Center message and }
    GetViewSettings(View);                  { write it to the screen }
    OutTextXY((View.x2-View.x1) div 2, (View.y2-View.y1) div 2, Message);
    ch := ReadKey;                          { Wait until a key is pressed }
    GUnpop;                                 { Remove the last window }
    ch := ReadKey;                          { Wait until a key is pressed }
    GUnpop;                                 { Remove the middle window  }
    ch := ReadKey;                          { Wait until a key is pressed }
    GUnpop;                                 { Remove the first window }
    CloseGraph;                             { Exit graphics mode }
end.
```

10

Interactive Drawing Tools

In this chapter we'll develop a set of interactive drawing tools that will allow us to use the mouse and keyboard to draw various figures on the screen. We'll use the BGI routines for drawing lines, polygons, circles, ellipses, and arcs as the core of our interactive drawing package. Our goal is to show you how you can interactively draw figures with the mouse or cursor keys rather than having to explicitly specify the screen coordinates of the shapes to be drawn.

This chapter is our final stop before we develop our paint and CAD programs in Chapters 11 and 12. The routines we develop here will provide the drawing capabilities for both of these programs. You'll find, however, that the interactive drawing tools will also be valuable in other interactive graphics packages that you create on your own.

Interactive Drawing

When we use the term *interactive drawing* we are referring to the technique of using an input device such as the mouse or the keyboard to draw graphics. As you start developing more sophisticated graphics programs, you'll realize that the user interaction aspect is often the most important feature of a program. The two primary reasons are that interactive routines encourage experimentation and that they generally make the drawing task easier.

By itself, the BGI does not include interactive drawing routines. We must, therefore, build routines around the BGI drawing routines in order to be able to draw figures with the mouse or the keyboard.

An Interactive Graphics Package

Our interactive drawing package includes 11 routines that extend from line drawing to spray can effects. The unit and source file that contains these routines is called **Draw.Pas** and is presented in Listing 10.1. The complete set of drawing routines in **Draw.Pas** is listed in Table 10.1.

Table 10.1. Interactive drawing routines included in Draw.Pas

Routine	Description
Pencil	Supports freehand drawing
Erase	Erases a portion of the screen
SprayCan	Provides a spray painting effect
DrawLines	Interactive line drawing routine
DrawPolygon	Interactive polygon drawing routine
DrawFillPoly	Allows user to draw filled polygons
DrawSquare	Draws squares interactively
DrawFillSquare	Draws filled squares interactively
DrawCircle	Draws circles interactively
DrawEllipse	Draws ellipses interactively
DrawArcs	Draws arcs interactively

Drawing Conventions

Each of the interactive drawing routines in the unit **Draw** follow several conventions. First, they assume that you'll be using the mouse tools developed in Chapter 7. Since our mouse package supports both the mouse and the keyboard, the drawing routines will work with either input device. You'll find, however, that the mouse provides the best performance.

In addition, the drawing routines restrict their output to a predefined window. Therefore, whenever one of the drawing routines is called, the current viewport is set to the drawing window and clipping is enabled. When the routine exits, the viewport is set back to the full screen. The boundaries of the drawing window must be initialized in the application program by setting the four global variables **wl**, **wt**, **wr**, and **wb** to the left, top, right, and bottom corners of the drawing window desired.

There are also four other global variables that must be set to initialize the drawing parameters that are used by the drawing routines. Table 10.2 contains a complete list of these variables.

Table 10.2. Global variables defined in an application program using Draw.Pas

Variable	Description
wl	Left column of drawing window
wt	Top of drawing window
wr	Right side of drawing window
wb	Bottom of drawing window
GlobalDrawColor	Defines the drawing color to be used in any of the drawing routines
GlobalFillColor	Defines the fill color to use
GlobalFillStyle	Defines the fill style to use
GlobalLineStyle	Defines the line style to use

The last four global variables should be set to the appropriate constants defined in **Graph**. For example, **GlobalFillStyle** can take on values of **SolidFill**, **EmptyFill**, or any of the other acceptable fill pattern values defined in **Graph**. Note that you must assign values in your application program to all of the global variables listed in Table 10.2 before calling any of the interactive drawing routines in **Draw.Pas**.

A Close Look at the Draw.Pas Tools

We're now ready to take a closer look at the interactive drawing routines. Some of these routines are similar to others, so we won't give them all the same attention; however, we'll at least provide a short description on how to use each routine.

Drawing with a Pencil

The **Pencil** procedure is probably the simplest drawing routine, so we'll start with that. **Pencil** is used to draw freehand figures. As you'll see in the upcoming sections, **Pencil** is similar to the other interactive drawing tools in **Draw.Pas** in that it does not require any parameters and does not return a value.

With **Pencil**, you can draw a continuous curve as long as the left mouse button is pressed. Whenever the mouse button is released, the drawing stops. To resume drawing, you simply hold down the left button again. This procedure is illustrated in Figure 10.1. To exit the routine, you click the left mouse button outside the drawing window. Presumably, this will be to select another drawing routine. We'll see how this technique works in Chapter 11 when we develop our paint program.

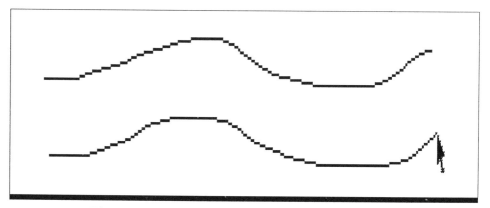

Figure 10.1. The Pencil routine draws freehand curves

The routine begins by setting the current viewport to the drawing window and resetting the drawing color as shown below.

```
SetViewPort(wl,wt,wr,wb,True);    { Set current viewport to }
                                  { drawing window, clip on }
SetColor(GlobalDrawColor);        { Use the global parameter }
                                  { to set the drawing color }
```

The drawing color must be reset to **GlobalDrawColor** because it may have been changed by another routine in the application program. In general, the routines in **Draw.Pas** must reset any of the drawing parameters that they use to the proper global variables listed in Table 10.2.

The core of **Pencil** consists of three **while** loops and a handful of other statements. The outer **while** loop is an infinite loop which ensures that the two inner **while** loops are continually executed. The only way out of the infinite loop and **Pencil** is through the **Exit** statement after the top-most inner **while** loop.

The first inner **while** loop is actually the empty loop as shown:

```
while not MouseButtonPressed(LeftButton) do ;
```

It continually calls **MouseButtonPressed** until the left mouse button is pressed at which time **MouseButtonPressed** returns True and the loop terminates. Recall from Chapter 7, that as long as the specified button, in this case the left button, is not pressed, **MouseButtonPressed** will return False.

Once the left button is pressed, the mouse coordinates are retrieved by a call to **GetMouseCoords** as shown next. These coordinates are checked against the drawing viewport to see if the user has clicked outside of the drawing window. If so, the viewport is reset to the full screen and **Pencil** is terminated.

```
GetMouseCoords(x,y);
if (x < wl) or (x > wr) or (y < wt) or (y > wb) then begin
   SetViewPort(0,0,GetMaxX,GetMaxY);
   Exit;
end;
```

The **Exit** statement shown above is the only way out of **Pencil**. All of the other interactive drawing routines are exited in a similar manner.

If the left mouse button is clicked while inside the drawing viewport, **Pencil** continues to the next **while** loop where the drawing action is performed.

The freehand curves drawn are created by connecting lines from the mouse's previous position to its current position. Therefore, as the mouse moves, the line grows. To avoid unnecessary screen writing, however, **Pencil** only draws lines if the mouse's position has changed. All these statements are included in the bottom-most **while** loop.

We will now show the bottom **while** loop in its entirety along with a couple of preliminary statements. The first two lines save the current location of the mouse in **OldX** and **OldY** so that later the routine can test whether the mouse has moved. Next, the BGI's **MoveTo** routine sets the current position to the mouse's current position. Later, we'll use a series of calls to **LineTo** to draw the freehand curve starting from this point. Note that the coordinates passed to **MoveTo** are adjusted by the left and top boundaries of the drawing viewport. This must be done since **MoveTo** uses coordinates that are relative to the current viewport, the drawing window, and the mouse coordinates, x and y, are always given in full-screen coordinates.

```
OldX := x;   OldY := y;
MoveTo(x-wl,y-wt);
while not MouseButtonReleased(LeftButton) do begin
   GetMouseCoords(x,y);
   if (x <> OldX) or (y <> OldY) then begin
     HideMouse;
     LineTo(x-wl,y-wt);
     ShowMouse;
     OldX := x;   OldY := y;
   end
end;
```

Once the preliminary work has been taken care of, the bottom **while** loop is entered. It draws the connected line segments that make up the freehand curve. Note that the boolean expression in the lower **while** loop continues until the left mouse button is released at which time **MouseButtonReleased** returns a nonzero value. When this occurs, the drawing stops and the routine climbs back to the top-most **while** loop which waits for the next press of the left button.

If the mouse button is still pressed, the current mouse coordinates are retrieved by **GetMouseCoords**. If these coordinates are different from the last occurrence (those saved in **OldX** and **OldY**), then a line is drawn from the previous mouse location to its current position using **LineTo**. Remember that calls to **HideMouse** and **ShowMouse** surround **LineTo** in order to prevent the mouse cursor from interfering with the screen. Once these statements have been executed, the values in **OldX** and **OldY** are updated to the current location of the mouse.

Erasing

Now that we've learned how to draw figures, let's see we how can remove them. For this, we'll use a routine called **Erase** which is designed to erase small portions of the screen. Images are erased by setting a rectangular region under the cursor to the background color. By holding down the left mouse button and moving the mouse around the drawing window, you can erase any area of the drawing window.

The **Erase** routine is similar to **Pencil** except that it draws small bars filled with the background color to the screen rather than a series of lines. In order to generate these small erasing blocks, the fill style is set to **SolidFill** and the fill and drawing colors are set to the background color by the statements:

```
SetColor(GetBkColor);
SetFillStyle(SolidFill,GetBkColor);
```

The routine draws these small solid-filled bars wherever the mouse cursor is located while the mouse button is pressed. Actually, as with **Pencil**, **Erase** does not erase the current location of the screen if the mouse has not been moved. This avoids unnecessary screen writes. The pixel dimensions of the eraser bar is specified by **EraseSize** which is a constant defined at the top of **Draw.Pas**. You might try making the eraser size a variable so that you can interactively change its size.

Spray Painting Effect

The **SprayCan** routine provides a simple spray painting effect by randomly setting pixels within a rectangular region to the current drawing color.

While the left mouse button is pressed, the spray painting action will occur as shown in Figure 10.2. To temporarily stop the spray painting you release the left

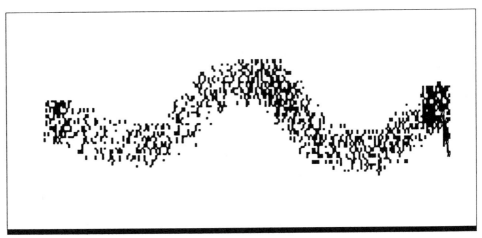

Figure 10.2. The spray can effect in Draw.Pas

mouse button, and to exit the spray painting routine, you move the mouse outside the drawing viewport and click the left button.

The spray painting effect is produced by two **for** loops contained within the **while** loop (shown below) that tests for the mouse button release.

```
{ Spray while left button is pressed }
while not MouseButtonReleased(LeftButton) do begin
   GetMouseCoords(x,y);
   HideMouse;
   for i := 1 to 8 do
     PutPixel(x-Random(SpraySize)+5-wl,y-Random(SpraySize)+5-wt,
              GlobalDrawColor);
   for i := 1 to 8 do
     PutPixel(x-Random(SpraySize-2)+3-wl, y-Random(SpraySize-2)+3-wt,
              GlobalDrawColor);
   ShowMouse;
end;
```

Each of the **for** loops is responsible for plotting 8 pixels in a rectangular region around the mouse cursor. The first **for** loop plots pixels away from the mouse cursor while the second **for** loop plots pixels closer. Note that the particular pixel that is painted by each iteration of the **for** loops is randomly selected using the Turbo Pascal function **Random**. This distributes the pixels evenly. The size of the spray region is partly determined by the constant **SpraySize** declared in **Draw.Pas**. However, the other integer values in the two **for** loops affect the distribution and location of the spray painting as well. You may want to experiment with other spray patterns.

Also note that **SprayCan** does not test to see if the mouse has been moved before drawing on the screen. This allows you to keep the mouse in one location and fill that region with painted pixels to the desired level. If the mouse is held in the same location long enough, the rectangular region becomes completely filled.

Drawing Lines

The next routine we'll look at is used to draw line segments. The **DrawLines** routine lets you a draw a single line by pointing to where the line is to begin, pressing and holding down the left mouse button, and then dragging the mouse to the line's endpoint. When the button is released, the line is frozen. However, while the button is pressed, **DrawLines** continues to draw the line from the initial location of the mouse when the button was pressed to the mouse's current position. Therefore, as the mouse is moved around the screen, the line will shrink and stretch as needed. This procedure for drawing lines is shown in Figure 10.3. This type of line is called a *rubber-banding* line because the line segment appears to be flexible like a rubber band. Anyway, to draw more lines you just repeat this simple process.

As you might expect, **DrawLines** is similar to the previously discussed routines. The first thing **DrawLines** does is set the viewport and drawing parameters by the statements:

```
SetViewPort(wl,wt,wr,wb,True);
SetLineStyle(GlobalLineStyle,0,NormWidth);
SetColor(GlobalDrawColor);
```

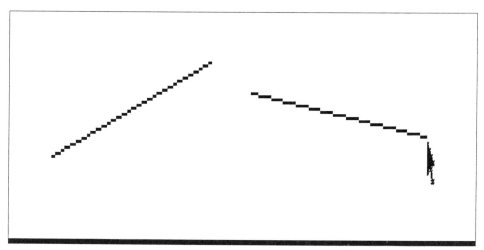

Figure 10.3. Using the DrawLines routine in Draw.Pas

The line style and drawing color must be reset to the proper global variables because we'll be using them when we draw our lines. You may notice that the line width is restricted to **NormWidth**. This is done to simplify the code. You may want to modify **Draw.Pas** so that the line width is a variable like **GlobalLineStyle** and **GlobalDrawColor**.

An important aspect of **DrawLines** is the rubber-banding line effect. The technique uses the exclusive-ORing feature provided by the BGI **SetWriteMode** procedure (see Chapter 6) to allow us to draw and move a line around the screen without permanently affecting what it overwrites. Once the exclusive OR mode is set, lines can be erased from the screen by writing over them with another line. The exclusive-OR feature is turned on after the left button is pressed by the line:

```
SetWriteMode(XorPut);
```

After this point, all lines are drawn by exclusive-ORing them to the screen. Sometimes you will see the effects of the exclusive-ORing as the line changes color as it crosses over other figures on the screen.

When you press the left mouse button while inside the drawing window, the exclusive-ORing mode is set as previously described and the first line is drawn, although at this time it is merely a point. While the mouse button is pressed, the code proceeds into the lower **while** loop in **DrawLines**.

Within this loop, you can see that the line drawing is performed by the two statements:

```
Line(x1-wl,y1-wt,OldX2-wl,OldY2-wt);
Line(x1-wl,y1-wt,x2-wl,y2-wt);
```

Since the exclusive-ORing mode is on, the first line erases the old line and the second line draws the line at the new position. Note that the first coordinate pair in each call to **Line** corresponds to the position on the screen where the user first pressed the mouse button. This point does not change. The only endpoint of the line that does change is the one that you drag around with the mouse. These two lines create the rubber-banding effect.

When the left mouse button is released, the bottom **while** loop terminates and the code proceeds to redraw the line using the following statements:

```
SetWriteMode(CopyPut);
HideMouse;
Line(x1-wl,y1-wt,x2-wl,y2-wt);
ShowMouse;
```

The line is redrawn with **SetWriteMode** taken out of the exclusive-OR mode, so that the line is drawn in its proper color. Remember that a figure exclusive-ORed with an object on the screen may change its color. This also explains why the **SetWriteMode** procedure must be included within the outer **while** loop rather than at the top of **DrawLines**—to set it back to the exclusive-OR mode.

Drawing Polygons

There are two routines in our toolset that allow you to draw polygons: **DrawPolygon** and **DrawFillPoly**. The first routine, **DrawPolygon**, is really nothing more than a variation of **DrawLines**. It allows you to draw a series of lines connected at their endpoints. The second routine, **DrawFillPoly**, is capable of drawing closed polygons using any of the predefined fill patterns.

Both routines operate in a similar manner although the way they work is slightly different than any of the routines previously discussed. These two procedures begin to draw a polygon after the first click of the mouse's left button. Next they draw a rubber-banding line as the mouse is moved around the screen, which defines one side of the polygon, until the left button is pressed again. The current line then becomes frozen and a new rubber-banding line is drawn starting from the current mouse location. This process, shown in Figure 10.4, can be repeated, to create additional sides to the polygon. When you want to close off the polygon, however, simply press the right mouse button and the closing side of the polygon is drawn. If **DrawFillPoly** is used, the interior of the polygon is filled.

The main difference between the two polygon drawing routines is that a **do** loop is used to replace the lower **while** loop. Recall that the lower loop is the one used to

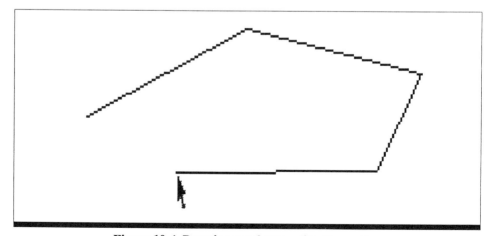

Figure 10.4. Drawing a polygon using Draw.Pas

test for the left button to be released and draws the graphics figure. In **DrawPolygon**, the **do** loop is used to test for the right button to be pressed and inside the **do** loop an if statement has been added which tests for the left button. If any left button presses occur, the mouse coordinates are saved, the current rubber-banding line is frozen and a new rubber-banding line is started at the previous line's endpoint. However, the right button is pressed, the polygon is closed off by tying it back to the first coordinate and then calling the appropriate polygon routine to draw the polygon.

Again the exclusive-ORing technique is used to create the rubber-banding effect by a call to **SetWriteMode** with **XorPut**. Therefore the complete polygon must then be redrawn with the write mode set to **CopyPut** after the user has closed off a polygon so that the correct colors will be displayed.

Drawing Squares

Now we'll develop two companion routines to interactively draw a square and a filled square. These routines are called **DrawSquare** and **DrawFillSquare**, respectively.

We'll use **GetImage** and **PutImage** to help us create the rubber-banding effect needed to draw boxes. We'll do this by saving the screen image where the box is to be drawn, so that later we can remove it from the screen by copying back to the screen with **PutImage**. In effect, we are doing nothing more than popping-up a window with the figure inside it. Let's begin by taking a closer look at **DrawSquare**.

The first thing you'll notice about **DrawSquare** is that it is much longer and probably more intimidating than any of the prior routines. Taken in pieces, the routine is actually similar to those discussed earlier. Note that **DrawSquare** is built around three **while** loops as in **Pencil** and **Erase**.

Now let's look at what makes **DrawSquare** unique. If you trace through the code, you'll discover several differences right from the start. The first statement, in fact, is a call to **GetMem** which allocates memory space to the pointer **Covered** that we'll use in our calls to **GetImage** when producing the rubber-banding effect. Since there is the possibility that the figure we want to draw encompasses the whole drawing window, we must allocate enough space to save the complete window. Remember from Chapter 2 that in some very high-resolution modes it may not be possible to save the whole image. The only way to avoid this is to ensure that your drawing window is not too large for the current graphics mode. If this situation occurs, a routine called **MallocError** is invoked. It is shown at the bottom of **Draw.Pas** and does nothing more than abort the program. You might want to modify this error handler to make the program more user friendly.

The next few statements set the drawing parameters and the drawing viewport coordinates. The code then proceeds through the outer **while** loop and the top-most **while** loop which waits for the left mouse button to be pressed. As before, drawing does not begin until the left button is pressed and held down. In addition, the only way to exit the drawing routine is to click the mouse outside of the drawing window. Note that on exit, the memory allocated for **Covered** is deallocated by calling the Turbo Pascal procedure **FreeMem**.

The next several lines initialize several important variables to the current coordinates of the mouse. We'll discuss these variables in a minute. Next, **GetImage** is called to save the screen located at the cursor. Although it is effectively saving only a point, this will begin our rubber-banding process.

Most of this complexity of the bottom **while** loop is due to the use of **GetImage** and **PutImage** to produce the rubber-banding effect. Keep in mind that these two routines do not clip their images relative to the current viewport. This means that we must perform the clipping ourselves. In addition, **GetImage** and **PutImage** require that the top-left and bottom-right coordinates of the image be properly supplied. While the mouse is dragging one corner of the rubber-banding square, it is possible that the top-left most coordinate can switch between the fixed corner of the square and the point being moved. This switch is illustrated in Figure 10.5.

The first set of **if** statements, shown next, clip the current coordinates of the mouse, given by **Right** and **Bottom**, to the drawing window. The process is illustrated in Figure 10.6.

```
if Right < wl then CRight := wl
  else if Right > wr then CRight := wr
    else CRight := Right;
```

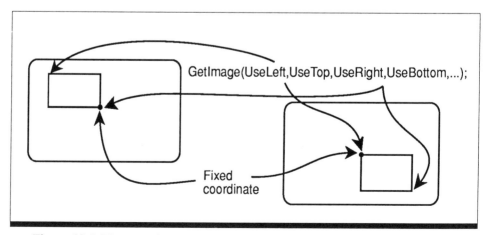

Figure 10.5. The coordinates passed to GetImage and PutImage may change

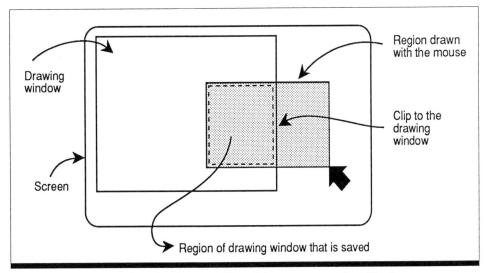

Figure 10.6. Rubber-banding objects may require clipping

```
if Bottom < wt then CBottom := wt
   else if Bottom > wb-1 then CBottom := wb - 1
     else CBottom := Bottom;
```

The clipped coordinates are saved in **CRight** and **CBottom**. We'll learn in a bit why the bottom coordinate is clipped differently from the rest.

The next **if** statement in **DrawSquare** tests whether the mouse has been moved from its previous position. Since the mouse's coordinates are given by the variables **Right** and **Bottom**, these two are checked to see if they have changed from **OldRight** and **OldBottom**. If so, the mouse has been moved and the rubber-banding square must be updated. Immediately after the **if** statement are two if-else statements to determine which coordinates are really the top left-most coordinates of the square being drawn. The correct ordering of the top-left and bottom-right coordinates are saved in the variables **UseLeft**, **UseTop**, **UseRight**, and **UseBottom**. These variables are used in the calls to **GetImage** and **PutImage** to define the region of the screen to be saved.

While looking over the code, you may have noticed that the **UseBottom** variable is offset by 1 and that the clipping of **Bottom** is made with respect to 1 pixel above the bottom of the window. The reason for these two minor adjustments is intertwined with the BGI's **Rectangle** routine. From a logical sense, it does not appear that these adjustments are necessary; however, **Rectangle** will leave traces of its edges if this is not done. If you look at **DrawFillSquare** these fudge factors are even more noticeable. In fact, here we have to add an extra pixel boundary around the whole square in order to assure that **GetImage** properly grabs the image of the square. The other key difference between **DrawSquare** and **DrawFillSquare** is that the latter uses calls to **Bard3D** to draw the filled square. Remember from Chapter 2 that **Bar3D** can draw a filled square if its depth is set to 0.

Drawing Circles

Now let's look at interactive routines to draw circles, ellipses, and arcs. Rather than go through these routines as we have in the past, we'll concentrate on the unique aspects of how they work.

As its name implies, **DrawCircle** is a routine that allows you to interactively draw a circle. The mouse action for **DrawCircle** is shown in Figure 10.7. As it demonstrates, the center of the circle is selected by pressing the left mouse button at the desired location. Then, by dragging the mouse to the right, the size of the circle is increased. Similarly, the size of the circle is reduced if the mouse is moved to the left.

As the mouse is moved, it doesn't directly change the coordinates used to draw the circle. Instead, the variables **AddRadius** and **Radius** keep track of the mouse movement which in effect specifies the radius of the circle. Therefore, as long as the left mouse button is pressed, the mouse routine **GetMouseMovement** is called to determine how much the mouse has moved and consequently what new size to make the circle. The mouse movement is returned in **AddRadius**. It specifies how much to change the size of the circle so it is added to the variable **Radius**. Since it is possible that **Radius** may become negative (if the mouse is continuously moved to

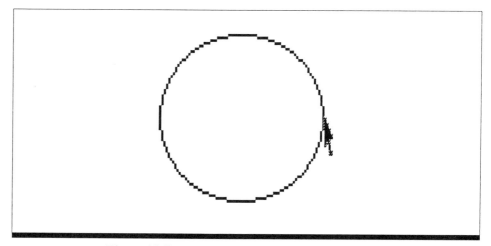

Figure 10.7. The DrawCircle routine in Draw.Pas

the left), the variable **AbsRadius** is used to hold the absolute value of the radius. It is this variable that will be used as the radius parameter in the call to the BGI procedure **Circle**.

Clipping for the circle is handled by the BGI; however, we must handle the clipping of our screen image used in the rubber-banding effect. This clipping is accomplished with four **if-else** statements which check to see if the radius extends beyond the edge of the drawing window. Since the aspect ratio of the screen may be different in the x and y directions, this routine may wind up saving too much of the drawing window, particularly in the y direction. However, this is not much of a problem.

Another point to note about **DrawCircle** is that it does not draw the circle if the radius is zero. This is needed because the BGI routine **Circle** will draw a circle of radius zero with a 1 pixel radius. Since this is not what we want, we avoid drawing such circles. We'll have to do the same type of tests for the ellipse and arc procedures, too.

Drawing Ellipses

Drawing an ellipse is accomplished by the **DrawEllipse** routine which is very similar to **DrawCircle**. The primary difference between the two is that **DrawEllipse** allows you to change both the x and y radius of the ellipse. As is the case with **DrawCircle**, the x radius is changed by dragging the mouse left and right, but now the y radius can also be changed by dragging the mouse up and down.

Drawing Arcs

The **DrawArcs** routine allows us to interactively draw a series of arcs. Unfortunately, the BGI **Arc** procedure is not suitable for an interactive arc drawing routine. The main difficulty is that it is cumbersome to come up with a way to interactively specify all of the parameters needed by the arc function, such as the center point, the radius, and the sweep angle. We'll sidestep the problem and create an extremely simple arc routine.

Our procedure, **DrawArcs**, always begins drawing arcs at the 3 o'clock position, but it allows you to change the sweep angle of the arc and alter the radius of the arc. The components used to draw an arc are shown in Figure 10.8. The center point of the arc is selected when the left mouse button is first pressed. Then by dragging the mouse right and left, with the left button pressed, the radius of the arc is increased and decreased, respectively. In addition, by moving the mouse down,

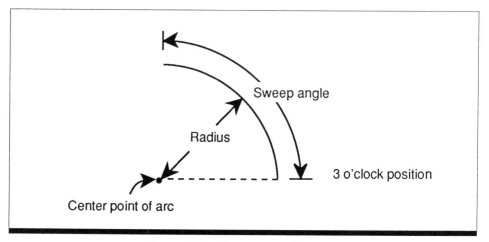

Figure 10.8. Components of an arc

the angle that the arc sweeps is increased. Similarly, when the mouse is moved up while the left button is pressed, the angle swept by the arc will decrease. The process for drawing an arc is illustrated in Figure 10.9.

As with **DrawCircle** and **DrawEllipse**, we'll track the mouse movement by calls to **GetMouseMovement** to determine how to change the radius and sweep angle of the arc. In addition, **GetImage** and **PutImage** are used to produce the exclusive-OR rubber-banding effect that we used in some of the other drawing routines. The **DrawArcs** routine saves a rectangular region large enough to contain the full 360 degree arc.

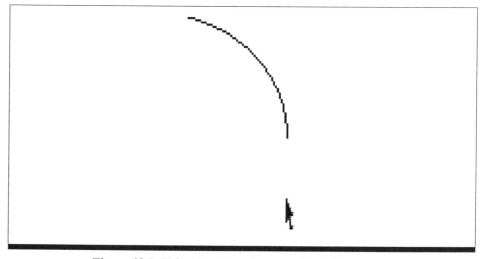

Figure 10.9. Using the DrawArcs routine in Draw.Pas

• Listing 10.1

```
unit Draw;
{ Draw.Pas -- interactive drawing utilities }
interface
uses
   Graph, MousePac;
const
   MaxPolySize = 40;              { A polygon can have this many edges }
   EraserSize: integer = 3;       { Half the size of the eraser }
   SpraySize: integer = 15;       { Size of spray can spray area }
{ The fill parameters, drawing colors, and so on are all kept as global variables.
  From time to time the current drawing, fill, and line styles may be changed, so
  before any drawing function make sure the various drawing parameters are reset to
  these global values.
}
var
   GlobalFillStyle: integer;      { Default fill style to use }
   GlobalFillColor: integer;      { Default fill color to use }
   GlobalDrawColor: integer;      { Default Drawing color to use }
   GlobalLineStyle: integer;      { Default line style to use }
   wl, wt, wr, wb: integer;       { Bounds of drawing window }
   LastScreen: pointer            { Pointers used to save drawing }
   CurrentScreen: pointer;        { window for UNDO operation }
{ These are the routines that are externally visible }
procedure Pencil;
procedure Erase;
procedure SprayCan;
procedure DrawLines;
procedure DrawPolygon;
procedure DrawFillPoly;
procedure DrawSquare;
procedure DrawFillSquare;
procedure DrawCircle;
procedure DrawEllipse;
procedure DrawArcs;
procedure SaveScreen;
procedure RestoreScreen;
procedure MallocError;
```

```pascal
implementation
procedure Pencil;
{ This routine emulates a pencil. While the left mouse button is pressed it will draw
  a trail of connected lines. When the mouse button is released, no drawing occurs. To
  avoid unnecessary drawing, lines are only drawn when mouse position changes.
}
var
   x, y, OldX, OldY: integer;

begin
   SetViewPort(wl, wt, wr, wb, True);              { Draw in this viewport }
   SetColor(GlobalDrawColor);                      { Use the Global color }
   while True do begin
      while not MouseButtonPressed(LeftButton) do ; { Wait until button pressed }
      GetMouseCoords(x, y);                        { Get coordinates of mouse}
      { If mouse location outside of window ...}
      if (x < wl) or (y < wt) or (y > wb) then begin
         SetViewPort(0, 0, GetMaxX, GetMaxY, True); { Restore viewport to full screen }
         Exit;                                      { Exit pencil routine }
      end;
      OldX := x;  OldY := y;
      MoveTo(x-wl, y-wt);              { Set current position where drawing is to begin }
      { As long as the mouse button is pressed, get its coordinates }
      while not MouseButtonReleased(LeftButton) do begin
         GetMouseCoords(x, y);
         { If mouse has been moved draw new line to it }
         if (x <> OldX) or (y <> OldY) then begin
            HideMouse;                              { Make sure to adjust mouse }
            LineTo(x-wl, y-wt);                     { coordinates to drawing viewport }
            ShowMouse;
            OldX := x;  OldY := y;                  { Save the current mouse location }
         end
      end
   end
end;

procedure Erase;
{ This routine resets a small block of the screen to the background color. The
  erasing is done by drawing a filled bar at the current mouse location as long
  as the left mouse button is pressed.
}
```

```
var
   x, y, OldX, OldY: integer;

begin
   SetViewPort(wl, wt, wr, wb, True);              { Use drawing window }
   SetColor(GetBkColor);                           { Use background color }
   SetFillStyle(SolidFill, GetBkColor);            { to erase the screen }
   while True do begin
      while not MouseButtonPressed(LeftButton) do ; { Wait for button press }
      GetMouseCoords(x, y);                        { Get mouse location }
      { If mouse clicked outside of drawing window, restore viewport and
        set Done flag to exit routine
      }
      if (x < wl) or (y < wt) or (y > wb) then begin
         SetViewPort(0, 0, GetMaxX, GetMaxY, True);
         Exit;
      end;
      OldX := x;  OldY := y;
      HideMouse;
      { Erase the screen where the mouse is }
      Bar(x-wl, y-wt, x-wl+EraserSize, y-wt+EraserSize);
      ShowMouse;
      { Continue erasing screen as long as mouse button pressed }
      while not MouseButtonReleased(LeftButton) do begin
         GetMouseCoords(x, y);
         if (x <> OldX) or (y <> OldY) then begin
            HideMouse;
            Bar(x-wl, y-wt, x-wl+EraserSize, y-wt+EraserSize);
            ShowMouse;
            OldX := x;  OldY := y;
         end
      end
   end
end;


procedure SprayCan;
{ The spraycan routine randomly paints pixels in a square region whenever the left
  mouse button is pressed
}
var
   i, x, y: integer;
```

```
begin
  { Init random function used to decide where to paint pixels }
  Randomize;
  SetViewPort(wl, wt, wr, wb, True);             { Use drawing window }
  while True do begin                            { Wait until the left button }
    while not MouseButtonPressed(LeftButton) do ; { is pressed }
    GetMouseCoords(x, y);
    { If mouse is outside of drawing window, restore viewport
      to the full screen and set Done flag to exit routine
    }
    if (x < wl) or (y < wt) or (y > wb) then begin
      SetViewPort(0, 0, GetMaxX, GetMaxY, True);
      Exit;
    end;
    { Spray as long as button is pressed }
    while not MouseButtonReleased(LeftButton) do begin
      GetMouseCoords(x, y);
      HideMouse;
      for i := 1 to 8 do
        PutPixel(x-Random(SpraySize)+5-wl,
                 y-Random(SpraySize)+5-wt, GlobalDrawColor);
      for i := 1 to 8 do
        PutPixel(x-Random(SpraySize-2)+3-wl,
                 y-Random(SpraySize-2)+3-wt, GlobalDrawColor);
      ShowMouse;
    end
  end
end;


procedure DrawLines;
{ Draw a line while left mouse button is pressed. Use XorPut to provide rubber-banding
  line feature. Once a line is to be fixed it is redrawn with CopyPut so that the
  color for the line will be drawn correctly, since XorPut won't guarantee this.
}
var
  x1, y1, x2, y2, OldX2, OldY2: integer;

begin
  SetViewPort(wl, wt, wr, wb, True);             { Use the drawing window }
  SetLineStyle(GlobalLineStyle, 0, NormWidth);   { and global }
  SetColor(GlobalDrawColor);                     { drawing settings }
```

```
   while True do begin
     while not MouseButtonPressed(LeftButton) do ;
     GetMouseCoords(x1, y1);
     if (x1 < wl) or (y1 < wt) or (y1 > wb) then begin
        SetViewPort(0, 0, GetMaxX, GetMaxY, True);
        SetWriteMode(CopyPut);
        Exit;
     end;
     SetWriteMode(XorPut);                          { Use XorPut to rubber-band lines }
     MoveTo(x1-wl, y1-wt);
     OldX2 := x1;  OldY2 := y1;
     while not MouseButtonReleased(LeftButton) do begin
        GetMouseCoords(x2, y2);
        if (x2 <> OldX2) or (y2 <> OldY2) then begin
           HideMouse;
           Line(x1-wl, y1-wt, OldX2-wl, OldY2-wt);
           Line(x1-wl, y1-wt, x2-wl, y2-wt);
           ShowMouse;
           OldX2 := x2;  OldY2 := y2;
        end
     end;
     SetWriteMode(CopyPut);                         { Redraw line when set }
     HideMouse;                                     { so color will be }
     Line(x1-wl, y1-wt, x2-wl, y2-wt);              { correct }
     ShowMouse;
   end
end;

procedure DrawPolygon;
{ Draw a polygon using rubber-banding }
var
   x1, y1, x2, y2, OldX2, OldY2, StartX, StartY: integer;
   t: boolean;

begin
   SetViewPort(wl,wt,wr,wb,True);
   SetLineStyle(GlobalLineStyle,0,NormWidth);
   SetColor(GlobalDrawColor);
   while True do begin
     while not MouseButtonPressed(LeftButton) do ;
```

```
      GetMouseCoords(x1,y1);
      if (x1 < wl) or (y1 < wt) or (y1 > wb) then begin
         SetViewPort(0,0,GetMaxX,GetMaxY,True);
         SetWriteMode(CopyPut);
         Exit;
      end;
      SetWriteMode(XorPut);                          { Use BGI exclusive-OR feature }
      MoveTo(x1-wl,y1-wt);
      x2 := x1;     y2 := y1;
      OldX2 := x2;   OldY2 := y2;
      StartX := x1;   StartY := y1;
      repeat
         GetMouseCoords(x2,y2);
         if (x2 <> OldX2) or (y2 <> OldY2) then begin
            HideMouse;
            Line(x1-wl,y1-wt,OldX2-wl,OldY2-wt);
            Line(x1-wl,y1-wt,x2-wl,y2-wt);
            ShowMouse;
            OldX2 := x2;   OldY2 := y2;
         end;
         if MouseButtonReleased(LeftButton) then begin
            t := MouseButtonPressed(LeftButton);
            SetWriteMode(CopyPut);                   { Draw line in permanently }
            HideMouse;
            Line(x1-wl,y1-wt,x2-wl,y2-wt);
            ShowMouse;
            SetWriteMode(XorPut);
            x1 := x2;   y1 := y2;
         end;
      until MouseButtonPressed(RightButton);
      SetWriteMode(CopyPut);                         { Draw line in permanently }
      HideMouse;
      Line(x1-wl,y1-wt,x2-wl,y2-wt);
      Line(x2-wl,y2-wt,StartX-wl,StartY-wt);
      ShowMouse;
   end
end;


procedure DrawFillPoly;
{ Draw a filled polygon using the global fill settings }
```

```
var
  x1, y1, x2, y2, OldX2, OldY2, p: integer;
  Poly: array[1..MaxPolySize] of PointType;
  t: boolean;

begin
  SetViewPort(wl, wt, wr, wb, True);
  SetLineStyle(GlobalLineStyle, 0, NormWidth);
  SetFillStyle(GlobalFillStyle, GlobalFillColor);
  SetColor(GlobalDrawColor);
  while True do begin
    while not MouseButtonPressed(LeftButton) do ;      { Wait for buttonpress }
    GetMouseCoords(x1, y1);
    if (x1 < wl) or (y1 < wt) or (y1 > wb) then begin  { If the mouse is not in }
      SetViewPort(0, 0, GetMaxX, GetMaxY, True);       { the drawing window, }
      SetWriteMode(CopyPut);                           { quit the routine }
      Exit;
    end;
    SetWriteMode(XorPut);                              { Use exclusive-OR feature }
    MoveTo(x1-wl, y1-wt);
    x2 := x1;              y2 := y1;
    OldX2 := x2;          OldY2 := y2;
    Poly[1].x := x1-wl;   Poly[1].y := y1-wt;
    p := 1;
    repeat                                             { Draw rubber-banding }
      GetMouseCoords(x2, y2);                          { sides of polygon until }
      if (x2 <> OldX2) or (y2 <> OldY2) then begin     { the right mouse button }
        HideMouse;                                     { is pressed }
        Line(x1-wl, y1-wt, OldX2-wl, OldY2-wt);
        Line(x1-wl, y1-wt, x2-wl, y2-wt);
        ShowMouse;
        OldX2 := x2;  OldY2 := y2;
      end;
      if MouseButtonReleased(LeftButton) then begin
        t := MouseButtonPressed(LeftButton);
        x1 := x2;  y1 := y2;
        Inc(p);
        Poly[p].x := x2-wl;   Poly[p].y := y2-wt;
      end;
    until MouseButtonPressed(RightButton);
```

```
    GetMouseCoords(x1, y1);
    Inc(p);
    Poly[p].x := x1-wl;        Poly[p].y := y1-wt;
    Inc(p);
    Poly[p].x := Poly[1].x;  Poly[p].y := Poly[1].y;
    SetWriteMode(CopyPut);                              { Restore drawing mode }
    HideMouse;
    FillPoly(p, Poly);                                  { Draw the filled polygon }
    ShowMouse;
    end
  end;


procedure MallocError;
{ If an error occurs in memory allocation call this routine and an error message will
  be displayed and the program will quit
}
begin
  CloseGraph;
  writeln('Not enough memory to run program');
  halt(1);
end;


procedure DrawSquare;
{ Interactively draw a square. Use GetImage/PutImage to provide rubber-banding effect
}
var
  Left, Top, Right, Bottom: integer;
  CRight, CBottom, OldRight, OldBottom: integer;
  UseLeft, UseTop, UseRight, UseBottom: integer;
  Covered: pointer;
  Size: word;

begin
  Size := ImageSize(wl, wt, wr,wb);
  GetMem(Covered, Size);
  if Covered = Nil then MallocError;
  SetColor(GlobalDrawColor);
  SetLineStyle(GlobalLineStyle, 0, NormWidth);
  SetViewPort(wl, wt, wr, wb, True);
  while True do begin
    while not MouseButtonPressed(LeftButton) do ;   { Wait for button to be pressed }
```

```
GetMouseCoords(Left, Top);
if (Left <= wl) or (Top <= wt) or (Top >= wb) then begin
   SetViewPort(0, 0, GetMaxX, GetMaxY, True);         { Quit routine if mouse }
   FreeMem(Covered, Size);                            { is outside of the }
   Exit;                                              { drawing window }
end;
OldRight := Left;    OldBottom := Top;
UseLeft := Left;     UseTop := Top;
UseRight := Left;    UseBottom := Top;
HideMouse;
GetImage(UseLeft-wl, UseTop-wt, UseRight-wl, UseBottom-wt+1, Covered^);
ShowMouse;
while not MouseButtonReleased(LeftButton) do begin
   GetMouseCoords(Right, Bottom);
   if Right < wl then CRight := wl                    { Clip drawing window }
   else if CRight > wr then CRight := wr
      else CRight := Right;
   if Bottom < wt then CBottom := wt
      else if Bottom > wb-1 then CBottom := wb-1
         else CBottom := Bottom;
   { Make sure coordinates passed to PutImage are in the correct order }
   if (Right<>OldRight) or (Bottom<>OldBottom) then begin
      HideMouse;
      PutImage(UseLeft-wl, UseTop-wt, Covered^, CopyPut);
      if Left > CRight then begin
         UseLeft := CRight;  UseRight := Left;
      end
      else begin
         UseLeft := Left;  UseRight := CRight;
      end;
      if Top > CBottom then begin
         UseTop := CBottom;   UseBottom := Top;
      end
      else begin
         UseTop := Top;  UseBottom := CBottom;
      end;
      GetImage(UseLeft-wl, UseTop-wt, UseRight-wl, UseBottom+1-wt, Covered^);
      RectAngle(Left-wl, Top-wt, Right-wl, Bottom-wt);      { Draw the rectangle }
      ShowMouse;
      OldRight := Right;  OldBottom := Bottom;
   end
```

```
        end
    end
end;

procedure DrawFillSquare;
{ Draw a filled square. Creates rubber-banding effect using GetImage and PutImage. }
var
    Left, Top, Right, Bottom: integer;
    CRight, CBottom, OldRight, OldBottom: integer;
    UseLeft, UseTop, UseRight, UseBottom: integer;
    Covered: pointer;
    Size: word;

begin
    Size := ImageSize(wl, wt, wr, wb);
    GetMem(Covered, Size);
    if Covered = Nil then MallocError;
    SetFillStyle(GlobalFillStyle, GlobalFillColor);
    SetLineStyle(GlobalLineStyle, 0, NormWidth);
    SetColor(GlobalDrawColor);
    SetViewPort(wl, wt, wr, wb, True);
    while True do begin
        while not MouseButtonPressed(LeftButton) do ;          { Wait for buttonpress }
        GetMouseCoords(Left, Top);
        if (Left <= wl) or (Top <= wt) or (Top >= wb) then begin
            SetViewPort(0, 0, GetMaxX, GetMaxY, True);
            FreeMem(Covered, Size);
            Exit;
        end;
        OldRight := Left;    OldBottom := Top;
        UseLeft := Left;     UseTop := Top;
        UseRight := Left;    UseBottom := Top;
        HideMouse;
        GetImage(UseLeft-1-wl, UseTop-1-wt, UseRight+1-wl, UseBottom+1-wt, Covered^);
        ShowMouse;
        while not MouseButtonReleased(LeftButton) do begin      { While button is pressed }
            GetMouseCoords(Right, Bottom);                      { draw a rubber-banding }
            { Clip to the drawing window }                      { rectangle }
            if (Right < wl+1) then CRight := wl + 1
                else if (Right > wr-1) then CRight := wr - 1
```

```
              else CRight := Right;
        if (Bottom < wt+1) then CBottom := wt + 1
          else if (Bottom > wb-1) then CBottom := wb - 1
              else CBottom := Bottom;
        { Make sure coordinates passed to PutImage are in the correct order }
        if (Right<>OldRight) or (Bottom<>OldBottom) then begin
          HideMouse;
          PutImage(UseLeft-1-wl, UseTop-1-wt, Covered^, CopyPut);
          if (Left > CRight) then begin
            UseLeft := CRight;  UseRight := Left;
          end
          else begin
            UseLeft := Left;  UseRight := CRight;
          end;
          if (Top > CBottom) then begin
            UseTop := CBottom;  UseBottom := Top;
          end
          else begin
            UseTop := Top;  UseBottom := CBottom;
          end;
          GetImage(UseLeft-wl-1,UseTop-wt-1,UseRight-wl+1,UseBottom-wt+1, Covered^);
          { Draw the filled rectangle }
          Bar3D(Left-wl, Top-wt, Right-wl, Bottom-wt, 0, False);
          ShowMouse;
          OldRight := Right;  OldBottom := Bottom;
        end
      end
    end
  end
end;


procedure DrawCircle;
{ Interactively draw a circle. Use GetMouseMovement to control the size of the
  circle's radius.
}
var
  CLeft, CTop, CRight, CBottom: integer;
  Radius, AbsRadius, AddRadius, Ignore: integer;
  CenterX, CenterY, OldLeft, OldTop: integer;
  Covered: pointer;
  Size: word;
```

```
begin
  Size := ImageSize(wl, wt, wr, wb);
  GetMem(Covered, Size);
  if Covered = Nil then MallocError;
  SetLineStyle(GlobalLineStyle, 0, NormWidth);
  SetColor(GlobalDrawColor);
  SetViewPort(wl, wt, wr, wb, True);
  while True do begin
    while not MouseButtonPressed(LeftButton) do ;   { Wait for button to be pressed }
    GetMouseCoords(CenterX, CenterY);
    GetMouseMovement(Ignore, Ignore);
    if (CenterX <= wl) or (CenterY <= wt) or (CenterY >= wb) then begin
      SetViewPort(0, 0, GetMaxX, GetMaxY, True);
      FreeMem(Covered, Size);
      Exit;
    end;
    Radius := 0;
    OldLeft := CenterX;  OldTop := CenterY;
    HideMouse;
    GetImage(OldLeft-wl, OldTop-wt, OldLeft-wl, OldTop-wt, Covered^);
    ShowMouse;
    while not MouseButtonReleased(LeftButton) do begin
      GetMouseMovement(AddRadius, Ignore);                 { Get amount of mouse }
      Inc(Radius, AddRadius);                              { movement. Use it to }
      if Radius < 0 then AbsRadius := -Radius              { calculate the radius }
        else AbsRadius := Radius;                          { of the circle. }
      if CenterX-AbsRadius < wl then CLeft := wl
        else CLeft := CenterX - AbsRadius;
      if CenterX+AbsRadius > wr then CRight := wr
        else CRight := CenterX + AbsRadius;
      if CenterY-AbsRadius < wt then CTop := wt
        else CTop := CenterY - AbsRadius;
      if CenterY+AbsRadius > wb then CBottom := wb
        else CBottom := CenterY + AbsRadius;
      if AddRadius <> 0 then begin
        HideMouse;
        PutImage(OldLeft-wl, OldTop-wt, Covered^, CopyPut);
        GetImage(CLeft-wl, CTop-wt, CRight-wl, CBottom-wt, Covered^);
        if AbsRadius <> 0 then
          Circle(CenterX-wl, CenterY-wt, AbsRadius);     { Draw the circle }
```

```
        ShowMouse;
          OldLeft := CLeft;  OldTop := CTop;
        end
      end
    end
end;

procedure DrawEllipse;
{ Draw an ellipse }
var
   CLeft, CTop, CRight, CBottom: integer;
   RadiusX, AbsRadiusX, AddRadiusX: integer;
   RadiusY, AbsRadiusY, AddRadiusY: integer;
   CenterX, CenterY, OldLeft, OldTop: integer;
   Covered: pointer;
   Size: word;

begin
   Size := ImageSize(wl, wt, wr, wb);
   GetMem(Covered,Size);
   if Covered = Nil then MallocError;
   SetLineStyle(GlobalLineStyle, 0, NormWidth);
   SetColor(GlobalDrawColor);
   SetViewPort(wl, wt, wr, wb, True);
   while True do begin
     while not MouseButtonPressed(LeftButton) do ;
     GetMouseCoords(CenterX, CenterY);
     GetMouseMovement(AddRadiusX, AddRadiusY);
     if (CenterX <= wl) or (CenterY <= wt) or (CenterY >= wb) then begin
       SetViewPort(0, 0, GetMaxX, GetMaxY, True);
       FreeMem(Covered, Size);
       Exit;
     end;
     RadiusX := 0;  RadiusY := 0;
     OldLeft := CenterX;  OldTop := CenterY;
     HideMouse;
     GetImage(OldLeft-wl, OldTop-wt, OldLeft-wl, OldTop-wt, Covered^);
     ShowMouse;
     while not MouseButtonReleased(LeftButton) do begin
       GetMouseMovement(AddRadiusX, AddRadiusY);
```

```pascal
      Inc(RadiusX, AddRadiusX);                              { Adjust the radius of the }
      if RadiusX < 0 then AbsRadiusX := -RadiusX            { ellipse based on the }
         else AbsRadiusX := RadiusX;                         { amount the mouse has }
      Inc(RadiusY, AddRadiusY);                              { been moved }
      if RadiusY < 0 then AbsRadiusY := -RadiusY
         else AbsRadiusY := RadiusY;
      if CenterX-AbsRadiusX < wl then CLeft := wl
         else CLeft := CenterX - AbsRadiusX;
      if CenterX+AbsRadiusX > wr then CRight := wr
         else CRight := CenterX + AbsRadiusX;
      if CenterY-AbsRadiusY < wt then CTop := wt
         else CTop := CenterY - AbsRadiusY;
      if CenterY+AbsRadiusY > wb then CBottom := wb
         else CBottom := CenterY + AbsRadiusY;
      if (AddRadiusX <> 0) or (AddRadiusY <> 0) then begin
         HideMouse;
         PutImage(OldLeft-wl, OldTop-wt, Covered^, CopyPut);
         GetImage(CLeft-wl, CTop-wt, CRight-wl, CBottom-wt, Covered^);
         if (AbsRadiusX <> 0) and (AbsRadiusY <> 0) then       { Draw the ellipse }
            Ellipse(CenterX-wl, CenterY-wt, 0, 360, AbsRadiusX, AbsRadiusY);
         ShowMouse;
         OldLeft := CLeft;  OldTop := CTop;
      end
   end
  end
end;


procedure DrawArcs;
{ Draw an arc }
var
  CLeft, CTop, CRight, CBottom: integer;
  Radius, AddRadius, Angle, AddAngle: integer;
  CenterX, CenterY, OldLeft, OldTop: integer;
  Covered: pointer;
  Size: word;

begin
  Size := ImageSize(wl, wt, wr, wb);
  GetMem(Covered,Size);
  if Covered = Nil then MallocError;
```

```
SetLineStyle(GlobalLineStyle, 0, NormWidth);
SetColor(GlobalDrawColor);
SetViewPort(wl, wt, wr, wb, True);
while True do begin
   while not MouseButtonPressed(LeftButton) do ;    { Wait for button to be pressed }
   GetMouseCoords(CenterX, CenterY);
   GetMouseMovement(AddRadius, AddAngle);
   if (CenterX <= wl) or (CenterY <= wt) or (CenterY >= wb) then begin
      SetViewPort(0, 0, GetMaxX, GetMaxY, True);
      FreeMem(Covered, Size);
      Exit;
   end;
   Radius := 0;  Angle := 0;
   OldLeft := CenterX;  OldTop := CenterY;
   HideMouse;
   GetImage(OldLeft-wl, OldTop-wt, OldLeft-wl, OldTop-wt, Covered^);
   ShowMouse;
   while not MouseButtonReleased(LeftButton) do begin
      GetMouseMovement(AddRadius, AddAngle);             { The size of the arc }
      Inc(Radius, AddRadius);                            { depends on how much the }
      if Radius < 0 then Radius := 0;                    { mouse has been moved }
      Inc(Angle,AddAngle);
      if Angle < 0 then Angle := 0;
      if CenterX-Radius < wl then CLeft := wl
         else CLeft := CenterX - Radius;
      if CenterX+Radius > wr then CRight := wr
         else CRight := CenterX + Radius;
      if CenterY-Radius < wt then CTop := wt
         else CTop := CenterY - Radius;
      if CenterY+Radius > wb then CBottom := wb
         else CBottom := CenterY + Radius;
      if (AddRadius <> 0) or (AddAngle <> 0) then begin
         HideMouse;
         PutImage(OldLeft-wl, OldTop-wt, Covered^, CopyPut);
         GetImage(CLeft-wl, CTop-wt, CRight-wl, CBottom-wt, Covered^);
         if (Radius > 0) and (Angle > 0) then            { Draw the arc }
            Arc(CenterX-wl, CenterY-wt, 0, Angle, Radius);
         ShowMouse;
         OldLeft := CLeft;  OldTop := CTop;
      end
```

```pascal
      end
    end
end;


procedure SaveScreen;
{ Save the drawing window in CurrentScreen }
var
   Temp: pointer;

begin
   Temp := LastScreen;
   LastScreen := CurrentScreen;
   CurrentScreen := Temp;
   HideMouse;
   GetImage(wl, wt, wr, wb, CurrentScreen^);
   ShowMouse;
end;


procedure RestoreScreen;
{ Restore the screen using LastScreen }
begin
   HideMouse;
   PutImage(wl, wt, LastScreen^, CopyPut);
   ShowMouse;
end;


end.
```

11

A Paint Program

This chapter has two interconnected goals. First, it will show you how to put together the complete paint program that we have been developing tools for in earlier chapters, and second it will serve as the user's guide for the paint program. By now, you should be armed with a powerful package of graphics programming tools, and, because building a useful paint program is not a trivial task, we'll be relying heavily on these tools to simplify the process. Before we complete this chapter, we'll also discuss several enhancements that you might try implementing so that you can create your own customized version of the paint program.

Overview of the Paint Program

Although our paint program uses many of the tools that we have developed throughout this book, we'll still need to develop more code in this chapter to create the program. The missing ingredients are handled by another source file, **Paint.Pas**, that provides the main program routines of our paint program. You'll find it in Listing 11.1 at the end of this chapter.

The **Paint.Pas** source file serves several purposes. First, it creates the environment for the paint program. It is responsible for arranging the icons, providing the pull-down menus, and segmenting off a portion of the screen for the drawing window. In addition, several miscellaneous routines are included to complete the paint program. Finally, **Paint.Pas** contains the main loop that handles the user interaction.

The Unit Files

As mentioned earlier, our paint program uses several of the tools that we developed in earlier chapters of the book. A listing of these units and the chapters in which they are discussed is shown in Table 11.1. Each of these will be added to the **uses** section of our paint program.

Table 11.1. Custom units used in the paint program

Source File	From Chapter	Description
MousePac.Pas	7	Mouse and keyboard utilities
GText.Pas	3	Text utilities in graphics mode
Object.Pas	5	Object-oriented utilities
GPopPac.Pas	9	Pop-up window package
Draw.Pas	10	Interactive drawing utilities

Setting Up the Environment

A complete version of the paint program's environment is shown in Figure 11.1. As you can see, the left side of the screen is reserved for the icons that represent the commands supported by the program. The top of the screen contains several keywords which are used to pull down various menus or select additional functions. At the bottom of the screen is a list of the fill patterns and the colors that are accessible in the current video mode. One important thing to realize is that each item described so far is designed to be handled as a graphics object on the screen by our object-oriented utility developed in Chapter 5. In other words, each of these screen objects (icons, words, etc.) has a predefined functionality that can be accessed by clicking on it with the mouse. The remainder of the screen is reserved for the drawing window.

All the components discussed above are created in the routine **SetupScreen** which is located near the end of **Paint.Pas**. Although this is a long routine, it is easy to follow if we break it up into manageable pieces. Let's examine how it works.

The first part of **SetupScreen** is responsible for setting up the main menu bar at the top of the screen. The menu bar is actually drawn by the following two statements:

```
Rectangle(0,0,GetMaxX,h);
OutTextXY(2, 2, "Undo  Text  Line  Clear  Quit");
```

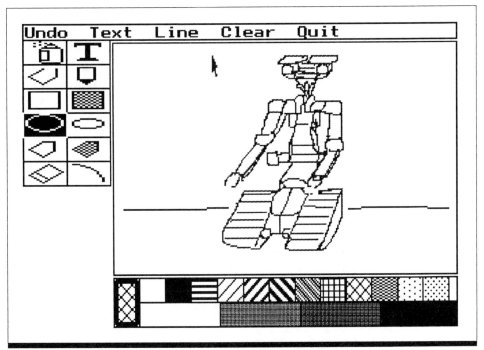

Figure 11.1. The Paint.Pas program

The processing of the menu bar is created in the lines that follow these two statements. The succeeding lines add each of the menu bar commands (*Undo*, *Text*, *Line*, etc.) to the list of objects that are on the screen. This is accomplished by using the object-oriented utility from Chapter 5. Therefore each of the main commands become, in effect, an icon that can be selected. We will later write routines to pull down the appropriate menu when one of these text icons is selected. Let's look in greater detail at how one of these menu words is added to the object list. By way of example, let's use the *Quit* option.

The *Quit* option is the last text icon added in the main menu bar. When this option is selected, we want the program to terminate. Program termination is handled by a procedure called **Quit** which is also in **Paint.Pas**. Our setup routine adds the text icon *Quit* to the list of objects by calling **AddObject**. The pointer to **Quit** is passed to **AddObject** so that it will be executed when the word *Quit* is selected. The line that performs all of this is:

```
AddObject(IconObj,'q',Offset,0,Offset+TextWidth('Quit'),
          TextHeight('Quit'), Quit);
```

To further illustrate how this routine works, let's look at each of its parameters. The first parameter, **IconObj**, specifies the type of object that is being added to the object list. In this case, although the object is really a word, we want the object routines to handle it as if it were actually an icon. The next parameter is the letter **q** which is the key that the user enters to quickly select the **Quit** command. The next four parameters specify the pixel boundaries for the string **Quit**. Finally, the last parameter is a pointer to the **Quit** procedure which is called when the *Quit* option is selected.

More complicated examples of the process just discussed occur with the **Text** and **Line** options. Each of these, when selected, are designed to bring down a pull-down menu. We'll look at the routines that create these pull-down menus later. However, it is important to note that the location under these words is saved in a pair of global variables in **SetupScreen** so that later we'll know where to place the pull-down menu. For example, in the case of the **Text** option, the pull-down menu appears at **TextWindowX** and **TextWindowY**.

The next 12 calls to the **AddObject** routine place each of the icons on the left side of the screen. Each of these icons are located in separate files and follow the naming convention that we introduced in Chapter 8 when we developed the icon editor.

Displaying an icon is a two step process. First, the icon is read from its file and displayed (this is accomplished in **ReadIcon** which is included in **Paint.Pas**). Next, the icon is added to the list of objects on the screen by calls to **AddObject**. Generally, these icons are used to invoke one of the drawing routines that we created in Chapter 10. The only exception is the **TypeText** routine which lets you type text in the drawing window. We'll look at this routine in greater detail later.

The next block of code in **SetupScreen** creates the fill patterns and color palette at the bottom of the screen. Because the size of the screen may vary according to the graphics mode in use, these routines are slightly more complicated than they would need to be otherwise. The primary thing to note is that each routine first calculates how wide each cell, for example a single fill pattern, needs to be in order for all of the cells to fit across the screen. A **for** loop is then used to sequence through each of the patterns or colors until all have been displayed. Note also that we are not adding each cell individually to our list of objects; instead we add the complete block of fill patterns and the block of colors as two individual objects. The procedure **ChangeFillPattern** or **ChangeFillColor** is invoked to decide which cell we selected and to make the appropriate action.

To the left of these fill styles is a rectangular region that displays the current fill pattern and color. This region is also added as an object, and it serves as a means for us to change the drawing color. For example, whenever you click on this region, the current fill color will become the current drawing color. This action is performed by the procedure **ChangeDrawColor**.

One last operation that **SetupScreen** performs is to calculate and draw the boundaries of the drawing window. As per the requirements of our **Draw.Pas** unit, these boundaries are saved in the global variables **wl**, **wt**, **wr**, and **wb**.

The Paint Routines

Now let's take a closer look at each of the support routines that our paint program needs. These routines are each listed with a short description in Table 11.2. We'll start by examining the procedure associated with the **Clear** option in the main menu bar and then we'll proceed through all of the other routines.

Table 11.2. Paint program support routines

Routine	Description
ClearWorkArea	Clears the drawing window when the **Clear** option is selected
Quit	Terminates the paint program
SaveScreen	Saves an image of the drawing window
RestoreScreen	Restores the drawing window to a saved image
SetupScreen	Allocates space to save screen images
ChangeFont	Selects a new font style
ChangeLineStyle	Selects a new line style
ChangeFillPattern	Selects a new painting pattern
ChangeFillColor	Selects a new painting color
TypeText	Controls text output

The Clear Screen Command

When the **Clear** option is selected, by clicking it on or typing the letter c, the paint program must clear the drawing window. This action is performed in the procedure **ClearWorkArea**. It is included in **Paint.Pas** and is quite short. It sets the viewport settings to the drawing window, calls the BGI routine **ClearViewPort**, and then returns the view settings to the full screen. Note that **ClearWorkArea** also toggles the mouse cursor on and off when updating the screen in order to prevent any conflict between the mouse cursor and what is on the screen.

Quitting the Program

The **Quit** routine is also very simple. When it is selected, it simply exits graphics mode and terminates the program by calling **Exit**. The **Quit** routine is the only path out of the program.

The Undo Operation

Another feature provided in the paint program is the ability to undo the last drawing operation. In order to accomplish this, the current image of the screen is saved before any drawing routine is invoked. Then, if you select the **Undo** option, the screen image is restored to its previous image. Actually, two sets of images are saved so that if you change your mind and want to undo the **Undo,** you can.

Two routines are included in **Paint.Pas** to save the drawing window of the screen and conversely restore it to its previous form. The routines are **SaveScreen** and **RestoreScreen**. Each of these routines is rather simple and uses the **GetImage/PutImage** pair to retrieve and restore the drawing window's image. The two screen images are saved in blocks of memory pointed at by **CurrentScreen** and **LastScreen**. Space for these arrays is allocated in the procedure **SetupScreen**.

Now that you've been introduced to these routines, you're probably wondering about how they are used. Basically, we need to call **SaveScreen** before each drawing routine is executed. We could do this by modifying our **Draw.Pas** utility; however, this would require many changes. An easier approach consists of modifying the **Object.Pas** unit so that before any paint command is executed the screen is saved so that it can later be restored if the **Undo** option is selected. Rather than show the entire **Object.Pas** file with this modification, let's just look at the required changes. Fortunately, we need only to modify two locations in the function **AnyToProcess**. More specifically, we must insert a call to **SaveScreen** before each of the **Exit** statements in the function. In addition, we must place a **uses** statement for the **Draw** unit in the file since this is where **SaveScreen** is defined. You can do this by adding the following lines after the **implementation** header in **Object.Pas**.

```
uses
   Draw;
```

The Pull-down Menus

As we stated earlier, the paint program uses pull-down menus for changing the text and line style. We could develop a general menu package to support pull-down menus, but this would lead to even more groundwork and would only delay our efforts to build a working paint program. Instead, we'll use a rather hard-coded approach in order to simplify the task of adding pull-down menus to our program.

The pull-down menus for the text and line styles are accessed by clicking on the words *Text* or *Line*. When one of these options is selected, either the routine **ChangeFont** or **ChangeLineStyle** is invoked through our object-oriented utility.

At the beginning of each of these routines are several statements that create the pull-down menus. The process begins by using **GPopup** (from the **GPopPac** unit) to pop-up the window for the menu. Next, a **for** loop is used to fill the window with the appropriate selections. For instance, if the **Text** option is selected, the different font styles are displayed so that you can select one. Similarly, if the line pull-down menu is chosen, a set of available line styles is shown. Figure 11.2 shows the paint environment with the *Line* pull-down menu visible.

The position of the pull-down menu options are hard-coded and defined within the routines **ChangeFont** and **ChangeLineStyle**. Therefore, when you click on one of the font styles (in the instance of the text menu) or one of the line segments (in the case of the line pull-down menu), the program can determine which option has been selected and take the appropriate action.

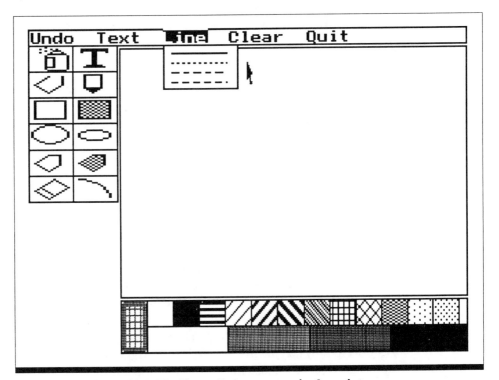

Figure 11.2. The line pull-down menu in the paint program

Determining which menu selection has been chosen is performed by the second **for** loop in **ChangeFont** and **ChangeLineStyle**. However, first, both of the routines wait for you to click the left mouse button with the statement:

```
while not MouseButtonPressed(LeftButton) do ;
```

Once the button is pressed, the mouse coordinates are retrieved and compared against the possible choices within the menu to see if one has been selected. If so, the appropriate text style or line style is changed and the function returns. If the mouse coordinates do not correspond to a menu selection then **ChangeFont** and **ChangeLineStyle** exit without performing any action.

Changing the Fill Style

At the bottom of the screen are a series of fill patterns and colors that can be used in the paint program. Remember from the previous discussion, that the patterns and the color palette are added to the object list as two objects and not as a series of smaller objects. Therefore, if you click the mouse within one of the fill patterns, for instance, no matter which one has been selected, **ChangeFillPattern** is called. Alternatively, if you select one of the color boxes, **ChangeFillColor** is called. These routines operate much like **ChangeFont** and **ChangeLineStyle**, in that they compare the mouse coordinates at the time of the button press with the locations of each of the regions. If the mouse has selected one of the boxes, the fill pattern or color from that box is used to set either **GlobalFillStyle** or **GlobalFillColor** which are two of the global drawing parameters defined in **Draw.Pas**.

The Text Routine

Another capability that our **Paint.Pas** file adds is the ability to type text within the drawing window by the procedure **TypeText**. The **TypeText** routine is similar to many of the other drawing routines that we developed for **Draw.Pas** in Chapter 10. Most notably, all of the text display is confined within an infinite **while** loop that is designed to continue until the user clicks the mouse somewhere outside of the drawing window. You can select where to begin typing text by moving the mouse to any location within the drawing window and clicking on the left mouse button. This will force a vertical bar to appear as a cursor at the current mouse location. Then as you type any text it will displayed left-to-right starting from the vertical bar. Once you start typing, you can move and click the mouse to another location and begin typing there if you choose.

The procedure **TypeText** also allows you to enter a series of carriage returns by pressing the enter key. The test for this feature can be found in the inner **while** loop of **TypeText**. It tests for a carriage return value, **CR**, and then simulates the carriage return by the statements:

```
if c = CR then begin
   Inc(y, TextHeight('S') + 2;
   MoveTo(x-wl,y-wt);
end;
```

If a carriage return is detected, the text cursor is moved down by the height of the text and the current position is set to the original x location and the new y location. Currently, the program does not support backspacing, vertical text, or many of the other power text features of the BGI.

User Interaction

The code used to process and control the user's inputs to the paint program is placed in the repeat-until loop at the bottom of the **mainline** in the **Paint.Pas** file. This infinite loop, shown below, calls the **MousePac** routine **WaitForInput** to get any user inputs, and then subsequently invokes **AnyToProcess** to perform the appropriate action if any.

```
repeat
   c = WaitForInput(LeftButton);
   AnyToProcess(c);
until False;
```

The **WaitForInput** function is found in the **MousePac.Pas** file that we developed in Chapter 9. As written, this function waits for either the left mouse button to be pressed or a key to be struck before it returns. The value of the action is returned in the integer variable **c**.

The input status code is passed to **AnyToProcess** which is a routine in **Object.Pas** from Chapter 5. It steps through the list of objects in the object lists and tests whether the user has clicked in the region bounding the object or has pressed its quick access key. If either is true, the routine invokes the appropriate routine associated with it.

Note that the **repeat** loop is an infinite loop. The infinite loop functions in what is commonly called an event-driven loop (an event can be a mouse click or a keyboard action). That is, the loop repeats as it waits for an event to occur. Because this loop repeats indefinitely, you're probably wondering how the program is terminated. Remember that the **Quit** procedure provides a path for exiting the program. Therefore, one of the events that can occur is that the user can select the *Quit* option or type in the letter q which in turn calls **Quit**.

Using the Paint Program

Now you are ready to compile your program and begin trying it out. After invoking the program from DOS, you should see the environment as it was shown in Figure 11.1. If you have any difficulty, make sure you have all of the icon files and graphics libraries in their appropriate location.

The program is easy to run. You can use the mouse or keyboard as outlined in Chapter 7 to move the cursor about the screen and you can use the various quick keys that were defined for the icons. The drawing routines should all work as described in Chapter 10. Most of the other routines that we have added have been described earlier in this chapter. The only one remaining is how to change the drawing color.

Remember that the palette on the bottom of the screen is used to directly change the fill color. To change the drawing color, you need to click on the box just to the left of the fill patterns which shows the current fill settings. By clicking on this box, which also was added as an object in **SetupScreen**, you will force the drawing color to be changed to the drawing color currently displayed within it.

Enhancing the Paint Program

Although the complete paint program is large, there are many features you might want to add. If you have some ideas, you should not have too much difficulty in carrying them out. This is in large part due to the fact that the program was designed so that additions could easily be made.

Let's look at what you need to do to add a new routine that would be accessible through an icon. For instance, let's say you want to add a routine that will use the flood fill operation to fill selected regions. Basically, there are three things that you will need to do:

1. Create an icon that reflects the functionality of the new feature using the icon editor from Chapter 8
2. Write a procedure to handle this new feature
3. Add a call to **AddObject** within **SetupScreen** to handle the new routine

You should refer to the routines already in **Paint.Pas** to see how these are done in particular.

Ideas to Experiment With

There are many additions you might make to the paint program. Probably the most useful would be to add routines to save the image of the current drawing window to disk and similarly read an image from disk. This way you can work on various pictures intermittently and can begin to archive your work. To add this feature, you will only need to write a function that writes the image already saved in **CurrentScreen** to disk and a complementary routine to read a disk image into **CurrentScreen**. These routines should be extremely easy to add. The difficult part is acquiring from the user the name of the file from which the disk is supposed to be written or read. For this you could try expanding on the **GReadStr** function included in **GText.Pas** and combining it with the pop-up window package to provide an easy to use input routine.

Another possibility is to expand some of the existing routines. For instance, you could modify the text routine, **TypeText**, so that the user can use the backspace key. In addition, you could modify **TypeText** so that it can type vertical text or text automatically scaled or justified. Each of these can be added with a minimal amount of effort.

Other enhancements might include improving the arc routines or some of the other drawing commands so that they would be more powerful. A final idea is to add a routine that allows the user to cut out a portion of the image and move it elsewhere. This feature could be implemented by letting the user mark off a region of the drawing window and then use **GetImage** and **PutImage** to move it to another location.

• Listing 11.1

```
program Paint;
{ This program exploits many of the BGI routines to build a simple, yet powerful paint
   program. Several of the tools built up earlier in the book are put to use in this
   program. The paint program will run on:
      All of the CGA modes
      EGALO and EGA64 (640 by 200 16 color)
      All the MCGA modes except MCGAHI
      All of the ATT400 modes except ATT400HI
      VGALO (640 by 200 16 color)
```

The program uses MousePac.Pas so it supports either the mouse or the keyboard automatically. The routines used in Paint.Pas are discussed in Chapters 9 and 10.

```pascal
}
uses
   Graph, MousePac, Object, GPopPac, Draw, GText, Crt;
const
   IconW = 16;                        { Icons are defined as 16 by 16 }
   IconH = 16;                        { pixel patterns }
   FillHeight = 16;                   { All 12 of the BGI fill patterns }
   NumFillsWide = 12;                 { are shown 16 pixel high in size }
   Border = 2;                        { A 2 pixel border is used }
   GDriver: integer = CGA;            { Use CGA by default }
   GMode: integer = CGAC3;
var
   TextWindowX: integer;              { Global values that specify where }
   TextWindowY: integer;              { font pull-down menu should appear }
   LineWindowX: integer;              { Specify where Line pull-down menu }
   LineWindowY: integer;              { will appear }
   { Holds an icon pattern read from a file }
   Icon: array[1..IconH,1..IconW] of byte;
   c: integer;                        { Miscellaneous variables used in mainline }
   t: boolean;


procedure ReadIcon(x, y: integer; FileName: string);
{ Read an icon from a file and display it. If the file is not found then print an
   error message and quit the program.
}
var
   IconFile: text;
   i, j, Width, Height, IconPixel: integer;

begin
   {$I-} Assign(IconFile, FileName);
   Reset(IconFile); {$I+}
   if IOResult = 0 then begin
     Readln(IconFile, Width, Height);     { Read file header }
     if (Width <> IconW) or (Height <> IconH) then begin
       CloseGraph;
       writeln('Incompatible icon file: ',FileName);
       halt(1);
     end;
```

```
    for j := 1 to IconH do begin                  { Read icon data }
      for i := 1 to IconW do begin
        Read(IconFile, IconPixel);
        if IconPixel = 1 then begin
          PutPixel(2*(i-1)+x, y+(j-1), White);
          PutPixel(2*(i-1)+1+x, y+(j-1), White);
        end
      end
    end;
    Close(IconFile);
    Rectangle(x, y, x+IconW*2, y+IconH);          { Draw box around icon }
  end
  else begin
    CloseGraph;
    writeln('Icon file not found: ',FileName);
    halt(1);
  end
end;

{$F+}                                   { Make these procedure declarations available }
                                        { so that pointers to them can be used }


procedure SaveScreen;
{ Save the drawing window in CurrentScreen }
var
  Temp: pointer;

begin
  Temp := LastScreen;
  LastScreen := CurrentScreen;
  CurrentScreen := Temp;
  HideMouse;
  GetImage(wl,wt,wr,wb,CurrentScreen^);
  ShowMouse;
end;


procedure RestoreScreen;
{ Restore the screen using LastScreen }
begin
  HideMouse;
```

```
      PutImage(wl,wt,LastScreen^,CopyPut);
      ShowMouse;
   end;

procedure Quit;
begin
   CloseGraph;
   halt(0);
end;

procedure ClearWorkArea;
{ Clear the drawing window }
begin
   SetViewPort(wl,wt,wr,wb,True);           { Set viewport to drawing window }
   HideMouse;
   ClearViewPort;                           { Erase drawing window }
   ShowMouse;
   SetViewPort(0,0,GetMaxX,GetMaxY,True);   { Restore viewport to full screen }
end;

procedure ChangeFillPattern;
{ User has selected one of the fill patterns, find which one it is and set
   GlobalFillStyle to this type
}
var
   x, y, i, mx, my: integer;
   FillWidth, FillType: integer;

begin
   FillWidth := (GetMaxX-1-IconW*4+2) div (NumFillsWide+1);
   FillType := 0;
   x := IconW * 4 + 2 + FillWidth;
   for i := 1 to NumFillsWide do begin
     GetMouseCoords(mx, my);
     if (MouseInBox(x,GetMaxY-FillHeight*2,x+FillWidth,
         GetMaxY-FillHeight,mx,my)) then begin
       GlobalFillStyle := FillType;
       SetFillStyle(GlobalFillStyle,GlobalFillColor);
       SetLineStyle(SolidLn,0,ThickWidth);
       HideMouse;
       { Show the new fill style }
```

```
         Bar3D(IconW*4+2+2,GetMaxY-FillHeight*2+2,
               IconW*4+2+FillWidth-2,GetMaxY-2,0,False);
         SetLineStyle(SolidLn,0,NormWidth);
         ShowMouse;
         Exit;
      end;
      Inc(FillType);
      Inc(x, FillWidth);
   end
end;


procedure ChangeFillColor;
{ User has selected one of the fill colors -- find which one it is and set
  GlobalFillColor to this value
}
var
   ColorWidth, FillColor, FillWidth: integer;
   i, x, y, mx, my: integer;


begin
   FillWidth := (GetMaxX-1-IconW*4+2) div (NumFillsWide+1);
   ColorWidth := (GetMaxX-1-IconW*4+2-FillWidth) div (GetMaxColor + 1);
   FillColor := 0;
   x := IconW*4+2+FillWidth;
   for i := 1 to GetMaxColor+1 do begin
      GetMouseCoords(mx,my);
      if MouseInBox(x,GetMaxY-FillHeight,x+ColorWidth, GetMaxY,mx,my) then begin
         GlobalFillColor := FillColor;
         SetFillStyle(GlobalFillStyle,GlobalFillColor);
         SetLineStyle(SolidLn,0,ThickWidth);
         HideMouse;
         Bar3D(IconW*4+2+2,GetMaxY-FillHeight*2+2,          { Show the new fill color }
         IconW*4+2+FillWidth-2,GetMaxY-2,0,False);
         SetLineStyle(SolidLn,0,NormWidth);
         ShowMouse;
         Exit;
      end;
      Inc(FillColor);
      Inc(x,ColorWidth);
   end
end;
```

```
procedure ChangeDrawColor;
{ User has selected the DrawColor block. Change GlobalDrawColor to the color used
  by GlobalFillColor which is the current color in the drawcolor block.
}
var
   FillWidth: integer;

begin
   FillWidth := (GetMaxX-1-IconW*4+2) div (NumFillsWide+1);
   GlobalDrawColor := GlobalFillColor;
   SetFillStyle(GlobalFillStyle,GlobalFillColor);
   SetLineStyle(SolidLn,0,ThickWidth);
   SetColor(GlobalDrawColor);
   HideMouse;
   { Make the border of the block the new color }
   Bar3D(IconW*4+2+2,GetMaxY-FillHeight*2+2,IconW*4+2+FillWidth-2,GetMaxY-2,0,False);
   SetLineStyle(SolidLn,0,NormWidth);
   ShowMouse;
end;


procedure TypeText;
{ Types text to the drawing window. Move cursor to location where text is to be typed,
  press the left button, and type the text. To start a new line, press carriage return
  or move the mouse to a new location, and press the left mouse button again.
}
var
   x, y, OldX, OldY, c: integer;
   SmallCursor: pointer;
   FirstLetter : boolean;
   Size: word;
   ch: char;
   S: string;

begin
   SetColor(GlobalDrawColor);
   SetTextJustify(LeftText,TopText);
   Size := ImageSize(1,1,1,1+TextHeight('S'));
   GetMem(SmallCursor,Size);
   if SmallCursor = Nil then MallocError;
   SetViewPort(wl,wt,wr,wb,True);
```

```
while not MouseButtonPressed(LeftButton) do ;
while True do begin
   GetMouseCoords(x, y);
   if (x < wl) or (y < wt) or (y > wb) then begin
      FreeMem(SmallCursor,Size);
      SetViewPort(0,0,GetMaxX,GetMaxY,True);
      Exit;
   end;
   FirstLetter := True;
   HideMouse;
   { Show cursor where mouse button was pressed }
   GetImage(x-wl,y-wt,x-wl,y+TextHeight('S')-wt,SmallCursor^);
   Line(x-wl,y-wt,x-wl,y+TextHeight('S')-wt);
   ShowMouse;
   OldX := x;  OldY := y;
   MoveTo(x-wl,y-wt);
   { For a better routine try integrating in GReadStr since it works
     with backspaces
   }
   repeat
      if KeyPressed then begin
         ch := ReadKey;
         if ch = CR then begin            { Do a carriage return and line feed }
            Inc(y,TextHeight('S') + 2);
            MoveTo(x-wl,y-wt);
         end
         else begin      { Show the letter typed by the user }
            HideMouse;
            { Erase the small cursor that marks the location where the text will start
              when the first letter is typed
            }
            if FirstLetter then begin
               PutImage(OldX-wl,OldY-wt,SmallCursor^,CopyPut);
               FirstLetter := False;
            end;
            S[0] := #1;  S[1] := Ch;
            GWrite(S);
            ShowMouse;
         end
      end;
   until MouseButtonPressed(LeftButton);
```

```
      while not MouseButtonReleased(LeftButton) do ;
      if FirstLetter then begin
        HideMouse;
        PutImage(OldX-wl,OldY-wt,SmallCursor^,CopyPut);
        ShowMouse;
      end
    end
end;

procedure ChangeFont;
{ User has selected text main menu option. Pull down the text menu and let
  user select one of the fonts. Load this new font, if any is selected.
}
const
  WindowLines = 5;
  FontStr: array[1..WindowLines] of string = ('Triplex',
    'Small', 'Sans Serif', 'Gothic', 'Default');
var
  SaveText: TextSettingsType;
  WindowWidth, WindowHeight, Offset, i, mx, my: integer;
  t: boolean;

begin
  GetTextSettings(SaveText);
  SetTextStyle(DefaultFont,HorizDir,1);
  WindowWidth := TextWidth('Sans Serif') + Border;
  WindowHeight := TextHeight('S') * WindowLines + 3 * Border;
  SetTextStyle(SaveText.Font,SaveText.Direction,SaveText.CharSize);
  HideMouse;
  t := GPopup(TextWindowX,TextWindowY,TextWindowX+WindowWidth+Border,
              TextWindowY+WindowHeight,SolidLn,GetMaxColor,SolidFill,Black);
  SetTextJustify(LeftText,TopText);
  SetTextStyle(DefaultFont,HorizDir,1);
  SetColor(GetMaxColor);
  Offset := Border;
  for i := 1 to WindowLines do begin                { Display menu choices }
    OutTextXY(Border,Offset,FontStr[i]);
    Inc(Offset,TextHeight(FontStr[i]));
  end;
  ShowMouse;
  while not MouseButtonPressed(LeftButton) do ;           { Get selection }
```

```
   GetMouseCoords(mx,my);
   Offset := Border;
   { Find which menu selection was chosen and switch load that font file }
   for i := 1 to WindowLines do begin
      if (MouseInBox(TextWindowX+Border,Offset, TextWindowX+TextWidth(FontStr[i]),
                  TextWindowY+Offset+TextHeight(FontStr[i]),mx,my)) then begin
         HideMouse;
         GUnpop;
         ShowMouse;
         SetTextStyle(i,HorizDir,1);
         Exit;
         { Clear out mouse button action/release if one of the }
         { items in the menu was selected }
         while not MouseButtonReleased(LeftButton) do ;
      end;
      Inc(Offset,TextHeight(FontStr[i]));
   end;
   HideMouse;
   GUnpop;
   ShowMouse;
end;

procedure ChangeLineStyle;
{ Pull-down line style menu. Change GlobalLineStyle to the line type selected from the
  menu, if any.
}
const
   LineHeight = 6;
   LineWidth = 40;
   MaxLineStyles = 4;
var
   WindowWidth, WindowHeight, Offset, i, mx, my: integer;
   t: boolean;

begin
   WindowWidth := LineWidth + Border * 6;
   WindowHeight := LineHeight * MaxLineStyles;
   HideMouse;
   t := GPopup(LineWindowX,LineWindowY,LineWindowX+WindowWidth+Border,LineWindowY+
             WindowHeight+LineHeight div 2,SolidLn,GetMaxColor,SolidFill,Black);
   SetColor(GetMaxColor);
```

```
   Offset := Border;
   for i := 0 to MaxLineStyles-1 do begin
     SetLineStyle(i,0,NormWidth);
     Line(Border*3,Offset+LineHeight div 2,Border*3+LineWidth,Offset+LineHeight div 2);
     Inc(Offset,LineHeight);
   end;
   ShowMouse;
   while not MouseButtonPressed(LeftButton) do ;          { Get selection }
   GetMouseCoords(mx,my);
   Offset := Border;
   for i := 0 to MaxLineStyles-1 do begin
     if MouseInBox(LineWindowX+Border*3,Offset-LineHeight div 2,LineWindowX+Border*3+
                   LineWidth,LineWindowY+Offset+LineHeight div 2,mx,my) then begin
       HideMouse;
       GUnpop;
       ShowMouse;
       SetLineStyle(i,0,NormWidth);
       GlobalLineStyle := i;
       while not MouseButtonReleased(LeftButton) do ;
       Exit;
     end;
     Inc(Offset,LineHeight);
   end;
   HideMouse;
   GUnpop;
   ShowMouse;
end;

{$F-}


procedure SetupScreen;
{ Set up the environment for the paint program }
var
   h, w, i, x, FillWidth, Offset, Space, FillType: integer;
   ColorWidth, MaxColors, FillColor: integer;

begin
{ Draw a main menu bar across the top of the screen. Each of the words in the menu bar
  will act as an icon that can be selected. Some of the words, such as Text and Line,
  will cause pull-down menus to appear if the user clicks on them.
}
```

```
HideMouse;
h := TextHeight('H') + 2;
Rectangle(0,0,GetMaxX,h);
OutTextXY(2,2,'Undo  Text  Line  Clear  Quit');

Space := TextWidth(' ');
Offset := 2;
AddObject(IconObj,'u',Offset,0,Offset+TextWidth('Undo'),
         TextHeight('Undo'),RestoreScreen);
Inc(Offset,TextWidth('Undo') + Space);
AddObject(IconObj,'t',Offset,0,Offset+TextWidth('Text'), TextHeight('Text'),
         ChangeFont);
TextWindowX := Offset;
TextWindowY := TextHeight('Text') + Border;

Inc(Offset, TextWidth('Text') + Space);
AddObject(IconObj,'l',Offset,0,Offset+TextWidth('Line'),TextHeight('Line'),
         ChangeLineStyle);
LineWindowX := Offset;
LineWindowY := TextHeight('Line') + Border;

Inc(Offset, TextWidth('Line') + Space);
AddObject(IconObj, 'c', Offset, 0, Offset +
     TextWidth('Clear'), TextHeight('Clear'), ClearWorkArea);
Inc(Offset, TextWidth('Clear') + Space);
AddObject(IconObj,'q',Offset,0,Offset+TextWidth('Quit'),TextHeight('Quit'),Quit);

{ Draw the icons on the left-hand side of the screen }
ReadIcon(0,h,'spray.icn');
AddObject(IconObj,'s',0,h,IconW*2,h+IconH,SprayCan);
ReadIcon(IconW*2,h,'letter.icn');
AddObject(IconObj,'c',IconW*2,h,IconW*4,h+IconH,TypeText);
ReadIcon(0,h+IconH,'line.icn');
AddObject(IconObj,'d',0,h+IconH,IconW*2,h+2*IconH,DrawLines);
ReadIcon(IconW*2,h+IconH,'pencil.icn');
AddObject(IconObj,'p',IconW*2,h+IconH,IconW*4,h+2*IconH,Pencil);
ReadIcon(0,h+2*IconH,'square.icn');
AddObject(IconObj,'s',0,h+2*IconH,IconW*2,h+3*IconH,DrawSquare);
ReadIcon(IconW*2,h+2*IconH,'fillbox.icn');
AddObject(IconObj,'r',IconW*2,h+2*IconH,IconW*4,h+3*IconH,DrawFillSquare);
```

```
ReadIcon(0,h+3*IconH,'circle.icn');
AddObject(IconObj, 'c', 0, h+3*IconH, IconW*2, h+4*IconH, DrawCircle);
ReadIcon(IconW*2, h+3*IconH, 'ellipse.icn');
AddObject(IconObj,'g',IconW*2,h+3*IconH,IconW*4,h+4*IconH,DrawEllipse);
ReadIcon(0, h+4*IconH, 'polygon.icn');
AddObject(IconObj,'p',0,h+4*IconH,IconW*2,h+5*IconH,DrawPolygon);
ReadIcon(IconW*2, h+4*IconH, 'fillpoly.icn');
AddObject(IconObj,'x',IconW*2,h+4*IconH,IconW*4,h+5*IconH,DrawFillPoly);
ReadIcon(0, h+5*IconH, 'eraser.icn');
AddObject(IconObj, 'e', 0, h+5*IconH, IconW*2, h+6*IconH, Erase);
ReadIcon(IconW*2, h+5*IconH, 'arc.icn');
AddObject(IconObj, 'a', IconW*2, h+5*IconH, IconW*4, h+6*IconH, DrawArcs);
{ Create the fill pattern box. This will appear on the lower }
{ portion of the screen }
FillWidth := (GetMaxX-1-IconW*4+2) div (NumFillsWide+1);
{ Start default fill color at MaxColor }
GlobalFillColor := GetMaxColor;
GlobalDrawColor := GlobalFillColor;
FillType := 0;
x := IconW * 4 + 2 + FillWidth;
for i := 1 to NumFillsWide do begin
   SetFillStyle(FillType, GlobalFillColor);
   Bar3D(x,GetMaxY-FillHeight*2,x+FillWidth,GetMaxY-FillHeight,0,False);
   Inc(FillType);
   Inc(x,FillWidth);
end;
Rectangle(IconW*4+2, GetMaxY-FillHeight*2, GetMaxX, GetMaxY);
AddObject(FillObj, 'w', IconW*4+2+FillWidth, GetMaxY -
FillHeight*2, GetMaxX, GetMaxY-FillHeight, ChangeFillPattern);
GlobalFillStyle := SolidFill;

MaxColors := GetMaxColor;
ColorWidth := (GetMaxX-1-IconW*4+2-FillWidth) div (MaxColors + 1);
FillColor := 0;
x := IconW * 4 + 2 + FillWidth;
for i := 1 to MaxColors+1 do begin
   SetFillStyle(SolidFill, FillColor);
   Bar3D(x,GetMaxY-FillHeight,x+ColorWidth,GetMaxY,0,False);
   Inc(FillColor);
   Inc(x,ColorWidth);
end;
```

```
AddObject (FillObj, 'z', IconW*4+2+FillWidth,
        GetMaxY-FillHeight, GetMaxX, GetMaxY, ChangeFillColor);
SetLineStyle (SolidLn, 0, ThickWidth);
SetFillStyle (GlobalFillStyle, GlobalFillColor);
Bar3D (IconW*4+2+2, GetMaxY-FillHeight*2+2,
      IconW*4+2+FillWidth-2, GetMaxY-2, 0, False);
AddObject (FillObj, 'y', IconW*4+2+2, GetMaxY-FillHeight*2+2,
        IconW*4+FillWidth-2, GetMaxY, ChangeDrawColor);
SetLineStyle (SolidLn, 0, NormWidth);

{ Draw main draw area window and calculate its size }
wl := IconW*4+2+1;     wt := h+2+1;
wr := GetMaxX-1;        wb := GetMaxY-FillHeight*2-2-1;
Rectangle (IconW*4+2, h+2, GetMaxX, GetMaxY-FillHeight*2-2);

{ Allocate memory for the Undo operation }
GetMem (LastScreen, ImageSize (wl, wt, wr, wb));
GetMem (CurrentScreen, Imagesize (wl, wt, wr, wb));
if (LastScreen = Nil) or (CurrentScreen = Nil) then begin
   CloseGraph;
   writeln ('Not enough memory for UNDO operation.');
   halt (1);
end;
GetImage (wl, wt, wr, wb, LastScreen^);
GetImage (wl, wt, wr, wb, CurrentScreen^);
GlobalFillStyle := SolidFill;
GlobalLineStyle := SolidLn;
ShowMouse;
end;


begin
   InitGraph (GDriver, GMode, '');
   t := InitMouse;
   SetupScreen;
   repeat
     c := WaitForInput (LeftButton);
     AnyToProcess (c);
   until False;
end.
```

12

A CAD Program

In Chapter 11 we developed a paint program that provides a graphics environment for drawing figures and shapes. In this chapter we'll extend the paint program so that it becomes a working CAD package. The differences between the two graphics programs may seem minor based on appearance; however, internally the two differ in several important ways. We'll explore these differences throughout this chapter as we discuss how the CAD program is written and how it functions. Finally, we'll end this chapter by outlining several enhancements that you might want to add to the CAD program to create your own custom version.

Painting versus Drafting

The environment for the CAD program is shown in Figure 12.1. Although the program looks like the paint program we developed in Chapter 11, the two have significant differences. For instance, the paint program is specifically designed to provide an environment for drawing pictures, while the CAD program is intended to be used to draw accurate representations of real world objects.

Internally, the programs differ in how they represent and process the figures they draw. The paint program, for example, stores objects as fixed images; therefore, the figures on the screen can't be easily manipulated. In the CAD program, however, a complete list of the graphics objects that are in its drawing window are maintained in a list in world coordinates. In addition, each object has attributes associated with it such as its size and location.

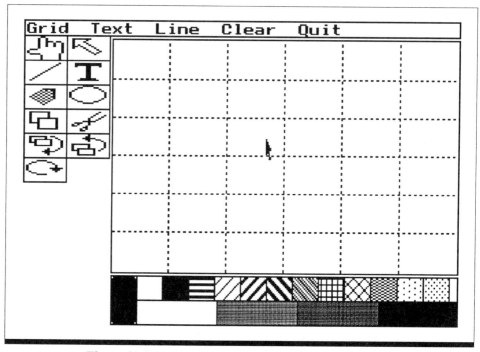

Figure 12.1. The environment of the Cad.Pas program

Each object in the drawing window is kept in an object list which is similar to the data structure used in processing the icons in the paint program. With this new object list, we can easily access, manipulate, and move each of the graphics objects in the drawing window.

The major enhancements included in the CAD program are:

1. All objects are stored in real world coordinates
2. Objects can be selected and moved
3. Graphics figures are saved in an object list
4. Supports a rotate and duplication feature
5. Draws dimensioning lines
6. Displays an alignment grid
7. The order that objects are drawn can be changed

In order to support each of these features, the CAD program will become rather large. Therefore, we'll develop two source files that support the specialized routines for the CAD program. These files, discussed in this chapter, are called **Cad.Pas** (Listing 12.1) and **CadDraw.Pas** (Listing 12.2). The **Cad.Pas** file contains several routines that are similar to the ones developed for the paint program in Chapter 11, so it will not be the primary focus of this chapter. Instead, we'll devote the majority of our discussions to **CadDraw.Pas**.

Because of the large size of the CAD program, only the line, polygon, circle and text drawing routines are supported. These routines provide enough power to make a useful CAD package. However, you could easily modify the CAD program to include several of the other drawing routines found in the paint program.

Setting up the Screen

Referring to Figure 12.1 you'll notice that the environment of the CAD program is slightly different than the paint program. There are several new icons and a grid pattern added to the drawing window. Each of these changes can be found in the **SetupScreen** procedure in **Cad.Pas** which is used to create the environment of the CAD program.

Let's start by examining the new icon patterns and their corresponding routines. If you review **Cad.Pas**, you'll notice several new routines and the modified calls to **AddObject** in **SetupScreen**.

A less visible change to **SetupScreen** is that the drawing window is set up to reflect real world coordinates that are 6 units wide and 6 units high. (You can consider the units to be of any type—inches, feet, kilometers, etc.) This is done by the following two statements in **SetupScreen**:

```
Set_Window(0.0, 0.0, 6.0, 6.0);
Set_ViewPort(wl, wt, wr, wb);
```

Both of these procedures were introduced in Chapter 5. To refresh your memory, they are used to set the relationship between real world coordinates and screen coordinates. The routine **Set_Window** defines the real world coordinate bounds to be between (0.0, 0.0) and (6.0, 6.0). The **Set_ViewPort** procedure (keep in mind that this routine is different than BGI's **SetViewPort**) defines the bounds of the drawing window for the **Matrix.Pas** unit.

A new feature added to the CAD program is the grid displayed in the drawing window. It is drawn by the **DrawGrid** procedure included in **CadDraw.Pas**. You'll find a call to this routine in **SetupScreen** after the window and viewports are initialized. The grid is designed to help you align objects in the drawing window. It consists of a series of horizontal and vertical dashed lines, spaced 1 unit apart in real world coordinates. After the line style is temporarily changed to dotted lines, the grid is drawn in **DrawGrid** with the two **for** loops as shown:

```
for j := 1 to 5 do begin
  WorldToPC(0.0, 0.0+j, x, y);
  Line(wl, y, wr, y);
end;
for i := 1 to 5 do begin
  WorldToPC(0.0+i, 0.0, x, y);
  Line(x, wt, x, wb);
end;
```

The top **for** loop sequences through the horizontal lines extending across the screen and the second **for** loop draws the vertical lines. Note that the index variables are added to real world coordinates which are then converted to screen coordinates by **WorldToPC** and then drawn. This ensures that the lines are spaced according to the dimensions of the world coordinates. When the grid is displayed, a global flag called **GridOn**, is set to True; otherwise it is False. This flag is used to determine when the grid should be displayed. To toggle the grid you can select the word *Grid* in the main menu bar of the program.

Now that we've looked at the major changes that are visible in the environment, let's turn to the unique internal parts of the CAD program.

The Object List

One of the major differences between the paint program in Chapter 11 and the CAD program is that the CAD program maintains a list of all of the objects in its drawing window. This list is much like the object-oriented list, found in **Object.Pas**, that we used to keep track of the various icons, pop-up menus, and commands on the screen in the paint program.

As is the case in **Object.Pas**, the list of objects is implemented as an array of records. Each structure is of type **GraphicsObj** as follows:

```
GraphicsObj = record
  ObjType: integer;           { Type of graphics object }
  Left, Top: integer;         { Pixels boundaries of object in }
  Right, Bottom: integer;     { full-screen coordinates }
  NumPoints: integer;         { Number of coordinate pairs in points }
  Points: WorldArray;         { Objects saved in WORLD coordinates }
  Str: string;                { Text strings are saved here }
  DrawColor: integer;         { Color used in object }
  LineStyle: integer;         { Line style used in object }
```

```
        FillStyle: integer;          { Fill style used in object }
        FillColor: integer;          { Fill color used in object }
        TextStyle: integer;          { Textstyle used in string }
        LeftArrow: boolean;          { True if left arrow on line }
        RightArrow: boolean;         { True if right arrow on lines }
      end;
```

The array of **GraphicsObjs** is called **GObjects** and is declared in **CadDraw.Pas** to be large enough to hold **NumGObjects** objects which is in turn defined to be 50.

The record **GraphicsObj** is used to store information about each of the objects that the CAD program can draw. However, the exact meanings of each of the fields in **GraphicsObj** may be slightly different depending on whether a line, polygon, circle, or text is being represented. In addition, not all the fields are always used when storing information about an object.

A graphics object is added to the **GObjects** array by a call to the procedure **AddGObject** which is also in the **CadDraw.Pas**. This routine is similar to the **AddObject** procedure in **Object.Pas**. One important point to note is that all of the graphics objects are saved in world coordinates. This is done so that the objects can easily be manipulated in the program. If you examine the code in **AddGObject**, you will see the conversions that are made between screen coordinates and world coordinates. In the next section we'll learn how objects are drawn and added to the graphics object list.

Drawing Objects

The CAD program supports a limited set of drawing routines. These include a line drawing procedure, a polygon routine, and a circle drawing procedure. Each of these routines has been modified from the paint program so that they add the figures that they draw to the **GObjects** array discussed in the last section. In addition, the text routine has been changed so that any text that is typed is handled as a graphics object. By doing this, we'll be able to select and move the text around the screen.

Although we won't discuss each drawing routine in detail, we'll now look at the new aspects of these routines.

Drawing Polygons and Circles

The polygon and circle drawing routine, **DrawFillPoly** and **DrawCircle** respectively, are similar to the drawing routines of the same names in the paint program. The significant difference is that they each have a call to **AddGObject** which adds each figure that they draw to the internal list of graphics objects, **GObjects**. Let's look at how this is done in **DrawFillPoly**.

You'll notice that there are two new lines added to **DrawFillPoly** immediately after the call to **FillPoly** which draws the finished polygon. These lines are:

```
GetPolyBounds(NumPoints,Points,Left,Top,Right,Bottom);
AddGObject(Poly,Left,Top,Right,Bottom,NumPoints,Points,'');
```

Both routines use the array **Points** which contains the vertices of the polygon in full-screen coordinates. The first routine, **GetPolyBounds**, determines the left, top, right, and bottom screen bounds of the polygon passed to it. These values along with the **Points** array and the number of coordinates in the array, **NumPoints**, are passed to **AddGObject** to add the object to the list of graphics objects. The first argument in **AddGObject** is the constant, **Poly**, which is defined at the top of the unit **CadDraw** and used to specify that the object being added is a polygon. Remember that within **AddGObject** the screen coordinates are mapped to world coordinates and saved in the **Points** field of the **GraphicsObj** record. The last parameter is a null string which is simply used as a place holder in this case. This parameter is solely used by the text input routine which we'll discuss later.

Adding a circle to the object list in the **DrawCircle** routine is done slightly differently. The main difference is due to the fact that a circle is specified by a center point and a radius instead of a list of points. Since the **GraphicsObj** record does not have fields to save the center and radius of the circle, we'll use the first three locations in the **Points** array instead. Index location 1 will hold the x and y coordinates of the center of the circle and the **x** field of the second component will holds its radius. Note that **Points** is an array of **PointType** which is a record with **x** and **y** integer fields. Therefore, the list of screen points passed to **AddGObject** in the array **Points** are set by the lines:

```
points[1].x := CenterX;      points[1].y := CenterY;
points[2].x := AbsRadius;    points[2].y := 1;
```

The last line simply places a dummy value into the **y** field of the second record in the array so that any later calculations that might be performed on it won't lead to unexpected overflow errors. We'll actually be ignoring this field value.

The call to **AddGObject** using the object type **Crcle** is:

```
AddGObject(Crcle,CenterX-AbsRadius,CenterY-Round(AbsRadius*AspectRatio),
          CenterX+AbsRadius,CenterY+Round(AbsRadius*AspectRatio),
          NumPoints,Points,'');
```

This procedure call is probably more complicated than expected. The reason is that the second, third, fourth, and fifth arguments include calculations to determine the boundaries of the circle. Since **AbsRadius** is the radius of the circle, it is easy to understand how the left side of the circle (specified by the second argument) is given by:

```
CenterX-AbsRadius
```

Similarly, the fourth argument calculates the right side of the circle as **CenterX+AbsRadius**. The other two calculations determine the top and bottom screen coordinates of the circle; however, they are complicated by the fact that we must adjust for the screen's aspect ratio. Remember that **AspectRatio** is a global variable calculated at the beginning of the program and is based on the values returned by **GetAspectRatio**.

Working with Lines

Drawing and adding lines to the object list is handled much the same way that it is done in **DrawFillPoly** and **DrawCircle**. The line segments are saved individually with each of the segments' endpoints placed in the **Points** field of a **GraphicsObj** record. Therefore, a line segment is added to the object list in **DrawLine** by the statement:

```
AddGObject (Ln,x1-3,y1-3,x2+3,y2+3,2,Points,'');
```

where the coordinates of the endpoints are given by (x1, y1) and (x2, y2). These values are passed to **AddGObject** to define the bounds of the line. Remember from **Object.Pas** that the boundaries of the object are used to determine which object the mouse has selected when one of its buttons is pressed. Also note that the boundary values are offset by 3 pixels. This is done so that when the line is horizontal or vertical it appears slightly larger and thus, easier to select.

Prior to the call to **AddGObject** is the statement:

```
DrawArrows (x1,y1,x2,y2,LeftArrow,RightArrow);
```

which calls the procedure **DrawArrows** in **CadDraw.Pas**. This routine appends arrowheads to the line segment if the user has selected this style. If you look at the **ChangeLineStyle** procedure, you'll see that three new line types have been added to support these arrows. The new pull-down menu for the Line menu option, which includes these new arrow line styles, is shown in Figure 12.2. Since two of the line styles are designed so that the arrow is on the leading or trailing edge of the line, it is important to maintain which side of the line the arrowhead is to be placed. Depending on the style of arrow selected, either **LeftArrow**, or **RightArrow**, or both are set to True. These are used in **DrawArrows** to select which arrows are displayed. The arrow size is specified by **ArrowSize** which is a constant defined in **CadDraw** to be 3 pixels in width and height.

The one difficult part in dealing with arrows is that the arrowhead must be rotated so that it is oriented at the same angle as the line segment to which it is attached. These adjustments are done in **DrawArrows**. We will now take a closer look at this.

The routine **DrawArrows** draws an arrow on the leading edge of the line segment, at (x1, y1), if **LeftArrow** is True and an arrow on the trailing edge of the line segment, at (x2, y2), if **RightArrow** is True. The arrowhead itself is made from two connected line segments which are joined to one of the ends of the line. The points describing this are contained in the array **ArrowHead**. The arrowhead figure is adjusted so that its angle matches that of the line segment, by first translating its center to the origin, rotating it, and then translating it back to the tip of the line segment. This process is performed by the lines:

```
PCTranslatePoly(3,ArrowHead,-x1+wl,-y1+wt);
PCRotatePoly(3,ArrowHead,Angle);
PCTranslatePoly(3,Arrowhead,x1-wl,y1-wt);
```

Finally, the arrow is drawn by the statement:

```
DrawPoly(3,ArrowHead);
```

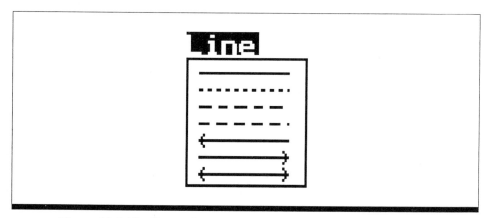

Figure 12.2. The line style pull-down menu includes arrow symbols

Text as a Graphics Object

In order to support text as a graphics object, a few changes have been made to the **TypeText** routine that appeared in the paint program. One change is the call to **AddGObject** which adds the text string you type to the object list. In addition, each line of text is broken into a separate graphics object. Otherwise, we would have to account for the carriage returns in the string when calculating its dimensions. Also, because we may be working with different text styles, the global variable **Global-TextStyle** has been added to the program and is saved in the **GraphicsObj** record. It specifies the text style used in the current text string.

When **AddGObject** is called to add a text object to the object list, the ASCII text is saved in the **Str** field of the **GraphicsObj** record. The starting screen coordinates of the text are specified in **TypeText** by **StartX** and **StartY**. These are passed to **AddGObject** and converted to world coordinates and saved in the **Points** field of the **GraphicsObj** record. Since the text string is justified to this point, it is actually the point that you use to select and move the text.

Displaying the Graphics Objects

Because the CAD program is designed so that you can modify the objects in the drawing window, it must have routines that are capable of redrawing the screen after the objects are changed. This is the purpose of the **CadDraw.Pas** routines listed in Table 12.1.

Table 12.1. Routines used to redraw graphics objects

Routine	Description
DisplayLine	Draws a single line object
DisplayPolygon	Displays a polygon
DisplayCircle	Draws a single circle object
DisplayText	Displays a text object

Each of these routines is designed to display an object in the **GObjects** array of a particular type. In addition, the routines **DisplayObject** and **DisplayAllObjects** are also included in **CadDraw.Pas** to draw a specific object in the **GObjects** array or all of the objects in the list. Each of these routines is fairly straightforward so we'll continue exploring the rest of the CAD program.

Deleting a Graphics Object

Now let's take a look at how to remove an object from the drawing window. Deleting an object from the screen involves two steps. First, the object is deleted from the internal object list, **GObjects**. Second, the whole screen is cleared and all remaining objects in **GObjects** are displayed.

The delete routine in the **CadDraw.Pas** source file is called **DeleteObj**. It removes the object indexed by the global variable **CurrentObj** which points to the current object being manipulated—in this case deleted. The routine centers around a **for** loop which rearranges **GObjects** so that the current object is moved to the end of **GObjects** and all records that were above it are moved down one index location. In order to accomplish this, a temporary pointer to the current object is saved in the local variable **Temp** and then the objects are shifted one location down in the array by the lines:

```
Temp := GObjects[CurrentObj];
for i := CurrentObj to NextObj-1 do
  GObjects[i] := GObjects[i+1];
GObjects[i] := Temp;
```

Next, the index pointer, **NextObj**, which points to the next available object location in **GObjects**, is decremented by one. In addition, a test is made to see if the last object is the one being deleted. If so, the **CurrentObj** index is also decremented. Finally, the screen is cleared and all of the objects in the object list are redrawn by calling the routines:

```
ClearWorkArea;
DisplayAllObjects;
```

The procedure **ClearWorkArea** clears the drawing window by using the BGI **ClearViewPort** routine and, in addition, draws a grid if the flag **GridOn** is True. The second routine, **DisplayAllObjects**, redraws all of the objects on the screen, except, of course, the object just deleted. Note that after the delete operation, the **CurrentObj** normally becomes the next object in the array **GObjects**.

The Duplicate Function

The CAD program also includes the procedure **Duplicate** which is used to duplicate objects in the object list. This routine is located in **CadDraw.Pas** and copies the object indexed by **CurrentObj** to the next free location in **GObjects** pointed to by the variable **NextObj**. Of course, simply duplicating all of the information about an object will cause the new figure to be displayed over the original object. To avoid this, **Duplicate** calls **WorldTranslatePoly** to translate the new object by 0.1 (in world coordinates) in the x and y directions. The translated copy of the current object and the rest of the object list are redrawn at the end of **Duplicate** by the routine **DisplayAllObjects**. Note that **Duplicate**, as written, does not allow text to be duplicated, although this would be simple to add.

The Rotate Command

Another function provided by the CAD program allows you to rotate objects about their center. This is accomplished by the routine **RotateObj**. The routine uses a series of calls to procedures in **Matrix.Pas** (see Chapter 5) to rotate the current object clockwise by 45 degree increments about its center point.

If the object is a polygon or a line (circles and text cannot be rotated in the CAD program) then the object's center is translated to the origin, the object is rotated, and then it is translated back to its original location. Once the object is rotated, its new screen boundaries are determined by calling the **CadDraw.Pas** procedure **Get-PolyBounds**. Finally, the screen is cleared and all objects are redrawn using **DisplayAllObjects** to show the rotation.

Changing the Drawing Order

Each time **DisplayAllObjects** is called it draws each of the objects in the **GObjects** array, starting from the 1 index and working toward the last location in the array which is just before the index **NextObj**. Since this drawing order is always followed, objects at the beginning of the list are always drawn first. Consequently, if two objects overlap, the object closer to the beginning of the **GObjects** array is always drawn below the other. The CAD program allows you to modify the order that the objects are displayed by swapping the positions of objects in **GObjects**. For instance, to move an object behind all other objects, it is simply a matter of moving the object to the beginning of the list. This is what is done in the procedure **FlipToBack**. Similarly, the routine **FlipToFront** moves an object from its current location to the tail of the list so that it will be displayed last and therefore, on top of all the other objects. Since both are similar, let's just look at the **FlipToFront** procedure.

The routine begins by testing whether the object list is empty. This is the case if **NextObj** is zero. If so, the routine simply exits with no action taken.

```
if Nextobj <= 1 then Exit;
```

Next, a temporary structure, **Temp**, is used to save the object pointed to by
CurrentObj. This is the object that will be moved to the end of the **GObjects** array.
Then each of the objects above **CurrentObj** is shifted down one position in the array
by the **for** loop:

```
for i := CurrentObj to NextObj-2 do
   GObjects[i] := GObjects[i+1];
```

Finally, the object, saved in **Temp**, is copied to the end of the object list and the
CurrentObj index is updated so it still points to the same object, even though it is
now at the end of the list.

```
GObjects[i] := Temp;
CurrentObj := i;
```

Once the object list is modified, the drawing window is updated by clearing the
screen and displaying all objects in **GObjects** by executing the two statements:

```
ClearWorkArea;
DisplayAllObjects;
```

This will cause the current object to be displayed on top of all the other graphics
objects in the drawing window.

Now that we have learned how to duplicate, rotate, and flip an object in the
object list, let's look at how we can select one and move it on the screen.

Selecting and Moving an Object

The CAD program allows you to select an object in the drawing window by moving
the mouse to the object and clicking on it. When this is done, a dashed rectangle will
appear around the figure and **CurrentObj** will be set to the index location its
corresponding object record. Consequently, this object will become the object
manipulated by any subsequent uses of routines such as **Duplicate** and **Rotate**. If
another object shares the same area on the screen as the currently selected object, it
can be selected instead by clicking on the mouse again in the same region. Similarly,
if there are other objects in the same area, you can sequence through them by clicking
the mouse several times.

The procedure **SelectObject** performs the actions described above. Rather than go through its code line-by-line, let's take a high-level view of it. Its main purpose is to change the **CurrentObj** index to the object pointed at by the mouse when the left mouse button is pressed. The routine **SelectObject** shows which object is the current object by calling the routine **MarkObject** which draws a rectangular box around it. The rectangle uses the **Left**, **Top**, **Right**, and **Bottom** components of the **GraphicsObj** record for the current object to determine its location. Note that **SetWriteMode** is set to **XorPut** so that the rectangle can be exclusive-ORed on the screen and therefore, easily moved. When **SelectObject** exits, the rectangle is erased by a final call to **MarkObject**.

Moving a selected object is done by clicking on the hand icon, moving the mouse to the object, and then pressing the left mouse button and dragging the object to its new location. When the mouse button is released, the entire screen is redrawn with the object at its new location.

This operation is performed in the routine **MoveObject** which is included in **CadDraw.Pas**. Moving an object is accomplished by keeping track of the amount that the mouse has been moved in the variables **MovedX** and **MovedY**. This amount is then mapped into world coordinates and used to translate the object. Once it is translated, the screen is erased and completely redrawn to reflect the change.

Extending the CAD Program

There are many ways to enhance the CAD program presented in this chapter. You might add routines to save the objects in the drawing window to a file, provide a facility to zoom in and out on the objects being displayed, or add the capability of grouping objects. Briefly, let's look at the first two suggestions.

If you want to be able to save the objects in the CAD program, all you'll need to do is save the **GObjects** array to a file. You could use the first line of the file to save the number of objects in the **GObjects** array and the index of the current object. The rest of the file can be used to save each of the **GraphicsObj** records in the **GObjects** array. Reading this information from a file into **GObjects** is similarly a very simple matter and would allow you to initialize the whole screen or read in selected objects.

Another feature you might want to add is the ability to zoom in and out on objects in the drawing window. The basic idea is to change the window size of the world coordinates that are displayed on the screen. For instance, to zoom in on objects in the drawing window you can set the window to between (0.0, 0.0) and (3.0, 3.0) as follows:

```
          procedure ZoomIn;
          begin
             Set_Window(0.0,0.0,3.0,3.0);
             Set_ViewPort(wl,wt,wr,wb);
             ClearWorkArea;
             DisplayAllObjects;
          end;
```

• Listing 12.1

```
program Cad;
{ This program exploits many of the BGI functions to build a simple yet powerful CAD
  program. Several of the tools built up earlier in the book are put to use in this
  program. The program will run on any of the following graphics modes:
       All CGA modes
       EGALo and EGA64 (640x200 16 color)
       All the MCGA modes except MCGAHI
       All of the ATT400 modes except ATT400HI
       VGALO (640x200 16 color)
}
uses
   Graph, MousePac, Object, GPopPac, CADDraw, Matrix, GText;
const
   GDriver: integer = CGA;
   GMode: integer = CGAC3;
   IconW = 16;
   IconH = 16;
   NumFillsWide = 12;
   FillHeight = 16;
   Border = 2;
var
   TextWindowX: integer;                        { Global values that specify where the }
   TextWindowY: integer;                        { font pull-down menu should appear }
   LineWindowX: integer;                        { Specify where the line pull-down menu }
   LineWindowY: integer;                        { should appear }
   Icon: array[1..IconH,1..IconW] of byte;  { Icon array }
   c: integer;
   t: boolean;
```

```
procedure ReadIcon(x, y: integer; FileName: string);
{ Reads an icon file }
var
   IconFile: text;
   i, j, Width, Height, IconPixel: integer;

begin
   {$I-} Assign(IconFile, FileName);
   Reset(IconFile); {$I+}
   if IOResult = 0 then begin
      Readln(IconFile, Width, Height);
      if (Width <> IconW) or (Height <> IconH) then begin
         CloseGraph;
         writeln(FileName,' is not a compatible icon file.');
         halt(1);
      end;
      for j := 1 to IconH do begin
         for i := 1 to IconW do begin
            Read(IconFile,IconPixel);
            if IconPixel = 1 then begin
               PutPixel(2*(i-1)+x, y+(j-1),White);
               PutPixel(2*(i-1)+1+x, y+(j-1),White);
            end
         end
      end;
      Close(IconFile);
      Rectangle(x,y,x+IconW*2,y+IconH);
   end
   else begin
      CloseGraph;
      writeln('Could not find icon file: ',FileName);
      halt(1);
   end
end;

{$F+}                    { Make the following procedures available so that }
                        { they can be passed as a parameter to AddObject }
procedure Quit;
{ Function to quit the program -- selected by Quit option in main menu bar
  of environment
}
```

```
begin
  CloseGraph;
  halt(0);
end;

procedure ChangeFillPattern;
{ Select one of the fill patterns at the bottom of the screen }
var
  x, y, i, mx, my, FillWidth, FillType: integer;

begin
  FillWidth := (GetMaxX-1-IconW*4+2) div (NumFillsWide+1);
  FillType := 0;
  x := IconW * 4 + 2 + FillWidth;
  for i := 1 to NumFillsWide do begin
    GetMouseCoords(mx,my);
    if MouseInBox(x,GetMaxY-FillHeight*2,x+FillWidth,
                  GetMaxY-FillHeight,mx,my) then begin
      GlobalFillStyle := FillType;
      SetFillStyle(GlobalFillStyle,GlobalFillColor);
      SetLineStyle(SolidLn,0,ThickWidth);
      HideMouse;
      Bar3D(IconW*4+2+2,GetMaxY-FillHeight*2+2,
            IconW*4+2+FillWidth-2,GetMaxY-2,0,False);
      SetLineStyle(SolidLn,0,NormWidth);
      ShowMouse;
      Exit;
    end;
    Inc(FillType);
    Inc(x,FillWidth);
  end;
end;

procedure ChangeFillColor;
{ Select one of the fill colors shown at the bottom of the screen }
var
  MaxColors, ColorWidth, FillColor, FillWidth: integer;
  i, x, y, mx, my: integer;

begin
  FillWidth := (GetMaxX-1-IconW*4+2) div (NumFillsWide+1);
```

```
    ColorWidth := (GetMaxX-1-IconW*4+2-FillWidth) div (GetMaxColor + 1);
    FillColor := 0;
    x := IconW * 4 + 2 + FillWidth;
    for i := 0 to GetMaxColor do begin
       GetMouseCoords(mx, my);
       if (MouseInBox(x,GetMaxY-FillHeight,x+ColorWidth,GetMaxY,mx,my)) then begin
          GlobalFillColor := FillColor;
          SetFillStyle(GlobalFillStyle,GlobalFillColor);
          SetLineStyle(SolidLn,0,ThickWidth);
          HideMouse;
          Bar3D(IconW*4+2+2,GetMaxY-FillHeight*2+2,
                IconW*4+2+FillWidth-2,GetMaxY-2,0,False);
          SetLineStyle(SolidLn,0,NormWidth);
          ShowMouse;
          Exit;
       end;
       Inc(FillColor);
       Inc(x,ColorWidth);
    end
end;


procedure ChangeDrawColor;
{ Change the global drawing color value when the user clicks on the rectangle to the
  left of the fill patterns. Set GlobalDrawColor to GlobalFillColor and redraw the
  border of this rectangle in the new drawing color.
}
var
   FillWidth: integer;

begin
   FillWidth := (GetMaxX-1-IconW*4+2) div (NumFillsWide+1);
   GlobalDrawColor := GlobalFillColor;
   SetFillStyle(GlobalFillStyle,GlobalFillColor);
   SetLineStyle(SolidLn,0,ThickWidth);
   SetColor(GlobalDrawColor);
   HideMouse;
   Bar3D(IconW*4+2+2,GetMaxY-FillHeight*2+2,IconW*4+2+FillWidth-2,GetMaxY-2,0,False);
   SetLineStyle(SolidLn,0,NormWidth);
   ShowMouse;
end;
```

```
procedure TypeText;
{ Allows user to enter text. Each line of text is added as a separate graphics object.
  No support is provided for carriage returns or backspaces.
}
const
  Txt = 0;                              { Text objects are of type 0 }
var
  x, y, StartX, StartY, c, i, j: integer;
  SmallCursor: pointer;
  S: string;
  Ignore: PCArray;                      { Use PCArray type to hold letters of text }
  Size: word;
  Done, FirstLetter: boolean;
  ch: char;

begin
  SetColor(GlobalDrawColor);
  SetTextJustify(LeftText,TopText);
  SetTextStyle(GlobalTextStyle,HorizDir,1);
  SetLineStyle(SolidLn,0,NormWidth);
  Size := Imagesize(1,1,1,1+TextHeight('S'));
  GetMem(SmallCursor,Size);
  if SmallCursor = Nil then MallocError;
  SetViewPort(wl,wt,wr,wb,True);
  while not MouseButtonPressed(LeftButton) do ;
  while True do begin
    GetMouseCoords(x,y);
    if (x < wl) or (y < wt) or (y > wb) then begin
      FreeMem(SmallCursor,Size);
      SetViewPort(0,0,GetMaxX,GetMaxY,True);
      Exit;
    end;
    HideMouse;
    GetImage(x-wl,y-wt,x-wl,y+TextHeight('S')-wt,SmallCursor^);
    Line(x-wl,y-wt,x-wl,y+TextHeight('S')-wt);
    ShowMouse;
    FirstLetter := True;
    StartX := x;   StartY := y;
    MoveTo(x-wl,y-wt);
    i := 0;
    c := WaitForInput(LeftButton);
```

```
      Done := False;
      while not Done and (c > 0) do begin
         if Char(c) = CR then Done := True
         else begin                              { End string if carriage return }
            HideMouse;
            { Erase the small cursor that marks the location where }
            { the text will start when the first letter is typed }
            if FirstLetter then begin
               PutImage(StartX-wl,StartY-wt,SmallCursor^,CopyPut);
               FirstLetter := False;
            end;
            GWriteCh(Char(c));
            ShowMouse;
            Inc(i);
            S[0] := Char(i); S[i] := Char(c);
         end;
         if not Done then c := WaitForInput(LeftButton);
      end;
      if FirstLetter then begin
         HideMouse;
         PutImage(StartX-wl,StartY-wt,SmallCursor^,CopyPut);
         ShowMouse;
      end
      else
         AddGObject(Txt,StartX,StartY,StartX,StartY,i,Ignore,S);
   end
end;


procedure ChangeFont;
{ Change the font by selecting one from the font pull-down menu }
const
   WindowLines = 5;
   FontStr: array[1..WindowLines] of string = ('Triplex',
      'Small', 'Sans Serif', 'Gothic', 'Default');
var
   SaveText: TextSettingsType;
   WindowWidth, WindowHeight, Offset, i, mx, my: integer;
   t: boolean;

begin
   GetTextSettings(SaveText);
```

```
   SetTextStyle(DefaultFont,HorizDir,1);
   WindowWidth := TextWidth('Sans Serif') + Border;
   WindowHeight := TextHeight('S') * WindowLines + 3 * Border;
   SetTextStyle(SaveText.Font,SaveText.Direction,SaveText.CharSize);
   HideMouse;
   t := GPopup(TextWindowX, TextWindowY,TextWindowX + WindowWidth + Border,
               TextWindowY+WindowHeight,SolidLn,GetMaxColor,SolidFill,Black);
   SetTextJustify(LeftText,TopText);
   SetTextStyle(DefaultFont,HorizDir,1);
   SetColor(GetMaxColor);
   Offset := Border;
   for i := 1 to WindowLines do begin
      OutTextXY(Border,Offset,FontStr[i]);
      Inc(Offset,TextHeight(FontStr[i]));
   end;
   ShowMouse;
   while not MouseButtonPressed(LeftButton) do ;
   GetMouseCoords(mx,my);
   Offset := Border;
   for i := 1 to WindowLines do begin
      if (MouseInBox(TextWindowX+Border, Offset,
      TextWindowX+TextWidth(FontStr[i]),
      TextWindowY+Offset+TextHeight(FontStr[i]),mx,my)) then begin
         HideMouse;
         GUnpop;
         ShowMouse;
         GlobalTextStyle := i;
         SetTextStyle(i,HorizDir,1);
         Exit;
      end;
      Inc(Offset,TextHeight(FontStr[i]));
   end;
   HideMouse;
   GUnpop;
   ShowMouse;
end;

procedure ChangeLineStyle;
{ Select a new line style from the line style pull-down menu. Note
  that arrows have been added to the menu from the Paint.Pas version.
}
```

```
const
   LineHeight = 6;
   LineWidth = 40;
   MaxLineStyles = 7;
var
   WindowWidth, WindowHeight, Offset, i, mx, my: integer;
   t: boolean;

begin
   WindowWidth := LineWidth + Border*6;
   WindowHeight := LineHeight * MaxLineStyles;
   HideMouse;
   t := GPopup(LineWindowX,LineWindowY,LineWindowX + WindowWidth + Border,LineWindowY+
              WindowHeight+LineHeight div 2,SolidLn,GetMaxColor,SolidFill,Black);
   SetColor(GetMaxColor);
   Offset := Border;
   for i := 0 to MaxLineStyles-1 do begin
      if i >= 4 then begin                         { Line styles 4, 5, and 6 have arrows }
         SetLineStyle(SolidLn,0,NormWidth);
         Line(Border*3,Offset+LineHeight div 2,Border*3+LineWidth,
             Offset+LineHeight div 2);
         case i of
            4 : begin
               Line(Border*3,Offset+LineHeight div 2,
                   Border*3+2,Offset+LineHeight div 2-2);
               Line(Border*3,Offset+LineHeight div 2,
                   Border*3+2,Offset+LineHeight div 2+2);
            end;
            5 : begin
               Line(Border*3+LineWidth,Offset+LineHeight div 2,
                   Border*3+LineWidth-2,Offset+LineHeight div 2-2);
               Line(Border*3+LineWidth,Offset+LineHeight div 2,
                   Border*3+LineWidth-2,Offset+LineHeight div 2+2);
            end;
            6 : begin
               Line(Border*3,Offset+LineHeight div 2,
                   Border*3+2,Offset+LineHeight div 2-2);
               Line(Border*3,Offset+LineHeight div 2,
                   Border*3+2,Offset+LineHeight div 2+2);
               Line(Border*3+LineWidth,Offset+LineHeight div 2,
                   Border*3+LineWidth-2,Offset+LineHeight div 2-2);
```

```
                Line(Border*3+LineWidth,Offset+LineHeight div 2,
                    Border*3+LineWidth-2,Offset+LineHeight div 2+2);
            end;
      end
   end
   else begin
      SetLineStyle(i,0,NormWidth);
      Line(Border*3,Offset+LineHeight div 2,Border*3+LineWidth,
          Offset+LineHeight div 2);
   end;
   Inc(Offset,LineHeight);
end;
ShowMouse;
LeftArrow := False;
RightArrow := False;
while not MouseButtonPressed(LeftButton) do ;
GetMouseCoords(mx,my);
Offset := Border;
for i := 0 to MaxLineStyles-1 do begin
   if (MouseInBox(LineWindowX+Border*3,Offset-LineHeight div 2,LineWindowX+
      Border*3+LineWidth,LineWindowY+Offset+LineHeight div 2,mx,my)) then begin
      HideMouse;
      GUnpop;
      ShowMouse;
      if i >= 4 then begin
         case i of
            4 : LeftArrow := True;
            5 : RightArrow := True;
            6 :  begin
               LeftArrow := True;
               RightArrow := True;
               end;
         end;
         i := SolidLn;
      end;
      SetLineStyle(i,0,NormWidth);
      GlobalLineStyle := i;
      Exit;
   end;
   Inc(Offset,LineHeight);
```

```
    end;
  HideMouse;
  GUnpop;
  ShowMouse;
end;

{$F-}

procedure SetupScreen;
{ Set up the environment for the CAD program }
var
  h, w, i, x, FillWidth, Offset, Space: integer;
  FillType, ColorWidth, MaxColors, FillColor: integer;

begin
{ Draw a main menu bar across the top of the screen. Each of the words in the menu bar
  will act as an icon that can be selected. Some of the words, such as Text and Line,
  will cause pull-down menus to appear if the user clicks on them.
}
  HideMouse;
  h := TextHeight('H') + 2;
  Rectangle(0, 0, GetMaxX, h);
  OutTextXY(2, 2, 'Grid  Text  Line  Clear  Quit');
  Space := TextWidth('  ');
  Offset := 2;
  AddObject(IconObj,'g',Offset,0,Offset+TextWidth('Grid'),
            TextHeight('Grid'),ToggleGrid);
  Inc(Offset, TextWidth('Grid') + Space);
  AddObject(IconObj,'t',Offset,0,Offset+TextWidth('Text'),
            TextHeight('Text'), ChangeFont);
  TextWindowX := Offset;
  TextWindowY := TextHeight('Text') + Border;
  Inc(Offset, TextWidth('Text') + Space);
  AddObject(IconObj, 'l', Offset, 0, Offset+TextWidth('Line'),
      TextHeight('Line'), ChangeLineStyle);
  LineWindowX := Offset;
  LineWindowY := TextHeight('Line') + Border;
  Inc(Offset, TextWidth('Line') + Space);
  AddObject(IconObj, 'c', Offset, 0, Offset+TextWidth('Clear'),
        TextHeight('Clear'), DeleteAllObjects);
  Inc(Offset, TextWidth('Clear') + Space);
```

```
AddObject(IconObj,'q',Offset,0,Offset+TextWidth('Quit'),TextHeight('Quit'),Quit);
{ Now draw the icons on the left-hand side of the screen }
ReadIcon(0, h, 'hand.icn');
AddObject(IconObj,'s',0,h,IconW*2,h+IconH,MoveObject);
ReadIcon(IconW*2,h,'pointer.icn');
AddObject(IconObj,'c',IconW*2,h,IconW*4,h+IconH,SelectObject);
ReadIcon(0,h+IconH,'line.icn');
AddObject(IconObj,'d',0,h+IconH,IconW*2,h+2*IconH,DrawLine);
ReadIcon(IconW*2,h+IconH,'letter.icn');
AddObject(IconObj,'p',IconW*2,h+IconH,IconW*4,h+2*IconH,TypeText);
ReadIcon(0,h+2*IconH,'fillpoly.icn');
AddObject(IconObj,'s',0,h+2*IconH,IconW*2,h+3*IconH,DrawFillPoly);
ReadIcon(IconW*2,h+2*IconH,'circle.icn');
AddObject(IconObj,'r',IconW*2,h+2*IconH,IconW*4,h+3*IconH,DrawCircle);
ReadIcon(0,h+3*IconH,'duplicat.icn');
AddObject(IconObj,'p',0,h+3*IconH,IconW*2,h+4*IconH,Duplicate);
ReadIcon(IconW*2,h+3*IconH,'scissor.icn');
AddObject(IconObj,'x',IconW*2,h+3*IconH,IconW*4,h+4*IconH,DeleteObj);
ReadIcon(0,h+4*IconH,'flipfrnt.icn');
AddObject(IconObj,'e',0,h+4*IconH,IconW*2,h+5*IconH,FlipToFront);
ReadIcon(IconW*2,h+4*IconH,'flipback.icn');
AddObject(IconObj,'x',IconW*2,h+4*IconH,IconW*4,h+5*IconH,FlipToBack);
ReadIcon(0,h+5*IconH,'rotate.icn');
AddObject(IconObj,'e',0,h+5*IconH,IconW*2,h+6*IconH,RotateObj);
{ Create the fill pattern box on the lower portion of the screen }
FillWidth := (GetMaxX-1-IconW*4+2) div (NumFillsWide+1);
GlobalFillColor := GetMaxColor; { Start fill color at maxcolor }
GlobalDrawColor := GlobalFillColor;
FillType := 0;
x := IconW * 4 + 2 + FillWidth;
for i := 0 to NumFillsWide-1 do begin
   SetFillStyle(FillType, GlobalFillColor);
   Bar3D(x,GetMaxY-FillHeight*2,x+FillWidth,GetMaxY-FillHeight,0,False);
   Inc(FillType);
   Inc(x,FillWidth);
end;
Rectangle(IconW*4+2, GetMaxY-FillHeight*2, GetMaxX, GetMaxY);
AddObject(FillObj, 'w', IconW*4+2+FillWidth, GetMaxY-FillHeight*2,
          GetMaxX, GetMaxY-FillHeight, ChangeFillPattern);
GlobalFillStyle := SolidFill;
```

```
   MaxColors := GetMaxColor;
   ColorWidth := (GetMaxX-1-IconW*4+2-FillWidth) div (MaxColors + 1);
   FillColor := 0;
   x := IconW * 4 + 2 + FillWidth;
   for i := 0 to MaxColors do begin
      SetFillStyle(SolidFill, FillColor);
      Bar3D(x, GetMaxY-FillHeight, x+ColorWidth, GetMaxY, 0, False);
      Inc(FillColor);
      Inc(x, ColorWidth);
   end;
   AddObject(FillObj, 'z', IconW*4+2+FillWidth,
        GetMaxY-FillHeight, GetMaxX, GetMaxY, ChangeFillColor);
   SetLineStyle(SolidLn, 0, ThickWidth);
   SetFillStyle(GlobalFillStyle, GlobalFillColor);
   Bar3D(IconW*4+2+2,GetMaxY-FillHeight*2+2,IconW*4+2+FillWidth-2,GetMaxY-2, 0, False);
   AddObject(FillObj, 'y', IconW*4+2+2, GetMaxY-FillHeight*2+2,
           IconW*4+FillWidth-2, GetMaxY, ChangeDrawColor);
   SetLineStyle(SolidLn, 0, NormWidth);
   { Create the drawing window }
   wl := IconW*4+2 + 1;  wt := h+2 + 1;
   wr := GetMaxX - 1;    wb := GetMaxY-FillHeight*2-2 - 1;
   Rectangle(IconW*4+2, h+2, GetMaxX, GetMaxY-FillHeight*2-2);
   { Set WORLD coordinate to screen coordinate relationship }
   Set_Window(0.0, 6.0, 0.0, 6.0);
   Set_ViewPort(wl, wr, wt, wb);
   GlobalFillStyle := SolidFill;
   GlobalLineStyle := SolidLn;
   GlobalTextStyle := SmallFont;
   GridOn := True;
   DrawGrid;
   LeftArrow := False;
   RightArrow := False;
   { Set the font here to what you want to use for the dimension labels.
     On the CGA in medium resolution mode, small font is good.
   }
   SetTextStyle(GlobalTextStyle, HorizDir, 1);
   ShowMouse;
end;


begin
   InitGraph(GDriver, GMode, '');
```

```
    GetAspectRatio(XAsp, YAsp);
    AspectRatio := XAsp / YAsp;
    t := InitMouse;
    SetupScreen;
    repeat
        c := WaitForInput(LeftButton);
        AnyToProcess(c);
    until False;
end.
```

• Listing 12.2

```
unit CadDraw;
{ Drawing and object support routines for CAD program }
interface
uses
    Graph, MousePac, Matrix, GText;
const
    NumGObjects = 50;              { Maximum number of graphics objects allowed }
    Txt = 0;                       { These four values are the types of }
    Poly = 1;                      { graphics objects that are supported }
    Crcle = 2;                     { in Cad.Pas }
    Ln = 3;
    ArrowSize = 3;                 { The arrow heads are this long }
    MaxPolySize = 40;
    { Objects in the drawing window are stored in structures of this type }
type
    WorldPoint = record
        x, y: real;
    end;
    GraphicsObj = record
        ObjType: integer;          { Type of graphics object }
        Left, Top: integer;        { Pixels boundaries of object in }
        Right, Bottom: integer;    { full-screen coordinates }
        NumPoints: integer;        { Number of coordinate pairs in points }
        Points: WorldArray;        { Objects saved in WORLD coordinates }
        Str: string;               { Text strings are saved here }
        DrawColor: integer;        { Color used in object }
        LineStyle: integer;        { Line style used in object }
```

```
    FillStyle: integer;            { Fill style used in object }
    FillColor: integer;            { Fill color used in object }
    TextStyle: integer;            { Textstyle used in string }
    LeftArrow: boolean;            { True if left arrow on line }
    RightArrow: boolean;           { True if right arrow needed on lines }
  end;
var
  GObjects: array[1..NumGObjects] of GraphicsObj;
  CurrentObj, NextObj: integer;
  LeftArrow, RightArrow: boolean;
  wl, wr, wt, wb: integer;         { Bounds of the drawing window }
  GlobalFillColor: integer;        { Drawing parameters used by program }
  GlobalDrawColor: integer;
  GlobalFillStyle: integer;
  GlobalLineStyle: integer;
  GlobalTextStyle: integer;
  GridOn: boolean;


procedure ToggleGrid;              { These routines are available }
procedure DrawGrid;                { to programs that "use" this unit }
procedure DeleteAllObjects;
procedure DeleteObj;
procedure MoveObject;
procedure SelectObject;
procedure ClearWorkArea;
procedure DrawFillPoly;
procedure DrawCircle;
procedure DrawLine;
procedure FlipToBack;
procedure FlipToFront;
procedure Duplicate;
procedure RotateObj;
procedure MallocError;
procedure AddGObject(ObjType, Left, Top, Right, Bottom: integer;
                 NumPoints: integer; PCPoly: PCArray; S: string);


implementation
procedure DisplayText(Obj: integer);
{ Draws a text object. Characters are stored in string field of GObjects structure.
  Number of character is in NumPoints field.

}
```

```
var
   j, x, y: integer;
   OldText: TextSettingsType;

begin
   WorldToPC(GObjects[Obj].Points[1].x,GObjects[Obj].Points[1].y,x,y);
   MoveTo(x-wl,y-wt);
   GetTextSettings(OldText);
   SetTextStyle(GObjects[Obj].TextStyle,HorizDir,1);
   HideMouse;
   for j := 1 to Length(GObjects[Obj].Str) do
      GWriteCh(GObjects[Obj].Str[j]);
   ShowMouse;
   SetTextStyle(OldText.Font,OldText.Direction,OldText.CharSize);
end;


procedure DisplayPolygon(Obj: integer);
var
   x, y, j: integer;
   Points: array[1..MaxPolySize] of PointType;

begin
   for j := 1 to GObjects[Obj].NumPoints do begin
      WorldToPC(GObjects[Obj].Points[j].x,GObjects[Obj].Points[j].y, x, y);
      Points[j].x := x - wl;  Points[j].y := y - wt;
   end;
   HideMouse;
   FillPoly(GObjects[Obj].NumPoints,Points);
   ShowMouse;
end;


procedure DisplayCircle(Obj: integer);
var
   x, y, Temp, Radius: integer;

begin
   WorldToPC(GObjects[Obj].Points[1].x,GObjects[Obj].Points[1].y, x, y);
   WorldToPC(GObjects[Obj].Points[2].x,0.0,Radius,Temp);
   HideMouse;
   Circle(x-wl,y-wt,Radius);
```

```
    ShowMouse;
end;

procedure DrawArrows(x1,y1,x2,y2: integer; LeftArrow,RightArrow: boolean);
{ Draw arrows to the line if needed. The mouse is already hidden when this routine
  is called.
}
var
    ArrowHead: PCArray;                   { An arrow is made from two lines offset }
                                          { 45 degrees on each side of the line }
    Angle: real;                          { Calculated slope of line }

    function ArcTan2(y, x: integer): real;
    { Returns the Arctan of y/x. }
    begin
       if x = 0 then begin
          if y < 0 then ArcTan2 := - Pi / 2.0
             else ArcTan2 := Pi / 2.0
       end
       else if x < 0 then ArcTan2 := ArcTan(y/x) + Pi
          else ArcTan2 := ArcTan(y/x);
    end;

begin
    if LeftArrow then begin          { Draw an arrow at the start of the line }
       ArrowHead[1].x := x1 + ArrowSize - wl;
       ArrowHead[1].y := y1 - ArrowSize - wt;
       ArrowHead[2].x := x1 - wl;
       ArrowHead[2].y := y1 - wt;
       ArrowHead[3].x := x1 + ArrowSize - wl;
       ArrowHead[3].y := y1 + ArrowSize - wt;
       Angle := ArcTan2(y2-y1,x2-x1) * 180.0 / Pi;
       PCTranslatePoly(3, ArrowHead, -x1+wl, -y1+wt);
       PCRotatePoly(3, ArrowHead, Angle);
       PCTranslatePoly(3, ArrowHead, x1-wl, y1-wt);
       DrawPoly(3, ArrowHead);           { Draw the arrow }
    end;
    if RightArrow then begin         { Draw an arrow at the end of the line }
       ArrowHead[1].x := x2 - ArrowSize - wl;
       ArrowHead[1].y := y2 - ArrowSize - wt;
```

```
      ArrowHead[2].x := x2 - wl;
      ArrowHead[2].y := y2 - wt;
      ArrowHead[3].x := x2 - ArrowSize - wl;
      ArrowHead[3].y := y2 + ArrowSize - wt;
      Angle :=  ArcTan2(y2-y1,x2-x1) * 180.0 / Pi;
      PCTranslatePoly(3, ArrowHead, -x2+wl, -y2+wt);
      PCRotatePoly(3, ArrowHead, angle);
      PCTranslatePoly(3, ArrowHead, x2-wl, y2-wt);
      DrawPoly(3, ArrowHead);  { Draw the arrow }
   end
end;


procedure DisplayLine(Obj: integer);
var
   x1, y1, x2, y2: integer;

begin
   WorldToPC(GObjects[Obj].Points[1].x,GObjects[Obj].Points[1].y,x1,y1);
   WorldToPC(GObjects[Obj].Points[2].x,GObjects[Obj].Points[2].y,x2,y2);
   HideMouse;
   Line(x1-wl,y1-wt,x2-wl,y2-wt);
   DrawArrows(x1,y1,x2,y2,GObjects[Obj].LeftArrow,GObjects[Obj].RightArrow);
   ShowMouse;
end;


procedure DisplayObject(Obj: integer);
{ Determine which object to display and call appropriate routine to display it }
begin
   { Set the drawing parameters for the object }
   SetLineStyle(GObjects[Obj].LineStyle,GObjects[Obj].DrawColor,NormWidth);
   SetFillStyle(GObjects[Obj].FillStyle,GObjects[Obj].FillColor);
   SetColor(GObjects[Obj].DrawColor);
   case GObjects[Obj].ObjType of                    { Draw the object }
     Txt : DisplayText(Obj);
     Poly: DisplayPolygon(Obj);
     Crcle: DisplayCircle(Obj);
     Ln: DisplayLine(Obj);
   end
end;
```

```
procedure DisplayAllObjects;
{ Display all of the graphics objects in the drawing window }
var
   Obj: integer;

begin
   SetViewPort(wl,wt,wr,wb,True);              { Use drawing window }
   SetWriteMode(CopyPut);
   for Obj := 1 to NextObj-1 do
      DisplayObject(Obj);
   SetViewPort(0,0,GetMaxX,GetMaxY,True);   { Restore viewport }
end;


procedure GetPolyBounds(NumPoints: integer; var PCpoly: PCArray;
                        var Left, Top, Right, Bottom: integer);
{ From the list of points in PCpoly, return its bounding box in Left, Top,
  Right, Bottom
}
var
   i: integer;

begin
   Left := GetMaxX;   Top := GetMaxY;
   Right := 0;        Bottom := 0;
   for i := 1 to NumPoints do begin
      if PCpoly[i].x < Left then Left := PCpoly[i].x;
      if PCpoly[i].x > Right then Right := PCpoly[i].x;
      if PCpoly[i].y < Top then Top := PCpoly[i].y;
      if PCpoly[i].y > Bottom then Bottom := PCpoly[i].y;
   end
end;


procedure DrawGrid;
{ Draws a background grid in the drawing window using a six horizontal and vertical
  dotted lines
}
var
   i, j, x, y, SaveColor: integer;
   SaveLine: LineSettingsType;
```

```
begin
   SaveColor := GetColor;
   GetLineSettings(SaveLine);
   SetLineStyle(DottedLn,0,NormWidth);
   SetColor(GetMaxColor);
   HideMouse;
   for j := 1 to 5 do begin
      WorldToPC(0.0,0.0+j,x,y);
      Line(wl,y,wr,y);
   end;
   for i := 1 to 5 do begin
      WorldToPC(0.0+i,0.0,x,y);
      Line(x,wt,x,wb);
   end;
   ShowMouse;
   SetLineStyle(SaveLine.LineStyle,SaveLine.Pattern,SaveLine.Thickness);
   SetColor(SaveColor);
end;

procedure ClearWorkArea;
{ Clear the drawing window and draw a grid if GridOn is True }
begin
   SetViewPort(wl,wt,wr,wb,True);
   HideMouse;
   ClearViewPort;
   ShowMouse;
   SetViewPort(0,0,GetMaxX,GetMaxY,True);
   if GridOn then DrawGrid;
end;

procedure ToggleGrid;
{ Turn grid off if on, otherwise redraw screen with grid }
begin
   if GridOn then GridOn := False
      else GridOn := True;
   ClearWorkArea;
   DisplayAllObjects;
end;

procedure AddGObject(ObjType, Left, Top, Right, Bottom: integer;
         NumPoints: integer; PCPoly: PCArray; S: string);
```

```
{ Adds an object to the list of graphic objects in the drawing window. ObjType
  indicates the type of object. It can be Txt, Poly, Crcle, or Ln. The next four
  values specify the bounds of the object that are used when trying to select the
  object from the screen using the mouse. The last two arguments
  specify the coordinates that make up the object.
}
var
  i: integer;
  WorldPoly: WorldArray;


begin
  GObjects[NextObj].ObjType := ObjType;          { Save various values }
  GObjects[NextObj].Left := Left;                { about the object in }
  GObjects[NextObj].Top := Top;                  { the next location }
  GObjects[NextObj].Right := Right;              { in the object list }
  GObjects[NextObj].Bottom := Bottom;
  GObjects[NextObj].NumPoints := NumPoints;
  GObjects[NextObj].DrawColor := GlobalDrawColor;
  GObjects[NextObj].LineStyle := GlobalLineStyle;
  GObjects[NextObj].FillColor := GlobalFillColor;
  GObjects[NextObj].FillStyle := GlobalFillStyle;
  GObjects[NextObj].TextStyle := GlobalTextStyle;
  GObjects[NextObj].LeftArrow := LeftArrow;
  GObjects[NextObj].RightArrow := RightArrow;
  if ObjType = Txt then begin                    { Object is a text string }
    { Save top-left coordinate of text location in index
      location 0 and 1 of the points array
    }
    PCToWorld(Left,Top,GObjects[NextObj].Points[1].x,GObjects[NextObj].Points[1].y);
    GObjects[NextObj].Str := S;
    Inc(GObjects[NextObj].Right,TextWidth(GObjects[NextObj].Str));
    Inc(GObjects[NextObj].Bottom,TextHeight(GObjects[NextObj].Str));
  end
  else begin
    PCPolyToWorldPoly(NumPoints,PCPoly,WorldPoly);
    CopyWorldPoly(NumPoints,WorldPoly,GObjects[NextObj].Points);
  end;
  CurrentObj := NextObj;
  Inc(NextObj);
end;
```

```pascal
procedure DeleteObj;
{ Delete an object from the graphics object list. Make the next object in the GObjects
  array the CurrentObj. Update the screen after deleting the object from the list, by
  erasing it and then redrawing all remaining objects.
}
var
  i: integer;
  Temp: GraphicsObj;

begin
  if NextObj <= 1 then Exit;                    { Empty list -- no objects }
  Temp := GObjects[CurrentObj];
  for i := CurrentObj to NextObj-1 do
    GObjects[i] := GObjects[i+1];
  GObjects[i] := Temp;
  Dec(NextObj);
  if (CurrentObj >= NextObj) and (CurrentObj > 1) then
    Dec(CurrentObj);                            { Deleted last, but not first }
  ClearWorkArea;
  DisplayAllObjects;
end;

procedure DeleteAllObjects;
{ Delete all objects in the object list by setting the index pointers to the beginning
  of the object list and clearing the drawing window
}

begin
  NextObj := 1;
  CurrentObj := 1;
  ClearWorkArea;
end;

procedure DrawFillPoly;
var
  x1, y1, x2, y2, OldX2, OldY2: integer;
  Left, Right, Top, Bottom, i, NumPoints: integer;
  Points: PCArray;
  t: boolean;
```

```
begin
    SetViewPort(wl,wt,wr,wb,True);                          { Use drawing window }
    SetLineStyle(GlobalLineStyle,0,NormWidth);
    SetColor(GlobalDrawColor);
    SetFillStyle(GlobalFillStyle,GlobalFillColor);
    while True do begin
        while not MouseButtonPressed(LeftButton) do ;
        GetMouseCoords(x1,y1);
        if (x1 < wl) or (y1 < wt) or (y1 > wb) then begin
            SetViewPort(0,0,GetMaxX,GetMaxY,True);
            SetWriteMode(CopyPut);
            Exit;
        end;
        SetWriteMode(XorPut);
        NumPoints := 1;
        Points[1].x := x1 - wl;  Points[1].y := y1 - wt;
        x2 := x1;                y2 := y1;
        OldX2 := x2;             OldY2 := y2;
        repeat
            GetMouseCoords(x2,y2);
            if (x2 <> OldX2) or (y2 <> OldY2) then begin
                HideMouse;
                { Erase current rubber-banding line and draw a new one }
                Line(x1-wl,y1-wt,OldX2-wl,OldY2-wt);
                Line(x1-wl,y1-wt,x2-wl,y2-wt);
                ShowMouse;
                OldX2 := x2;  OldY2 := y2;
            end;
            if MouseButtonReleased(LeftButton) then begin
                HideMouse;                       { Fix this polygon edge }
                SetWriteMode(CopyPut);
                Line(x1-wl,y1-wt,OldX2-wl,OldY2-wt);
                ShowMouse;
                SetWriteMode(XorPut);
                x1 := x2;  y1 := y2;      { Start next polygon edge at this edge's end }
                Inc(NumPoints);
                Points[NumPoints].x := x2 - wl;  Points[NumPoints].y := y2 - wt;
            end;
            t := MouseButtonPressed(LeftButton);     { Clear button press flags }
            t := MouseButtonPressed(RightButton);
```

```
      until MouseButtonReleased(RightButton);
      Inc(NumPoints);
      Points[NumPoints].x := x2 - wl;
      Points[NumPoints].y := y2 - wt;
      SetWriteMode(CopyPut);
      HideMouse;
      FillPoly(NumPoints,Points);                { Draw the filled polygon }
      ShowMouse;
      { Save polygon in full-screen coordinates as an object }
      for i := 1 to NumPoints do begin
        Inc(Points[i].x,wl);
        Inc(Points[i].y,wt);
      end;
      GetPolyBounds(NumPoints,Points,Left,Top,Right,Bottom);
      AddGObject(Poly,Left,Top,Right,Bottom,NumPoints,Points,'');
   end
end;


procedure MallocError;
{ Memory allocation error -- exit program }
begin
   CloseGraph;
   writeln('Not enough memory to run program.');
   halt(1);
end;


procedure DrawCircle;
var
   CLeft, CTop, CRight, CBottom: integer;
   Radius, AbsRadius, AddRadius, Ignore: integer;
   CenterX, CenterY, OldLeft, OldTop: integer;
   Covered: pointer;
   Points: PCArray;
   Size: word;

begin
   Size := ImageSize(wl,wt,wr,wb);
   GetMem(Covered, Size);
   if Covered = Nil then MallocError;
   SetLineStyle(GlobalLineStyle,0,NormWidth);
```

```
SetColor(GlobalDrawColor);
SetViewPort(wl,wt,wr,wb,True);
while True do begin
   while not MouseButtonPressed(LeftButton) do ;
   GetMouseCoords(CenterX,CenterY);
   { Initialize mouse movement counter to zero }
   GetMouseMovement(Ignore,Ignore);
   if (CenterX <= wl) or (CenterY <= wt) or (CenterY >= wb) then begin
      SetViewPort(0,0,GetMaxX,GetMaxY,True);
      FreeMem(Covered,Size);
      Exit;
   end;
   Radius := 0; OldLeft := CenterX;  OldTop := CenterY;
   HideMouse;
   GetImage(OldLeft-wl,OldTop-wt,OldLeft-wl,OldTop-wt,Covered^);
   ShowMouse;
   while not MouseButtonReleased(LeftButton) do begin
      GetMouseMovement(AddRadius,Ignore);
      Inc(Radius,AddRadius);
      AbsRadius := Abs(Radius);
      if CenterX-AbsRadius < wl then CLeft := wl
         else CLeft := CenterX - AbsRadius;
      if CenterX+AbsRadius > wr then CRight := wr
         else CRight := CenterX + AbsRadius;
      if CenterY-AbsRadius < wt then CTop := wt
         else CTop := CenterY - AbsRadius;
      if CenterY+AbsRadius > wb then CBottom := wb
         else CBottom := CenterY + AbsRadius;
      if AddRadius <> 0 then begin
         HideMouse;
         PutImage(OldLeft-wl,OldTop-wt,Covered^,CopyPut);
         GetImage(CLeft-wl,CTop-wt,CRight-wl,CBottom-wt,Covered^);
         if AbsRadius <> 0 then Circle(CenterX-wl,CenterY-wt,AbsRadius);
         ShowMouse;
         OldLeft := CLeft;  OldTop := CTop;
      end
   end;
   Points[1].x := CenterX;    Points[1].y := CenterY;
   Points[2].x := AbsRadius;  Points[2].y := 1;
   AddGObject(Crcle,CenterX-AbsRadius,
```

```
         CenterY-Round(AbsRadius*AspectRatio),CenterX+AbsRadius,
         CenterY+Round(AbsRadius*AspectRatio),2,Points,'');
   end
end;

procedure DrawLine;
{ The function to interactively draw lines. It adds each line as a separate object to
  the list of graphics objects in the drawing window.
}
var
   x1, x2, y1, y2: integer;
   OldX2, OldY2, Left, Right, Top, Bottom: integer;
   Points: PCArray;

begin
   SetViewPort(wl,wt,wr,wb,True);
   SetLineStyle(GlobalLineStyle,0,NormWidth);
   SetColor(GlobalDrawColor);
   while True do begin
     while not MouseButtonPressed(LeftButton) do ;
     GetMouseCoords(x1,y1);
     if (x1 < wl) or (y1 < wt) or (y1 > wb) then begin
        SetViewPort(0,0,GetMaxX,GetMaxY,True);
        SetWriteMode(CopyPut);
        Exit;
     end;
     SetWriteMode(XorPut);
     MoveTo(x1-wl,y1-wt);
     OldX2 := x1;   OldY2 := y1;
     while not MouseButtonReleased(LeftButton) do begin
        GetMouseCoords(x2,y2);
        if (x2 <> OldX2) or (y2 <> OldY2) then begin
          HideMouse;
          Line(x1-wl,y1-wt,OldX2-wl,OldY2-wt);
          Line(x1-wl,y1-wt,x2-wl,y2-wt);
          ShowMouse;
          OldX2 := x2;   OldY2 := y2;
        end
     end;
     SetWriteMode(CopyPut);
```

```
      HideMouse;
      Line(x1-wl,y1-wt,x2-wl,y2-wt);
      DrawArrows(x1,y1,x2,y2,LeftArrow,RightArrow);
      ShowMouse;
      Points[1].x := x1;   Points[1].y := y1;
      Points[2].x := x2;   Points[2].y := y2;
      GetPolyBounds(2,Points,Left,Top,Right,Bottom);
      AddGObject(Ln,Left-3,Top-3,Right+3,Bottom+3,2,Points,'');
   end
end;

procedure FlipToBack;
{ Move the current object to the back by copying it to the head of the object list.
  After the operation the same object is the current object.
}
var
   i: integer;
   Temp: GraphicsObj;

begin
   if NextObj <= 1 then Exit;
   Temp := GObjects[CurrentObj];
   for i := CurrentObj downto 2 do
     GObjects[i] := GObjects[i-1];
   GObjects[1] := Temp;
   CurrentObj := 1;
   ClearWorkArea;
   DisplayAllObjects;
end;

procedure FlipToFront;
{ Move the object to the front by putting it at the end of the object list and
  redrawing all of the objects. After the operation the same object is the current
  object.
}
var
   i: integer;
   Temp: GraphicsObj;

begin
   if NextObj <= 1 then Exit;
```

```pascal
    Temp := GObjects[CurrentObj];
    for i := CurrentObj to NextObj-2 do
      GObjects[i] := GObjects[i+1];
    GObjects[NextObj-1] := Temp;
    CurrentObj := NextObj-1;
    ClearWorkArea;
    DisplayAllObjects;
end;


procedure Duplicate;
{ Duplicate CurrentObj. Make a copy of the current object in the drawing window. New
  object appears offset from the original by translating it (.1, .1). Make sure the
  object is saved in WORLD coordinates.
}
var
  i, NumPoints, Left, Top, Right, Bottom: integer;
  Points: PCArray;


begin
  { Make sure there are objects in list and it is not text }
  { and the object list is not full }
  if (NextObj <= 1) or (GObjects[CurrentObj].ObjType = Txt) or
     (NextObj > NumGObjects) then Exit;
  GObjects[NextObj].ObjType := GObjects[CurrentObj].ObjType;
  GObjects[NextObj].NumPoints := GObjects[CurrentObj].NumPoints;
  GObjects[NextObj].DrawColor := GObjects[CurrentObj].DrawColor;
  GObjects[NextObj].LineStyle := GObjects[CurrentObj].LineStyle;
  GObjects[NextObj].FillColor := GObjects[CurrentObj].FillColor;
  GObjects[NextObj].FillStyle := GObjects[CurrentObj].FillStyle;
  GObjects[NextObj].NumPoints := GObjects[CurrentObj].NumPoints;
  GObjects[NextObj].LeftArrow := GObjects[CurrentObj].LeftArrow;
  GObjects[NextObj].RightArrow := GObjects[CurrentObj].RightArrow;
  NumPoints := GObjects[CurrentObj].NumPoints;
  CopyWorldPoly(NumPoints,GObjects[CurrentObj].Points, GObjects[NextObj].Points);
  CurrentObj := NextObj;              { New object becomes current object }
  Inc(NextObj);
  case GObjects[CurrentObj].ObjType of
    Ln, Poly : begin
        WorldTranslatePoly(NumPoints,GObjects[CurrentObj].Points,0.1,0.1);
        WorldPolyToPCPoly(NumPoints,GObjects[CurrentObj].Points,Points);
```

```
            GetPolyBounds(NumPoints,Points,Left,Top,Right,Bottom);
            if GObjects[CurrentObj].ObjType = Ln then begin
               Dec(Left,3); Inc(Right,3);
               Dec(Top,3);  Inc(Bottom,3);
            end;
        end;
     Crcle: begin
        WorldTranslatePoly(1, GObjects[CurrentObj].Points, 0.1, 0.1);
        WorldPolytoPCpoly(NumPoints,GObjects[CurrentObj].Points,Points);
        Left := Points[1].x - Points[2].x;                    { CenterX - Radius }
        Top := Points[1].y - Round(Points[2].x * AspectRatio);  { CenterY - Radius }
        Right := Points[1].x + Points[2].x;                   { CenterX + Radius }
        Bottom := Points[1].y + Round(Points[2].x * AspectRatio); { CenterY + Radius }
     end;
  end;
  GObjects[CurrentObj].Left := Left;
  GObjects[CurrentObj].Top := Top;
  GObjects[CurrentObj].Right := Right;
  GObjects[CurrentObj].Bottom := Bottom;
  SetViewPort(wl,wt,wr,wb,True);
  SetWriteMode(CopyPut);
  DisplayObject(CurrentObj);
  SetViewPort(0,0,GetMaxX,GetMaxY,True);
end;

procedure RotateObj;
{ Rotate the current object about its center point }
var
  x, y, Left, Top, Right, Bottom: integer;
  CenterX, CenterY: real;
  Points: PCArray;

begin
  if NextObj <= 1 then Exit;     { Make sure there are objects in the list }
  x := (GObjects[CurrentObj].Left + GObjects[CurrentObj].Right) div 2;
  y := (GObjects[CurrentObj].Top + GObjects[CurrentObj].Bottom) div 2;
  PCToWorld(x, y, CenterX, CenterY);
  case GObjects[CurrentObj].ObjType of
     Ln, Poly :begin
       WorldTranslatePoly(GObjects[CurrentObj].NumPoints,
                      GObjects[CurrentObj].Points,-CenterX,-CenterY);
```

```
            WorldRotatePoly (GObjects [CurrentObj] .NumPoints,
               GObjects [CurrentObj] .Points, 45.0) ;
            WorldTranslatePoly (GObjects [CurrentObj] .NumPoints,
               GObjects [CurrentObj] .Points, CenterX, CenterY) ;
            WorldPolyToPCpoly (GObjects [CurrentObj] .NumPoints,
               GObjects [CurrentObj] .Points, Points) ;
            GetPolyBounds (GObjects [CurrentObj] .NumPoints, Points, Left, Top, Right, Bottom) ;
            if GObjects [CurrentObj] .ObjType = Ln then begin
               Dec (Left, 3) ;   Inc (Right, 3) ;
               Dec (Top, 3) ;    Inc (Bottom, 3) ;
            end;
            GObjects [CurrentObj] .Left := Left;
            GObjects [CurrentObj] .Top := Top;
            GObjects [CurrentObj] .Right := Right;
            GObjects [CurrentObj] .Bottom := Bottom;
            end;
      end;
   ClearWorkArea;
   DisplayAllObjects;
end;


procedure MarkObject (Obj: integer) ;
{ Highlight an object by drawing a dashed rectangle around its border }
var
   SaveLine: LineSettingsType;
   SaveColor: integer;

begin
   SaveColor := GetMaxColor;
   GetLineSettings (SaveLine) ;
   SetWriteMode (XorPut) ;
   SetColor (GetMaxColor) ;
   SetLineStyle (DashedLn, 0, NormWidth) ;
   HideMouse;
   Rectangle (GObjects [Obj] .Left-wl, GObjects [Obj] .Top-wt,
      GObjects [Obj] .Right-wl, GObjects [Obj] .Bottom-wt) ;
   ShowMouse;
   SetLineStyle (SaveLine.LineStyle, SaveLine.Pattern, SaveLine.Thickness) ;
   SetColor (SaveColor) ;
end;
```

```
procedure SelectObject;
{ Select an object by encompassing it with a rectangle. An object can be selected by
  pressing the Left mouse button while over the object. To select another object in
  the same region, click the mouse button again. On exiting, the currently marked
  object becomes the CurrentObj which is used in all succeeding operations.
}
var
   x, y, TestObj, LastObj: integer;
   Done: boolean;

begin
   if NextObj <= 1 then Exit;                    { Make sure there are objects in the list }
   SetViewPort(wl,wt,wr,wb,True);
   TestObj := CurrentObj + 1;
   if TestObj >= NextObj then TestObj := 1;
   MarkObject(CurrentObj);                       { Mark object }
   LastObj := CurrentObj;
   while True do begin
     while not MouseButtonPressed(LeftButton) do ;
     GetMouseCoords(x,y);
     if (x <= wl) or (y <= wt) or (y > wb) then begin
       MarkObject(CurrentObj);                   { Unmark object }
       SetViewPort(0,0,GetMaxX,GetMaxY,True);
       SetWriteMode(XorPut);
       Exit;
     end;
     while not MouseButtonReleased(LeftButton) do ;
     GetMouseCoords(x,y);
     Done := False;
     repeat
     if (((x>=GObjects[TestObj].Left) and (x<=GObjects[TestObj].Right)) or
         ((x>=GObjects[TestObj].Right) and (x<=GObjects[TestObj].Left))) and
        (((y>=GObjects[TestObj].Top) and (y<=GObjects[TestObj].Bottom)) or
         ((y>=GObjects[TestObj].Bottom) and (y<=GObjects[TestObj].Top))) then begin
       MarkObject(LastObj);                       { Unmark object }
       MarkObject(TestObj);                       { Mark object }
       LastObj := TestObj;
       CurrentObj := TestObj;
       Inc(TestObj);
       if TestObj >= NextObj then TestObj := 1;
```

```
          Done := True;
       end
       else begin
          Inc(TestObj);
          if TestObj >= NextObj then TestObj := 1;
       end;
     until (TestObj = CurrentObj) or Done;
     end
end;

procedure MoveObject;
{ Move the current object (CurrentObj) by pressing the Left mouse button while over
  the object and then dragging the mouse. Once the mouse button is released the object
  is translated to its new coordinates and the screen is redrawn.
}
var
   x, y, OldX, OldY, MoveX, MoveY, MovedX, MovedY: integer;
   Left, Top, Right, Bottom, SaveColor: integer;
   OriginalX, OriginalY, TranslateX, TranslateY: real;
   SaveLine: LineSettingsType;

begin
   if NextObj <= 1 then Exit;    { Make sure objects are in the list }
   SetViewPort(wl,wt,wr,wb,True);
   MarkObject(CurrentObj);
   SaveColor := GetColor;
   GetLineSettings(SaveLine);
   SetLineStyle(DashedLn,0,NormWidth);
   SetColor(GetMaxColor);
   { Should assume already marked in fact it must be marked }
   Left := GObjects[CurrentObj].Left;
   Top := GObjects[CurrentObj].Top;
   Right := GObjects[CurrentObj].Right;
   Bottom := GObjects[CurrentObj].Bottom;
   while True do begin
     while not MouseButtonPressed(LeftButton) do ;
     GetMouseCoords(x, y);
     if (x <= wl) or (y <= wt) or (y > wb) then begin
       MarkObject(CurrentObj);
       SetViewPort(0,0,GetMaxX,GetMaxY,True);
```

```
        SetLineStyle(SaveLine.LineStyle,SaveLine.Pattern,SaveLine.Thickness);
        SetColor(SaveColor);
        SetWriteMode(CopyPut);
        Exit;
    end;
    SetWriteMode(XorPut);
    GetMouseCoords(x, y);
    if (x>=Left) and (x<=Right) and (y>=Top) and (y<=Bottom) then begin
        MovedX := 0;  MovedY := 0;
        OldX := x;    OldY := y;
        while not MouseButtonReleased(LeftButton) do begin
            GetMouseCoords(x, y);
            MoveX := x - OldX;  MoveY := y - OldY;
            if (MoveX <> 0) or (MoveY <> 0) then begin
                HideMouse;
                Rectangle(Left-wl,Top-wt,Right-wl,Bottom-wt);
                Inc(Left,MoveX);    Inc(Right,MoveX);
                Inc(Top,MoveY);     Inc(Bottom,MoveY);
                Inc(MovedX,MoveX);  Inc(MovedY,MoveY);
                Rectangle(Left-wl,Top-wt,Right-wl,Bottom-wt);
                ShowMouse;
                OldX := x;  OldY := y;
            end
        end;
        PCToWorld(GObjects[CurrentObj].Left,
                  GObjects[CurrentObj].Top,OriginalX,OriginalY);
        PCToWorld(Left,Top,TranslateX,TranslateY);
        TranslateX := TranslateX - OriginalX;
        TranslateY := TranslateY - OriginalY;
        case GObjects[CurrentObj].ObjType of
            Ln, Poly : WORLDtranslatepoly(GObjects[CurrentObj].NumPoints,
                       GObjects[CurrentObj].Points,TranslateX,TranslateY);
            Txt, Crcle: WORLDtranslatepoly(1,GObjects[CurrentObj].Points,
                       TranslateX,TranslateY);
        end;
        Inc(GObjects[CurrentObj].Left,MovedX);
        Inc(GObjects[CurrentObj].Top,MovedY);
        Inc(GObjects[CurrentObj].Right,MovedX);
        Inc(GObjects[CurrentObj].Bottom,MovedY);
        ClearWorkArea;
```

```
      DisplayAllObjects;
      { Restore settings for object box, because DisplayAllObjects }
      { may have changed them }
      SetViewPort(wl,wt,wr,wb,True);
      SetLineStyle(DashedLn,0,NormWidth);
      SetColor(GetMaxColor);
      SetWriteMode(XorPut);
      MarkObject(CurrentObj);
    end
    else
      while not MouseButtonReleased(LeftButton) do ;
  end
end;


begin
  NextObj := 1;           { Initialize index pointers to Graphics }
  CurrentObj := 1;        { object list }
end.
```

13

Three-Dimensional Graphics

In this chapter we will explore three-dimensional graphics. Our goal is to develop a graphics package that displays three-dimensional wire-frame objects from any vantage point. We'll begin by defining some of the terminology used in three-dimensional graphics. Next, we'll discuss various components of the three-dimensional viewing package and explain how it works. Finally, we'll give you a few sample three-dimensional object files for you to display and suggest some extensions you might try adding to the program.

Adding the Third Dimension

In the preceding chapters we have been limiting our discussion to programs with two-dimensional objects. For example, in the CAD program presented in Chapter 12, the objects that we created were all defined in world coordinates using only the x and y dimensions. This gave us objects with specific heights and widths. Now we will add depth to our objects by including a third dimension, z.

In the following sections, we'll develop a program called **ThreeD.Pas** that will allow us to view wire-frame objects as shown in Figure 13.1. In order to develop the three-dimensional program, however, we'll be developing a handful of new tools and explore various issues related to three-dimensional graphics.

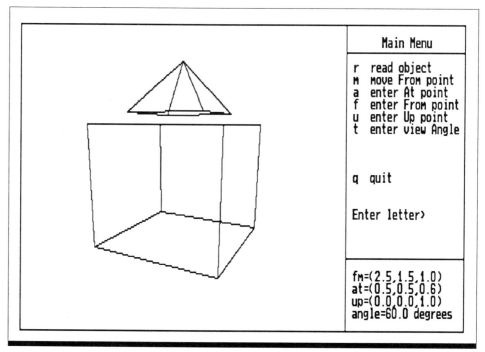

Figure 13.1. The environment of the ThreeD.Pas program

Using a Camera Model

Generating a scene of a three-dimensional object is similar to taking a picture of an object with a camera in that they both create a two-dimensional view of a three-dimensional object. In fact, we'll be using a camera model to help us specify how objects are to be displayed.

Basically, we will assume that we are using a pinhole camera where everything in view is in focus. In addition, we'll assume that the camera is located somewhere in world coordinates at a location called the *from* point, and that it is looking directly toward a location called the *at* point. The camera model also specifies a viewing angle that acts much like a lens in that it defines how much of the scene will actually be displayed. Finally, our camera model includes a parameter called an *up* vector that defines the orientation of the viewing plane with relation to the coordinate system. Figure 13.2 illustrates each of these viewing parameters as they appear in world coordinates.

Actually, since we are interested in how objects appear with respect to the screen, we will be using another coordinate system, called *eye coordinates*. It has

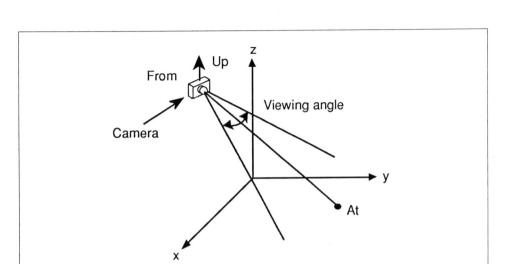

Figure 13.2. The viewing parameters in world coordinates

its origin at the *from* point and the *at* point on the positive z axis as shown in Figure 13.3. The name "eye coordinates" comes from the fact that coordinate system is oriented with respect to the viewer—in our case the camera.

Finally, our camera model uses a perspective projection of all objects. In other words, we will project all objects onto the viewing plane along rays that extend out from the from point as shown in Figure 13.4. Because we will be using perspective projection objects will appear distorted as illustrated in Figure 13.1. This gives a natural sensation of depth.

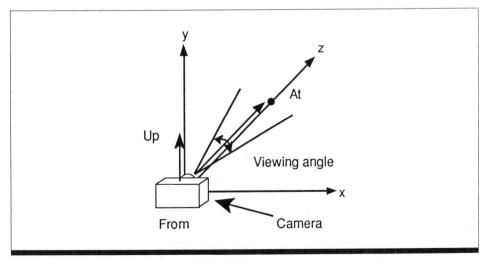

Figure 13.3. The viewing parameters as they appear in eye coordinates

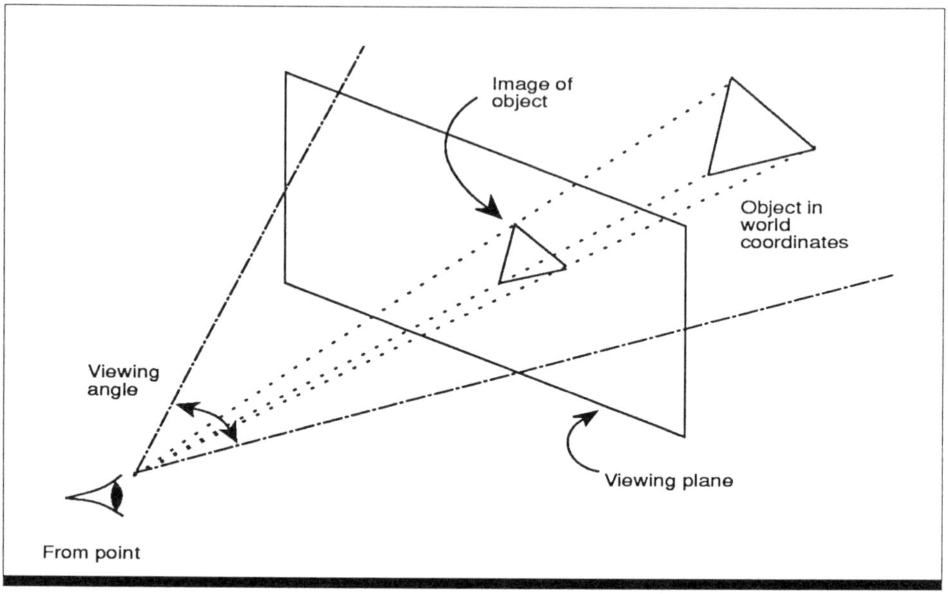

Figure 13.4. Projecting a three-dimensional object into two dimensions

Objects in Three Dimensions

To keep things simple, we'll be dealing exclusively with three-dimensional wire-frame objects like that shown in Figure 13.1. Consequently, each object is represented by a series of three-dimensional coordinate triplets that are connected by line segments to create the outlines of an object being displayed.

Each point, or *vertex*, as it is usually called, is specified as an (x,y,z) coordinate in world coordinates. The goal of a three-dimensional graphics package, therefore, is to transform these coordinates into two-dimensional screen coordinates and then connect them with line segments. This process requires numerous steps that we'll cover in the next several sections.

Transforming from World to Eye Coordinates

As mentioned before, we'll represent each object as a series of connected vertices where each point specifies an x, y, and z value in world coordinates. However, we are not so much interested in where these points are located in world coordinates as we are in where they are with respect to the viewer—the eye coordinates. In fact, one of our first steps will be to transform object points from the world coordinate system to an eye coordinate system. By doing this we will easily be able to determine what objects are in view and how they appear.

Unfortunately, transforming a three-dimensional point from world coordinates to eye coordinates is not a trivial matter. Basically, what we need to do is to apply a series of transforms that can align the world coordinate system with the eye coordinate system. This can be broken up into the following steps:

1. Translate the world coordinate system so that the location of the viewer (the from point) is at the origin of the eye coordinate system
2. Rotate x axis so that the at point will lie on the positive z axis
3. Rotate y axis similarly
4. Rotate z axis

At this point, objects can be projected onto the viewing plane which is situated along the z axis. The projection process is described in greater detail later.

Although the steps just described can be used to transform between world and eye coordinates, they require numerous mathematical operations. On a PC these calculations can make a system too slow to be practical.

Instead, we'll use a vector algebra technique that reduces the number of mathematical operations that must be made. The process begins, as before, by translating the viewer in the world coordinate system to the origin of the eye coordinates; however, to align the coordinate axes, we will not use a series of rotations. Instead, we'll replace these three steps by one as shown in Figure 13.5. We won't derive the matrix expression V that replaces the rotations described above, but let's look at what it is doing. Essentially, the matrix V specifies how the unit vectors A_1, A_2, and A_3 can be aligned to the eye coordinate system as Figure 13.6 illustrates. Therefore, by applying the matrix V shown in Figure 13.5 after translating the world coordinates, we can transform all world coordinates to eye coordinates.

In addition, we will apply the matrix:

$$\begin{bmatrix} D & 0 & 0 & 0 \\ 0 & D & 0 & 0 \\ 0 & 0 & 1 & 0 \\ 0 & 0 & 0 & 1 \end{bmatrix}$$

where D is

$$\frac{1}{\tan(viewing\_angle/2)}$$

Step 1: Translate points by $(-f_x, -f_y, -f_z)$

Step 2: Multiply result from Step 1 by V_{4x4} where

$$V = \begin{bmatrix} a_{1x} & a_{2x} & a_{3x} & 0 \\ a_{1y} & a_{2y} & a_{3y} & 0 \\ a_{1z} & a_{2z} & a_{3z} & 0 \\ 0 & 0 & 0 & 1 \end{bmatrix}$$

$(A_1) \quad (A_2) \quad (A_3)$

To compute A_1, A_2, and A_3, let A' be a vector where $A' = A - F$

and

$$A_3 = \frac{A'}{\| A' \|} \qquad A_1 = \frac{A' \times U}{\| A' \times U \|}$$

$$A_2 = \frac{(A' \times U) \times A'}{\| (A' \times U) \times A' \|}$$

Figure 13.5. Operations to convert world to eye coordinates

after converting points to eye coordinates. The purpose of this matrix operation is to adjust the scene according to the viewing angle so that the object extends between the lines $y=z$, $y=-z$, $x=z$, and $x=-z$ and as a result makes clipping a lot easier. We'll look at this presently.

Fortunately, we can combine the operations shown in Figure 13.5 and the matrix shown above into a handful of equations. These resulting equations are used in the procedure **TransformSeg** to transform lines from world to eye coordinates in the three-dimensional program. Many of the values in **TransformSeg** are calculated in the routine **SetEye** which must be called prior to transforming any line segments. You'll notice that **SetEye** performs most of the calculations outlined in Figure 13.5. Since many of these operations are vector operations, we have included a separate utility called **Vector.Pas** (see Listing 13.1) to perform these operations. A list of the routines in **Vector.Pas** is shown in Table 13.1.

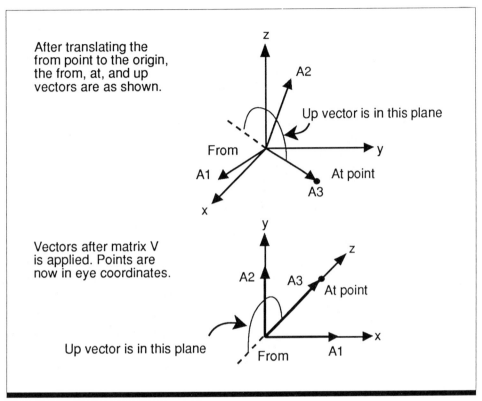

After translating the from point to the origin, the from, at, and up vectors are as shown.

Up vector is in this plane

From

A1

At point

A3

Vectors after matrix V is applied. Points are now in eye coordinates.

Up vector is in this plane

From

At point

A3

A2

A1

Figure 13.6. Vectors before and after the vector V is applied

Table 13.1. Routines in Vector.Pas

Routine	Description
Subtract	Subtracts two vectors
Divide	Divides a vector by a scalar
Mag	Returns the magnitude of a vector
Cross	Calculates the cross product of two vectors

Clipping in Three Dimensions

Thus far we have been fortunate in that the BGI has provided us with clipping algorithms to handle clipping of graphics figures as they are displayed. However, now we must develop our own code to clip objects in three dimensions. Essentially, what we want to do is to ignore all objects that do not project onto the projection plane or clip edges of objects that extend out beyond the border of the viewport on the projection plane.

To accomplish this, **ThreeD.Pas** (see Listing 13.2) includes the routines **Clip3D** and **Code** which clip three-dimensional line segments in *eye coordinates* to a *viewing pyramid* as shown in Figure 13.7. Note that all objects within the viewing pyramid will be projected onto the viewing plane and displayed on the screen. This is done at the end of **Clip3D**. We'll get back to this, but first, let's look at how the clipping algorithm works.

After we transform a line segment from world coordinates to eye coordinates, we'll pass it through the clipping process which begins by calling **Clip3D**. Then **Clip3D** calls **Code** to determine on which side of the viewing pyramid the endpoints of the line segment fall. If one of the coordinates falls outside of the viewing pyramid, an appropriate bit in the variable **C** is set to indicate that the line may cross the edge of the viewing pyramid and must be clipped. The clipping is done in **Clip3D** by calculating where the line segment intersects the viewing pyramid. This intersection is then used as the new endpoint of the line and the resulting line is passed through the process again until it is broken up into a segment that is completely within the viewing pyramid. Then the line is displayed. As mentioned before, this is done at the end of **Clip3D**. Let's now examine how this is done.

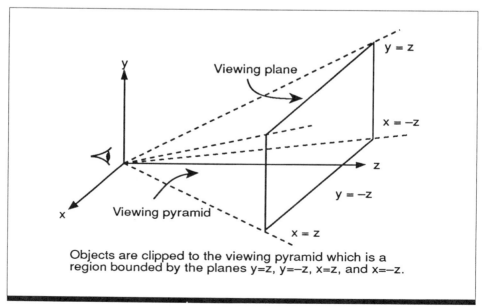

Objects are clipped to the viewing pyramid which is a region bounded by the planes y=z, y=−z, x=z, and x=−z.

Figure 13.7. The viewing pyramid is used to clip objects in three dimensions

Perspective Projection

All objects in the three-dimensional viewing program are displayed using perspective projection. The basic idea is to project all objects onto the viewing plane as shown earlier in Figure 13.4. Note that objects will be displayed only if a line connecting them and the viewer passes through the viewport on the viewing plane. Objects that do not intersect this region are clipped as described in the last section.

Assuming that we have a line segment that is within the viewport on the viewing plane, how do we know what size to draw it? Fortunately, we can use a simple geometric property of similar triangles as shown in Figure 13.8. Based on these values, a point (x,y,z) maps to $(x/z,y/z)$ on the viewing plane. This point is then converted to PC coordinates using the routine **WorldToPC** as is done in **Clip3D**. Note that we need to make sure z is not zero, so that we don't divide by zero! Once the points are converted to PC screen coordinates, the line segment is displayed using **Line**.

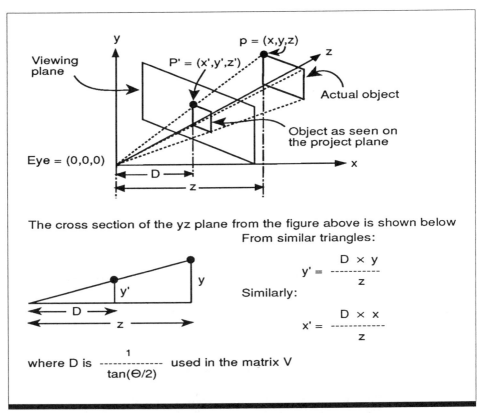

Figure 13.8. Projecting objects onto the viewing plane

Object Files

The three-dimensional viewing program does not let you interactively create objects like the CAD program in Chapter 12. Instead, **ThreeD.Pas** is intended to merely display three-dimensional objects. Therefore, the program reads the objects that it displays from object files. This is done in the function **Read3DObject**.

In order to save space and simplify modifications, three-dimensional objects are saved in a special format. The file begins with a header that specifies the number of vertices in the object and the number of connections between the vertices, respectively. After the header is a list of the vertices that make up the object where each vertex is represented by three **real** values that correspond to the x, y, and z values of the point in world coordinates. The number of vertices in this list is specified by the first value in the header as mentioned earlier. Next is a series of indexes into this list of vertices that specifies which vertices should be connected to which ones. Essentially, they describe how the points read in above should be connected to draw the object. For example, if our object is a triangle with the vertices:

$$(0.0, 1.0, 0.1) \quad \text{vertex 1}$$
$$(1.0, 0.0, 0.1) \quad \text{vertex 2}$$
$$(1.0, 0.1, 1.0) \quad \text{vertex 3}$$

and we wanted them connected in this order, then the list of connections would appear as

    1 2 3 -1

This indicates that vertex 1 is connected to vertex 2 which is connected to vertex 3 which in turn is connected to vertex 1. Note that the last value is negative. This is a special marker in the connection list that indicates that the object has ended or at least that this face of the object is complete. The number of connections that must be read in is specified by the second number in the file header.

The function **Read3DObject** reads these values into the global variables listed in Table 13.2. Later, the values in **Points** are accessed according to the order specified in the array **Connect** to draw the object.

Displaying a Three-Dimensional Object

Now that we know how a three-dimensional object is read from a file, let's see how **Points** and **Connect** are used to display an object. This is accomplished by the nested **while** loops in the routine **View** as shown next.

Table 13.2 Global variables which store objects

Variable	Description
Vertices	Number of vertices in object
Length	Number of connections in vertices
Points	Array of vertices that are stored in world coordinates
Connect	Array of indexes into the **Points** array which specify how the vertices are to be connected

```
i := 1;
while i < Length do begin
   Start := i;
   Inc(i);
   while Connect[i] > 0 do begin
      TransformSeg(Points[Connect[i1]],Points[Connect[i]]);
      Inc(i);
   end;
   TransformSeg(Points[Connect[i-1]],Points[-Connect[i]]);
   TransformSeg(Points[-Connect[i]],Points[Connect[Start]]);
   Inc(i);
end;
```

The outer **while** loop sequences through the list of vertex connections contained in **Connect**. Remember that the negative values in **Connect** are used to denote the end of a series of connected points. The inner **while** loop sequences through the list of connected vertices until a negative marker is found. For each pair of connected points, **TransformSeg** is called as shown below to transform the two points and display a line connecting them if it is visible:

```
Transformseg(Points[Connect[i-1]],Points[Connect[i]]);
```

When a negative value is reached in the **Connect** array, the current pair of points is displayed and then the last point is connected back to the first by the lines:

```
TransformSeg(Points[Connect[i-1]],Points[-Connect[i]]);
TransformSeg(Points[-Connect[i]],Points[Connect[Start]]);
```

This process continues until all values in the **Connect** are used.

Setting the Viewing Parameters

There are several parameters that must be set for the three-dimensional viewing package to work properly. For instance, before an object can be viewed the **From**, **At**, **Up**, and **Angle** variables must be all set. To simplify things, each of these are given default values or are designed to automatically calculate values that can be used. For example, the *at* location is set by **SetAt** each time a new object is read in. It calls the routine **MinMax** to determine the bounds of the object and then it sets the *at* point to the middle of the object. Similarly, **SetFrom** sets the *from* point so that it is far enough away from the object that the entire object will appear in the viewport.

In addition, there are several routines that allow you to interactively specify each of these values. They can be changed by selecting the appropriate options in the program menu.

Using the Three-Dimensional Program

After you have your three-dimensional program compiled, you're ready to try displaying an object. In the next section, there are file listings for two three-dimensional objects. To display each of these objects, first type the data into two separate files and give them the names as indicated. The files can then be read by the three-dimensional program by selecting the read file command which is done by typing the letter r. A pop-up window will appear in the center of the screen prompting you to enter the name of the file to be read. You should type this file name and press return. Once you press return, the object file is read and the object is displayed. That's all there is to it.

You can experiment with each of the viewing parameters by selecting the appropriate menu options from the screen. For instance, to change the *from* point, you can type the letter f which will cause a pop-up window to prompt you for a new *from* point. For example, try changing the *from* point to the world coordinates (2, 2, 2) or even (0, 0, 0). The latter value should take you inside the object!

One other area that you might want to try experimenting with is changing the viewing angle. This can be done in two different ways. One approach is to select the t menu option which prompts you for a new viewing angle. Alternatively, you can incrementally change the viewing angle by selecting the z menu option. It will incrementally change the viewing angle whenever you press the up or down arrow keys on the keypad. This will effectively allow you to zoom in and out on the object. There is a similar incremental function, selectable through the m option, that lets you move the *from* point along the x axis.

Sample Objects

This section lists two data files for objects that you should try with your three-dimensional program. Here is the data file, called **Test1.Dat** for the object shown in Figure 13.9:

```
13 40
1.0    1.0    1.0    1.0    1.0    0.0
1.0    0.0    0.0    1.0    0.0    1.0
0.0    1.0    1.0    0.0    1.0    0.0
0.0    0.0    0.0    0.0    0.0    1.0
0.8    0.2    1.1    0.8    0.8    1.1
0.2    0.8    1.1    0.2    0.2    1.1
0.5    0.5    1.5
1   5   8   -4   5   6   7   -8   6   2   3   -7   1   4   3   -2
8   7   3   -4   6   5   1   -2   9   10   -13   10   11   -13   11   12
-13   12   9   -13   12   11   10   -9
```

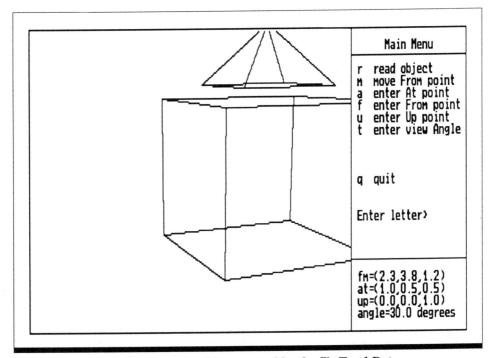

Figure 13.9. The object created by the file Test1.Dat

The next data file, called **Test2.Dat**, generates the object shown in Figure 13.10.

```
38 54
1.0   1.0   1.0   1.0   1.0   0.0
1.0   0.0   0.0   1.0   0.0   1.0
0.0   1.0   1.0   0.0   1.0   0.0
0.0   0.0   0.0   0.0   0.0   1.0
0.25  0.0   0.25  0.25  0.0   0.75
0.75  0.0   0.75  0.75  0.0   0.7
0.3   0.0   0.7   0.3   0.0   0.5
0.6   0.0   0.5   0.6   0.0   0.45
0.3   0.0   0.45  0.3   0.0   0.25
1.0   0.3   0.2   1.0   0.3   0.3
1.0   0.6   0.3   1.0   0.6   0.5
1.0   0.3   0.5   1.0   0.3   0.8
1.0   0.7   0.8   1.0   0.7   0.7
1.0   0.4   0.7   1.0   0.4   0.6
1.0   0.7   0.6   1.0   0.7   0.2
0.4   0.3   1.0   0.4   0.6   1.0
0.2   0.6   1.0   0.2   0.7   1.0
0.8   0.7   1.0   0.8   0.6   1.0
0.5   0.6   1.0   0.5   0.3   1.0
1   5   8   -4   5   6   7   -8   6   2   3   -7   1   4   3   -2
8   7   3   -4   6   5   1   -2   9   10   11   12   13   14   15   16
17   -18   19   20   21   22   23   24   25   26   27   28   29   -30   31   32   33   34
35   36   37   -38
```

Extending the Program

There are several enhancements that you might try adding to the three-dimensional viewing package. Probably, the first thing you might want to try adding is putting in routines to interactively draw three-dimensional objects. The difficulty here is in coming up with a clean way of interactively drawing the object. You will probably want to use several viewports that show the object at different perspectives in order to give yourself a good idea of the object that you are drawing.

Another possible extension of the program would be to add color, or fill patterns to the objects that are drawn. Since our file format groups edges of the objects into faces by use of the **Connect** array, you can try using **FillPoly** to draw the faces of the object rather than drawing them a line at a time. This way you'll be able to make

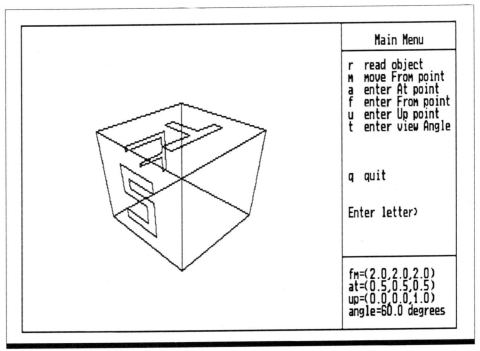

Figure 13.10. The object created by Test2.Dat

the faces of the objects solid. However, you'll find that the order that faces are painted is important in drawing the object correctly. Generally, this becomes a problem of hidden surface removal. For the ambitious, this is probably the direction you want to try.

• Listing 13.1

```
unit Vector;
{ A set of vector manipulation routines used in ThreeD.Pas }
interface
uses
   Graph;
type
   VectorType = record
      x, y, z: real;
   end;
```

```
{ These functions are available to external routines }
function Mag(V: VectorType): real;
procedure Subtract(V1, V2: VectorType; var S: VectorType);
procedure Cross(V1, V2: VectorType; var C: VectorType);
procedure Divide(V: VectorType; Num: real; var D: VectorType);


implementation
function Mag(V: VectorType): real;
{ Calculate the magnitude of the vector }
begin
   Mag := Sqrt(v.x * v.x + v.y * v.y + v.z * v.z);
end;


procedure Subtract(V1, V2: VectorType; var S: VectorType);
{ Subtract two vectors }
begin
   S.x := V1.x - V2.x;
   S.y := V1.y - V2.y;
   S.z := V1.z - V2.z;
end;


procedure Cross(V1, V2: VectorType; var C: VectorType);
{ Cross multiply the two vectors v1 and v2 }
begin
   C.x := V1.y * V2.z - V2.y * V1.z;
   C.y := V1.z * V2.x - V2.z * V1.x;
   C.z := V1.x * V2.y - V2.x * V1.y;
end;


procedure Divide(V: VectorType; Num: real; var D: VectorType);
{ Divide the scalar number into the vector v }
begin
   if Num <> 0 then begin
     D.x := V.x / Num;
     D.y := V.y / Num;
     D.z := V.z / Num;
   end
   else begin
     CloseGraph;
     writeln('Divide by 0 in Matrix Divide Operation');
```

```
        halt(1);
    end
end;

end.
```

• Listing 13.2

```
program ThreeD;
{ ThreeD.Pas -- wire-frame viewing package. Displays wire-frame three-dimensional
  views of objects using perspective projection. Objects are read from files and
  displayed according to the settings of the from, at, up, and viewing angle.
}
uses
    Graph, GText, Matrix, GPopPac, Vector, Crt;
const
    NumConnections = 100;
    NumVertices = 150;
    PCL: integer = 1;              { Border of viewing region on }
    PCR: integer = 469;            { the screen }
    PCT: integer = 1;
    PCB: integer = 198;
    UpKey = #72;
    DownKey = #80;
    prompt: string[14] = 'Enter letter> ';
var
    a, b, c, d, DVal: real;
    From, At, Up: VectorType;      { Viewing parameters }
    Angle: real;                   { The viewing angle }
    a1, a2, a3: VectorType;        { Used in three-dimensional transform }
    Connect: array[1..NumConnections] of integer;   { Vertex connections }
    Points: array[1..NumVertices] of VectorType;     { Vertices }
    Length: integer;               { Number of vertex connections }
    Vertices: integer;             { Number of vertices }
    ObjXMin, ObjXMax: real;        { Extent of three-dimensional object }
    ObjYMin, ObjYMax: real;
    ObjZMin, ObjZMax: real;
    TFrom: real;                   { Controls from-at point distance }
    OffsX, OffsY, OffsZ: real;     { Transform variables }
```

```
      Dist: VectorType;                          { Distance to from-at point }
      MaxX, MaxY: integer;                       { Size of the screen }
      ch: char;


   function MaxOf(Val1, Val2: real): real;
   begin
      if Val1 > Val2 then MaxOf := Val1
         else MaxOf := Val2;
   end;


   procedure WorldToPC(xw, yw: real; var xpc, ypc: integer);
   { Converts clipped world coordinates to screen coordinates }
   begin
      xpc := Round(a * xw + b);
      ypc := Round(c * yw + d);
   end;


   procedure Init3DGraphics;
   { Must be called before program begins main execution }
   const
      GDriver: integer = Detect;
   var
      GMode: integer;
   begin
      InitGraph(GDriver, GMode, '');
      MaxX := GetMaxX;  MaxY := GetMaxY;
      a := (PCR - PCL) / (1 + 1);               { Set viewport/window }
      b := PCL - a * (-1);                      { mapping variables }
      c := (PCT - PCB) / (1 + 1);
      d := PCB - c * (-1);
      { Set default values for From, At, Up vectors }
      From.x := 1.0;  From.y := 0.0;  From.z := 0.0;
      At.x := 0.0;    At.y := 0.0;    At.z := 0.0;
      Up.x := 0.0;    Up.y := 0.0;    Up.z := 1.0;
      Angle := ToRadians(60);                   { Use 60 degree viewing angle }
      TFrom := 1.0;
   end;


   procedure MinMax;
   { Return the minimum and maximum values in the point array for the x, y, and z values
   }
```

```
var
   i: integer;

begin
   ObjXMin := 32000;  ObjYMin := 32000;  ObjZMin := 32000;
   ObjXMax := -32000; ObjYMax := -32000; ObjZMax := -32000;
   for i := 1 to Vertices do begin
      if Points[i].x > ObjXMax then ObjXMax := Points[i].x
         else if Points[i].x < ObjXMin then
      ObjXMin := Points[i].x;
      if Points[i].y > ObjYMax then ObjYMax := Points[i].y
         else if Points[i].y < ObjYMin then
      ObjYMin := Points[i].y;
      if Points[i].z > ObjZMax then ObjZMax := Points[i].z
         else if Points[i].z < ObjZMin then
      ObjZMin := Points[i].z;
   end
end;

procedure SetAt;
{ Routine to provide a default value for the at point. It is set to the midpoint of
  the extents of the object.
}
begin
   MinMax;
   At.x := (ObjXMin + ObjXMax) / 2.0;
   At.y := (ObjYMin + ObjYMax) / 2.0;
   At.z := (ObjZMin + ObjZMax) / 2.0;
end;

procedure SetFrom;
{ Routine that provides a default value for the from point. It is dependent on the at
  point and the view angle.
}
const
   Width: real = 1.73205;                  { Ratio used to determine from point }
                                           { It is based on the size of the object }
begin
   From.x := At.x + (ObjXMax-ObjXMin) / 2.0 + Width *
   MaxOf((ObjZMax-ObjZMin)/2.0, (ObjYMax-ObjYMin)/2.0);
```

```
    From.y := At.y;  From.z := At.z;
end;


procedure SetEye;
{ There must be a valid object in the Points array before calling this function. It
  sets up the various variables used in transforming an object from world to eye
  coordinates.
}
var
  AMarkMag, TempMag: real;
  Temp: VectorType;

begin
  DVal := Cos(Angle/2.0) / Sin(Angle/2.0);
  Subtract(At, From, Dist);
  AMarkMag := Mag(Dist);
  Divide(Dist, AMarkMag, a3);
  Cross(Dist, Up, Temp);
  TempMag := Mag(Temp);
  Divide(Temp, TempMag, a1);
  Cross(a1, a3, Temp);
  TempMag := Mag(Temp);
  Divide(Temp, TempMag, a2);
  OffsX := -a1.x * From.x - a1.y * From.y - a1.z * From.z;
  OffsY := -a2.x * From.x - a2.y * From.y - a2.z * From.z;
  OffsZ := -a3.x * From.x - a3.y * From.y - a3.z * From.z;
end;


procedure Clip3D(x1, y1, z1, x2, y2, z2: real);
{ Clips line segment in three-dimensional coordinates to the viewing pyramid }
const
  NoEdge: byte      = $00;
  LeftEdge: byte    = $01;
  RightEdge: byte   = $02;
  BottomEdge: byte  = $04;
  TopEdge: byte     = $08;

var
  c, c1, c2: byte;
  x, y, z, t: real;
  xpc1, ypc1, xpc2, ypc2: integer;
```

```
function Code(x, y, z: real): byte;
{ Returns a code specifying which edge in the viewing pyramid
  was crossed. There may be more than one.
}
var
  c: byte;

begin
  c := NoEdge;
  if x < -z then c := c or LeftEdge;
  if x > z then c := c or RightEdge;
  if y < -z then c := c or BottomEdge;
  if y > z then  c := c or TopEdge;
  Code := c;
end;

begin
  c1 := Code(x1, y1, z1);
  c2 := Code(x2, y2, z2);
  while (c1 <> NoEdge) or (c2 <> NoEdge) do begin
    if (c1 and c2) <> NoEdge then Exit;
    c := c1;
    if c = NoEdge then c := c2;
    if (c and LeftEdge) = LeftEdge then begin
      { Crosses left edge }
      t := (z1 + x1) / ((x1 - x2) - (z2 - z1));
      z := t * (z2 - z1) + z1;
      x := -z;
      y := t * (y2 - y1) + y1;
    end
    else if (c and RightEdge) = RightEdge then begin
      { Crosses right edge }
      t := (z1 - x1) / ((x2 - x1) - (z2 - z1));
      z := t * (z2 - z1) + z1;
      x := z;
      y := t * (y2 - y1) + y1;
    end
    else if (c and BottomEdge) = BottomEdge then begin
      { Crosses bottom edge }
      t := (z1 + y1) / ((y1 - y2) - (z2 - z1));
```

```
        z := t * (z2 - z1) + z1;
        x := t * (x2 - x1) + x1;
        y := -z;
      end
    else if (c and TopEdge) = TopEdge then begin
      { Crosses top edge }
      t := (z1 - y1) / ((y2 - y1) - (z2 - z1));
      z := t * (z2 - z1) + z1;
      x := t * (x2 - x1) + x1;
      y := z;
    end;
    if c = c1 then begin
      x1 := x;  y1 := y;  z1 := z;
      c1 := Code(x, y, z);
    end
    else begin
      x2 := x;  y2 := y;  z2 := z;
      c2 := Code(x, y, z);
    end
  end;
  if z1 <> 0 then begin
    WorldToPc(x1/z1, y1/z1, xpc1, ypc1);
    WorldToPc(x2/z2, y2/z2, xpc2, ypc2);
  end
  else begin
    WorldToPc(x1, y1, xpc1, ypc1);
    WorldToPc(x2, y2, xpc2, ypc2);
  end;
  { Draw the line after it has been clipped }
  Line(xpc1, ypc1, xpc2, ypc2);
end;

procedure TransformSeg(v1, v2: VectorType);
{ Transform the segment connecting the two vectors into the viewing plane. 3DClip
  clips and draws the line if visible.
}
var
  x1, y1, z1, x2, y2, z2: real;

begin
  x1 := (v1.x * a1.x + a1.y * v1.y + a1.z * v1.z + offsx) * DVal;
```

```
    y1 := (v1.x * a2.x + a2.y * v1.y + a2.z * v1.z + offsy) * DVal;
    z1 :=   v1.x * a3.x + a3.y * v1.y + a3.z * v1.z + offsz;
    x2 := (v2.x * a1.x + a1.y * v2.y + a1.z * v2.z + offsx) * DVal;
    y2 := (v2.x * a2.x + a2.y * v2.y + a2.z * v2.z + offsy) * DVal;
    z2 :=   v2.x * a3.x + a3.y * v2.y + a3.z * v2.z + offsz;
    Clip3D(x1, y1, z1, x2, y2, z2);
end;


procedure View;
{ Index through the Points array which contains the vertices of the object
  and display them as you go. This will draw out the object.
}
var
   i, Start: integer;

begin
   i := 1;
   while i < Length do begin
      Start := i;
      Inc(i);
      while Connect[i] > 0 do begin
         TransformSeg(Points[Connect[i-1]], Points[Connect[i]]);
         Inc(i);
      end;
      TransformSeg(Points[Connect[i-1]], Points[-Connect[i]]);
      TransformSeg(Points[-Connect[i]], Points[Connect[Start]]);
      Inc(i);
   end;
end;


procedure Clear_Viewport;
{ Clear the viewport }
begin
   SetViewPort(PCL,PCT,PCR,PCB,True);
   ClearViewPort;
   SetViewPort(0,0,GetMaxX,GetMaxY,True);
end;


function VectorToStr(V: VectorType): string;
{ Text output routine used to write vector values to graphics screen }
```

```
begin
   VectorToStr := RealToStr(V.x, 3, 1) + ' ' +
   RealToStr(V.y, 3, 1) + ' ' + RealToStr(V.z, 3, 1);
end;

procedure ShowValues;
{ Show the from, at, up, and angle values in a window on
  the bottom right of the screen
}
begin
   { Erase the area where the values are to be written }
   SetFillStyle(SolidFill,0);
   Bar3D(PCR+1,19*8,GetMaxX,GetMaxY,0,False);
   GWriteXY(60*8,19*8+TextHeight('F'),'fm='+VectorToStr(From));
   GWriteXY(60*8,19*8+2*TextHeight('F'),'at='+VectorToStr(At));
   GWriteXY(60*8,19*8+3*TextHeight('F'),'up='+VectorToStr(Up));
   GWriteXY(60*8,19*8+4*TextHeight('F'),
           'angle='+RealToStr(Angle/0.017453293, 3, 1)+' degrees');
end;

procedure PopupError(Message: string);
{ Pop-up an error message }
const
   Press: string[25] = ' Press ENTER to Continue ';
var
   Width: integer;
   ch: char;
   t: boolean;

begin
   Width := TextWidth(Message);
   if Width < TextWidth(Press) then Width := TextWidth(Press);
   t := GPopup(MaxX div 2,MaxY div 2+20,MaxX div 2+width+10,
               MaxY div    2+20+3*TextHeight('H'),SolidLn,GetMaxColor,SolidFill,0);
   GWriteXY(5,5,Message);
   GWriteXY(5,5+TextHeight('H'),Press);
   ch := ReadKey;
   GUnpop;
end;
```

```
function GetVector(Title, Message: string; var Nu: VectorType): boolean;
begin
   if GPopup(MaxX div 2 - TextWidth(Title) div 2-5,
      MaxY div 2-4*TextHeight('H'),MaxX div 2+TextWidth(Title) div 2+5,
      MaxY div 2+4*TextHeight('H'),SolidLn,GetMaxColor,SolidFill,0) then begin
      GWriteXY(5,5,Title);
      GWriteXY(5,5+2*TextHeight('H'),'Enter x y z coordinates');
      GWriteXY(5,5+3*TextHeight('H'),Message);
      GWriteXY(5,5+4*TextHeight('X'),'x> ');
      GWriteXY(5,5+5*TextHeight('X'),'y> ');
      GWriteXY(5,5+6*TextHeight('X'),'z> ');
      MoveTo(5+TextWidth('x> '),5+4*TextHeight('H'));
      if GReadReal(Nu.x) then begin
         MoveTo(5+TextWidth('y> '),5+5*TextHeight('H'));
         if GReadReal(Nu.y) then begin
            MoveTo(5+TextWidth('z> '),5+6*TextHeight('H'));
            if GReadReal(Nu.z) then begin
               GetVector := True;
               Exit;
            end;
         end
      end
   end;
   GetVector := False
end;

procedure GetFrom;
{ Interactively specify the from coordinates. It cannot be the same as the at point. }
var
   Nu: VectorType;

begin
   if GetVector('    Change the From Point     ',
                'of new From point.', Nu) then begin
      GUnpop;
      if (Nu.x = At.x) and (Nu.y = At.y) and (Nu.z = At.z) then begin
         PopupError(' Invalid From Point ');
         Exit;
      end;
      From.x := Nu.x;  From.y := Nu.y;  From.z := Nu.z;
```

```
      Clear_Viewport;
      SetEye;
      View;
    end
    else
      GUnpop;
end;

procedure GetAt;
{ Let the user change the at point. The at point should not be the same as the from
  point or the up vector.
}
var
  Nu: VectorType;

begin
    if GetVector('    Change the At Point    ', 'of new At point.', Nu) then begin
      GUnpop;
      if ((Nu.x = From.x) and (Nu.y = From.y) and (Nu.z = From.z)) or
        ((Nu.x = Up.x) and (Nu.y = Up.y) and (Nu.z = Up.z)) then begin
        PopupError(' Invalid At Point ');
        Exit;
      end;
      At.x := Nu.x;  At.y := Nu.y;  At.z := Nu.z;
      Clear_Viewport;
      SetEye;
      View;
    end
    else
      GUnpop;
end;

procedure GetUp;
{ Change the up vector coordinate to the user coordinates indicated. It should not be
  the same as the at point.
}
var
  Nu: VectorType;

begin
    if GetVector('    Change the Up Vector    ','of new Up vector.', Nu) then begin
```

```
      GUnpop;
      if (Nu.x = At.x) and (Nu.y = At.y) and (Nu.z = At.z) then begin
        PopupError(' Invalid Up Vector ');
        Exit;
      end;
      Up.x := Nu.x;  Up.y := Nu.y;  Up.z := Nu.z;
      SetEye;
      Clear_Viewport;
      View;
    end
    else
      GUnpop;
end;

procedure GetAngle;
{ Ask the user for a viewing angle. It must be between 0 and 180 degrees. }
const
  Title: string[34] = '    Change the Viewing Angle    ';
var
  nut: real;
  t: boolean;

begin
  t := GPopup(MaxX div 2-TextWidth(Title) div 2-5,
      MaxY div 2-3*TextHeight('H'),MaxX div 2+TextWidth(Title) div 2+5,
      MaxY div 2+4*TextHeight('H'),SolidLn,GetMaxColor,SolidFill,0);
  GWriteXY(5,5,Title);
  GWriteXY(5,5+2*TextHeight('H'),'Enter a new angle between');
  GWriteXY(5,5+3*TextHeight('H'),'0 and 180 degrees.');
  GWriteXY(5,5+4*TextHeight('X'),'> ');
  MoveTo(5+TextWidth('> '),5+4*TextHeight('H'));
  if not GReadReal(Nut) then begin
    GUnpop;
    Exit;
  end;
  GUnpop;
  if (Nut > 0) and (Nut < 180) then begin
    Angle := ToRadians(Nut);
    SetEye;
    Clear_Viewport;
```

```
      View;
   end
   else
      PopupError(' Angle must be between 0 and 180 ');
end;

procedure MoveFrom;
{ Interactively move the from point toward or away from the at point depending on
  the user input
}
const
  FromInc: real = 0.1;
var
  Nufx, Nufy, Nufz: real;
  StartV: VectorType;

begin
  StartV.x := From.x;  StartV.y := From.y;  StartV.z := From.z;
  TFrom := 1.0;
  GWriteXY(60*8,15*8,'Up arrow moves in ');
  GWriteXY(60*8,16*8,'Down to move away ');
  GWriteXY(60*8,17*8,'Any key to quit   ');
  ch := ReadKey;
  while ch = #0 do begin
    ch := ReadKey;
    if (ch = UpKey) or (ch = DownKey) then begin  { Move in or out }
      if ch = UpKey then begin
        if (TFrom > FromInc) then TFrom := TFrom - FromInc
      end
      else
        TFrom := TFrom + FromInc;
      Nufx := At.x + TFrom * (StartV.x - At.x);
      Nufy := At.y + TFrom * (StartV.y - At.y);
      Nufz := At.z + TFrom * (StartV.z - At.z);
      if (Nufx = At.x) and (Nufy = At.y) and (Nufz = At.z) then
        PopupError(' Cannot move to here ')
      else begin
        From.x := Nufx;  From.y := Nufy;  From.z := Nufz;
        SetEye;
        Clear_Viewport;
```

```
        View;
        ShowValues;
      end
    end;
    ch := ReadKey;
  end;
  SetFillStyle(SolidFill, Black);
  Bar(60*8,15*8,MaxX-2,18*8-1);
end;


procedure Zoom;
{ By changing the viewing angle, zoom in and out toward the object }
const
  ZoomInc: real = 0.17453293;                    { Inc this many radians }
var
  ch: char;


begin
  GWriteXY(60*8,15*8,'Up arrow zooms in ');
  GWriteXY(60*8,16*8,'Down to zoom out  ');
  GWriteXY(60*8,17*8,'Any key to quit   ');
  ch := ReadKey;
  while ch = #0 do begin
    ch := ReadKey;
    if ch = UpKey then begin                     { Zoom in }
      if Angle > ZoomInc then begin
        Angle := Angle - ZoomInc;
        SetEye;
        Clear_Viewport;
        View;
        ShowValues;
      end
      else
        PopupError(' Cannot zoom in any closer. ');
    end
    else if ch = DownKey then begin              { Zoom out }
      if Angle < ToRadians(179) - ZoomInc then begin
        Angle := Angle + ZoomInc;
        Clear_Viewport;
        SetEye;
```

```
            View;
            ShowValues;
          end
        else
          PopupError(' Cannot zoom out any more. ');
      end;
        ch := ReadKey;
  end;
  SetFillStyle(SolidFill, Black);
  Bar(60*8,15*8,MaxX-2,18*8-1);
end;


function Read3DObject(FileName: string): boolean;
{ Read in a file describing a polygon which adheres to standard described above.
  Returns True if file is read successfully; otherwise it returns False.
}
var
  InFile: text;
  i: integer;

begin
  {$I-} Assign(InFile, FileName);
  Reset(InFile); {$I+}
  if IOResult <> 0 then begin
    PopupError('Could not open file.');
    Read3DObject := False;
    Exit;
  end;
  Readln(InFile, Vertices, Length);
  if (Vertices > NumVertices) or (Length > NumConnections) then begin
    PopupError('Object in file is too large.');
    Read3DObject := False;
    Exit;
  end;
  for i := 1 to Vertices do
    Read(InFile,Points[i].x,Points[i].y,Points[i].z);
  for i := 1 to Length do
    Read(InFile, Connect[i]);
  Close(InFile);
  Read3DObject := True;
end;
```

```
procedure Read3DObjectFile;
{ Prompts for the file name of the file to be read and then calls Read3DObject to
  read it. If the file is successfully read, it is displayed by calling view after
  setting the viewing parameters.
}
const
    Title: string[28] = '  Reading a 3D Object File  ';
var
    FN: string;
    t: boolean;

begin
    t := GPopup(MaxX div 2-TextWidth(Title) div 2-5,
         MaxY div 2-3*TextHeight('H'),MaxX div 2+TextWidth(Title) div 2+5,
         MaxY div 2+4*TextHeight('H'),SolidLn,GetMaxColor,SolidFill,0);
    GWriteXY(5,5,Title);
    GWriteXY(5,5+2*TextHeight('H'),'Enter filename:');
    MoveTo(5,5+3*TextHeight('X'));
    GWrite('> ');
    if GReadStr(FN) then begin
      if Read3DObject(FN) then begin
        GUnpop;
        SetAt;
        SetFrom;
        SetEye;
        Clear_Viewport;
        View;
      end
      else
        GUnpop;
    end
    else
      GUnpop;
end;

procedure MainMenu;
{ Listing for the main menu }
begin
    Rectangle(PCR+1,0,MaxX,19*8);
    GWriteXY(60*8,1*8,'    Main Menu');
```

```
   Rectangle(PCR+1,0,MaxX,TextHeight('M')*2+2);
   GWriteXY(60*8,3*8,'r   read object');
   GWriteXY(60*8,4*8,'m   move From point');
   GWriteXY(60*8,5*8,'z   zoom in/out');
   GWriteXY(60*8,6*8,'a   enter At point');
   GWriteXY(60*8,7*8,'f   enter From point');
   GWriteXY(60*8,8*8,'u   enter Up point');
   GWriteXY(60*8,9*8,'t   enter view Angle');
   GWriteXY(60*8,12*8,'q   quit');
end;

begin
   Init3DGraphics;
   Rectangle(PCL-1,PCT-1,PCR+1,PCB+1);
   MainMenu;
   ShowValues;
   repeat
     GWriteXY(60*8,15*8,Prompt);
     MoveTo(60*8+TextWidth(Prompt),15*8);
     ch := ReadKey;
     case(ch) of
        'm' : MoveFrom;
        'z' : Zoom;
        'r' : Read3DObjectFile;
        'a' : GetAt;
        'f' : GetFrom;
        'u' : GetUp;
        't' : GetAngle;
     end;
     ShowValues;
   until ch = 'q';
   CloseGraph;
end.
```

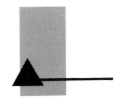

Index

Disk Order Form

The real fun in computer graphics is running programs—not typing them in. To help, we are making available a set of diskettes that contain all the source code presented in this book.

To order your disks, fill out the form below and mail it along with $15 in check or money order (orders outside the U.S. add $5 for shipping and handling) to:

> Loren Heiny
> Turbo Pascal Graphics Disks
> P.O. Box 122
> Tempe, AZ 85280

- -

Please send me _____ copies of the Turbo Pascal Graphics Disks at $15 each (orders outside the U.S. add $5 shipping and handling). Please make checks payable to Loren Heiny.

_____
Name

_____
Address

_____
City   State   Zip Code

_____
Telephone

A Special Offer From Wiley

Don't miss out on the book that takes you inside Turbo C's powerful graphics features and provides you with numerous useful programs.

• Please send me _____ copy(ies) of **Power Graphics Using Turbo C** (1-61909-4) @ $22.95 plus applicable sales tax.

NAME _____

COMPANY _____

ADDRESS _____

CITY _____ STATE/ZIP _____

TELEPHONE _____

Method of Payment (please make payment to John Wiley & Sons)
❏ Payment Enclosed (Wiley pays postage)   ❏ Bill me   ❏ Bill Company
❏ VISA   ❏ MASTERCARD (Sales tax, postage and handling will be added.)

Expiration Date _____/_____/_____   Card No. _____

SIGN HERE: _____
Order invalid if not signed. Offer good in U.S. and Canada only.

- -

To get the most out of Turbo C graphics, you'll want to add the following book written by the authors of *Power Graphics Using Turbo Pascal* to your personal library:

✓ *Power Graphics Using Turbo C*— provides an in-depth look at how practical graphics programs are developed with Borland's BGI. This book will help you master the art of crafting graphics tools for a variety of applications from presentation graphics to CAD programs.

To order, fill out the form above and mail it along with your payment to:

John Wiley & Sons, Inc.
Order Department
1 Wiley Drive
Somerset, NJ 08850-1272